St.Helens Libraries

This book is due for return on or before the last date shown.
Fines are charged on overdue books. Renewal may be made by
personal application, post or telephone, quoting membership
number and name.

2 6 AUG 2005		
2 9 MAY 2007		
2 8 MAY 2010		
3 0 DEC 2010		

Crosland - Taylor, W.J.
Crosville - The sowing and the Harvest.

TR388.322 C

CROSVILLE

THE SOWING AND THE HARVEST

W. J. CROSLAND-TAYLOR,
M.C., M.Inst.T.

With Foreword by
EDMUND VALE

Edited and Revised 1987

by

John A. Senior

© Transport Publishing Company Ltd

March 1987

086317 136 2

Produced for the Publishers by
Mopok Graphics
128 Pikes Lane
Glossop, Derbyshire
Printed in Great Britain

Publisher's Note

The *Sowing and the Harvest* was first published in 1948 and many of the references in the text, which we have not wished to alter, relate to that publication date.

Edmund Vale, a lifelong family friend and childhood neighbour, contributed the original Foreword, which we have naturally retained. He remembers the Crosland-Taylors as 'a remarkable family, brimful of original ideas; in the forefront of every modern trend, yet doing things in a totally different way from anybody else'.

The illustrations in this revised edition have been most carefully selected and captioned by our editor, drawing largely from first hand knowledge of former Company employees. We have tried to present the information as we feel W. J. Crosland Taylor would have wished it.

In 1986, the 75th year of its motor bus operation, the great Crosville company was divided between the Welsh and the English—it took an Order in Council to achieve it though!

FOREWORD

To the student of transportation this book has an obvious value. To the general reader it will also make an appeal because it has a certain quality which might well be unlooked for in a work of this kind; a quality which crops out continually, making a mere treatise into a readable and very humane narrative. It is a sense of romance in its most basic form.

The author sees romance not only in the building and planning of a great transportation concern in which he has taken so large a part himself, but in all the elements that make it up; and his gift is that he can impart his feelings simply and naturally to the reader.

The story is as true an adventure as any of those sagas of Elizabethan mariners collected by Master Hakluyt at the end of the sixteenth century. But it might not be easy to see it in that light without the usual lapse of time, which makes all old-world things seem glamorous, were it not for all those singular touches of side-light on machines, money, and men which the author has supplied so deftly. The "commercial proposition" and that uncompromising attitude towards things expressed by the term "business is business" are all there, but their drabness is continually pierced and enlivened by penetrating sallies, suddenly revealing the inner meanings of things. And there is never a serious situation, except one tragic moment, whose funny side is not shown up. Exclamation-marks and other sign-posts for those who can't see a joke at first sight are not used, the drollery always falls from unsmiling lips.

Not the least interesting part of the narrative is that dealing with Wales. That there is a great gulf fixed between Saxon and Celt is not often apprehended, nor any attempt made (particularly by English commercial venturers) to gauge its depth. Crosville not only fathomed but bridged it and got the best instead of the worst out of the Welshman, his tribal instinct of pride in his chief, his fabulous loyalty. Even his natural and abundant courtesy was mobilised successfully in the interests of the bus passenger—to say nothing of his amazing resourcefulness in the coaxing of refractory machines. Not only is a tribute to the goodness of these native qualities (so seldom found out and acknowledged by the Englishman) set down in print, but also to the genius of Wales herself, mountain, sky, coast and torrent, that might have come from the pen of a mystic.

In one outstanding thing a private enterprise differs from a state-run business. It is susceptible to the leaven of personality and enthusiasm if they should be found at the head of affairs, and in the history of the Crosville firm three men have succeeded each other as leaders who have possessed both these sovereign qualities. So that, as a passenger, travelling in any remote outpost area of the Company, one has the feeling of being in a family concern of which members are proud of each other and of the tribe and all its doings. And in this book one does not lose interest, for the same reason.

EDMUND VALE

The men behind the story—Edward, Claude and James with George, Edward's son, photographed in Chester in 1922.

DEDICATED

TO

MY FATHER,

GEORGE CROSLAND TAYLOR

without whose special brand of Yorkshire tenacity the Crosville Company would surely have gone under in the struggle for existence during the early years.

ALSO TO MY BROTHER

CLAUDE

who unfortunately did not live to see the full ripening of his early work.

G. CROSLAND
TAYLOR,
F.R.G.S.
*Founder and
Chairman,
1906-1923.*
Died January, 1923

C. CROSLAND
TAYLOR.
Chairman, 1923-1929.
*Managing Director,
1930-1935.*
Died March, 1935.

PREFACE

F orty years! A short time in the history of most nations, and a mere flea-bite out of the age of Christianity, but the *first* forty years count a great deal in the lifetime of any industry—and Crosville is a fair average section of the passenger road transport business.

Although stage coaches were running two hundred years ago, there were not many motor coaches in 1906, or even 1910 when we ran our first passenger vehicle, and so I have come to the conclusion that some account should be drawn up of the activities of the Crosville Company during its first forty years of existence. If it is not done now it never will be, and the Government's Nationalisation Programme, with the best intentions in the world, will swamp our identity, and the record of our achievements will be lost for all time. There must be many of our 5,000 employees who would not like this to occur, and many too of our passengers to whom our name is so familiar, that they would like to know how it all happened and what in fact did take place at various stages of our existence.

The tale of the first forty years of our Company has some fascination, too. We must mention a few statistics, though they are confined as far as possible to appendices which can be studied by those who are interested. In the main, however, I have tried to make it into a narrative of human achievement—to portray some of the lovable characters who have played their part in these doings, and to record just a few of the incidents that have gone to make up our history.

Some readers of these notes may get rather a shock when they see the first chapter headed "1857-1911". We certainly had no existence ninety years ago, but it was then that the founder of the Company came into the world—in Yorkshire, and he did not just start the ball rolling and float it on to the public in the approved manner of company promoters who so often take their profit from the new shareholders and then say "good-bye". He backed it when all the rules said that it should be closed down. He was generous to it when, in order to help, he renounced sums of money which were properly owing to him. The Company in return provided occupation and a living for his three sons and a large number of other people, so I think we must start at the beginning—in 1857—if we are to give a true picture.

1911-1919 was a period of change from losses to profits and stands by itself since the war prevented any expansion.

From 1919 we get the first stage of major development lasting ten years, at the end of which time we were taken over by the London Midland & Scottish Railway Company although we still retained our name.

The fourth chapter shows a further change back again to a Company in the Tilling and British Group, still with our old name and traditions wisely maintained by a Board which knew their value. Claude was still there to keep up the continuity, but with his death in 1935 we start on the last two chapters which take us right through the recent war and up to the present day, including the change of control in December, 1942, which made us a member of the Tilling Group of Companies under the Chairmanship of Sir J. Frederick Heaton, another Yorkshireman, whose wide and long experience particularly fitted him to guide us through the final years leading towards the present Government's Nationalisation proposals.

I have made this a chronological narrative as described above since it is more readable than a series of articles on the Company's activities in the various branches that make up the industry. Then again, it is impossible for any one person to do justice to all the items that go to make up such a history, so I can only hope that I have not missed out too much that should have been told or stressed other aspects more than I ought to have done.

There are only sparse details available for the first machines we had, but in 1911 we began to favour Dennis. The next year Daimler brought out a chassis with the "Silent Knight" sleeve-valve engine which had been so successful on their motor cars since 1909 or 1910. We obtained one, fitted it with a body which had plenty of standing room and called it the "Flying Fox". I drove it many miles in 1919 and it was followed by a number of others. A few Lacres joined the fleet as a result of a successful venture with a coach of that make called the "Grey Knight", but they were very poor fish compared with the Daimlers.

One day, while working on the story, I was wondering how I could get a clearer picture of the period between 1910 and 1919. All available evidence seemed to be exhausted when I suddenly thought of Bob Walmsley, a man who had worked for us as a fitter for well over thirty years—he would surely remember something. He came into the office and stood there hat in hand wondering why I had asked him to come.

"Sit down, Bob," I said, "and stick your hat somewhere."

No reply, and then he suddenly saw that I was talking to him.

"I'm as deaf as a post—you'd better shout."

The next half hour was bedlam, but we finished up with quite a lot of information down on paper. I showed him a picture of some twelve vehicles at Queensferry munition works in 1917. He fastened on to it like a dog on to a bone.

"That's Percy Potter's No. 17, and there's No. 12 too. Which numbers were the Lacres did you say? I'll soon tell you that. I know them all." And he did.

"And what about this A.E.C., Bob?"

"Them things—I never held with them things. There was three of them, Nos. 26, 27 and 28, always running big ends. We fitted 'em with Daimler engines afterwards."

"Do you remember any registered numbers?" I asked.

"Never could remember number plates," was the answer.

"How long have you been here?" was the next question. I knew the answer, but also knew that Old Bob would never be happy if he didn't get the chance to tell me how the Company had kept two days' wages in hand over thirty years ago, and never paid him yet.

"1916 was when I came—but Andrew Reynolds says it was 1915. Mr. Claude—he told me when he paid me on Friday it was only till the previous Tuesday and he was keeping two days' in hand. Now Mr. James—I've never had that two days."

"Look, Bob," I bawled at the top of my voice, "when you leave, if ever you do—and not before—you'll get paid right up. But you won't go and you won't die, so what can I do?"

He grinned. This answer always finished him off, but I was grateful for his help. The collection of old photographs always fascinates the old hands. They gaze lingeringly at No. 6 or whatever it may be, with memories of more generous and better days crowding back before their eyes—and so the information comes to light, and the picture is put together as near as we can.

In 1921 came the first two Leylands—sturdy G7s—known as the Edinburgh type, followed the next years by seventeen more like them, and so the Leyland age came into being only to be broken twenty-one years later by the necessity of having some Guys during the war, to be followed by a number of Bristols when we joined the Tilling Group of Companies.

In 1925 all Leylands and most Daimlers were converted to pneumatic tyres and everybody wondered how they had ever tolerated the old solid tyred machines for so long.

It should be noticed about the operators whose businesses and vehicles we bought, that their buses had generally seen their best days. Probably that was why they sold. The variety of makes was astounding and often led to trouble resulting in a desire to get out if a reasonable price could be agreed. We had no sentiment about what we had bought. As many machines as possible were scrapped at once. Odd makes are expensive to run and we had no money to waste. Leylands and A.E.C.s were kept and added to our standard fleet.

During the last war we had to hire 134 double-deckers, all of which had to be returned, and annual mileage had increased permanently by 30%, so that when new deliveries started in 1946 we had endless leeway to make up, but try as we would we never seemed to catch up with our requirements. In the meantime many buses are over twenty years old and the average age per vehicle for the whole fleet is over twelve years. This effort to meet our obligations is probably good for us, but the struggle is and will remain keen for quite a long time yet.

We have been blessed for the most part with a loyal and competent staff, and the good British Public has paid its pennies to buy our tickets and thus enable us to live and pay some return on our capital, which is what we set out to get it to do, and whatever happens in the future will go on turning merrily, bringing us security in our jobs and providing travel for our public.

What more can a man want?

W. J. CROSLAND-TAYLOR
M.C., M.Inst.T.
General Manager 1935 onwards

CONTENTS

Sunday morning in Llanidloes in 1925, and relief conductor
Higgs stands proudly by his new Leyland. The solid tyres
will give a bumpy ride but the bus is smart in its new grey
paint and he's just swept it out for the day's work.
Pneumatic tyres were fitted to the majority of the fleet
during that same year and the riding and handling
qualities were greatly improved.

How it all started
1857-1911

W e must look back into the last century really to get to the bottom of Crosville history. To be exact, we must turn back the calendar to Saturday evening, the 30th January, 1857, and go into the house of Henry Dyson Taylor, just outside Huddersfield, where an event was pending which should with luck provide that gentleman with a son to carry on the Worsted Coating Mill. Such a desire was entirely in keeping with good Yorkshire practice in these matters, and the fact that the eldest child had been a girl only intensified their wish for a son.

It was nearly midnight and Henry walked up and down the dining room floor just like anybody else in such a case. Perhaps it would be Sunday—well, it didn't matter so long as all went satisfactorily with Sarah. Indeed, by now it didn't matter even if it were another girl. But he needn't have worried. They brought him word early on Sunday morning, the 31st January, that it was really a boy, and that his name was George.

"Why George?" asked Henry.

"Your wife said so," replied the doctor, "and if I were you I should agree. After all, St. George and the Dragon, you know."

"I shall add Crosland—Sarah's maiden name—and then he'll be George Crosland Taylor," said Henry, and poured out two glasses of port wine, which in those days was always in evidence at that type of house.

Thus came Crosland into the world. By some peculiar chance they never called him George, although that was his first name.

Sarah was to have two more children, James and Hannah.

All went well with them and at the age of sixteen Crosland had his first taste of the mill. 6.30 a.m. every morning like everybody else. The machinery fascinated him and he set himself to master its intricacies as best he could. The office work and financial side of the business had also to be learned, and he did this with a good grace, but most of his time was spent in the actual mill. Chemistry, too, drew him like a magnet, and Henry was well pleased with his eldest son.

In his early twenties he was sent to Australia by sailing ship, presumably to get to know the wool merchants, since that country has always been our main source of supply, but the development of electricity had already fascinated him and he was determined to do something in that line. What his father thought about it has never been recorded, but he must have been a little disappointed. In any case he died in the early eighties and Crosland was able to put money into what was now his favourite industry and really set to work.

Thus we have the British Insulated & Helsby Cable Company, founded at Neston in Cheshire in 1882 after a visit to the Paris Exhibition in 1881. The old buildings were solidly built of sandstone and are now occupied by Neston Laundry. The original company has now become the British Insulated Callenders Cables since its amalgamation with Tom Callender's Company a short time ago.

The rapid development in design and manufacture of electric cables absorbed all his energies for some years, and there is no doubt that he was energetic in spite of a weakness in one lung that caused him some trouble and eventually killed him. If the days were spent at the works, the evenings were mostly occupied in making endless drawings and designs in his room at Ravenscar, the family home which he had designed and which stood on the great sandstone bluff of Helsby Hill. From its windows one could see the ships passing up and down the newly opened Manchester Ship Canal.

Something new—all the time it had to be something new—and in 1899 it was the internal combustion engine that began to draw his thoughts and, of course, he must have a motor car. A 10 h.p. Wolseley with a horizontal twin cylinder engine, chain driven, and fitted with a four-seater body. This was a grand toy. His brother, James, who was with him in the Cable business, bought one exactly the same. I can remember both cars although I was only five at the time, and as we lived half way up Helsby Hill there was always the excitement and gamble as to whether it would get back to the house once it had gone down to the main road.

This was the forerunner of lots of other cars, a motor tricycle, and several Belgian motor bikes, and the question of their commercial possibilities began to loom large in the scheme of things. It took him three years to get to this stage, and in 1902 he went off to Brussels to review the situation on the continent.

My eldest brother, Edward, has sent me a few notes as to what happened in those years up to the time he left the country in 1911, and we cannot do better than give his story in his own words:-

THE ORIGIN OF THE CROSVILLE MOTOR SERVICES

"It would be correct to say that the origin of the Crosville arises from a visit to Paris. In 1903 my father and I went to the Motor Exhibition in Paris, which was a very large affair. My father had previously become interested in the commercial side of motor cars in 1902 when he bought several cars and several motor cycles in Brussels and took them back to Helsby, where they were sold.

"In 1904 we again went to the Paris Motor Show, and in 1905 we repeated the visit. On this occasion we met a Frenchman called Georges Ville, who had some designs for cars, samples of which had been made by a firm in Paris called Morane, and who were also interested in the early attempts to manufacture aeroplanes.

"In 1906 my father finally bought two sample cars from Monsieur Ville, and a chassis of another, together with all drawings, and some patterns relating to these cars; the designs included a very modern looking vehicle of about 50 h.p. with a circular radiator.

"Late in 1906, and I am open to correction on the date, my father rented the present Crane House and warehouse from the Shropshire Union Railway and Canal Company and installed a small machine shop there. We intended to assemble cars of this French design and sell them. After a few months' operation it was found that a much larger shop would have to be built, so a company was formed, the Crosville Motor Company Limited, there being two shareholders, my father and a Mr. Catt of Belper, Derbyshire. A modern shop was built across the access lane to Crane Wharf, which was the nucleus of the present repair shops of Crosville Motor Services.

"This brings us to 1908, when work was started on the new car. We bought the parts from various manufacturers and one car was finally put together, this being of the 50 h.p. circular radiator design; another car of 20 h.p. was assembled from parts bought from Paris.

"I will now, for the sake of the record, give some details of the cars, and there were only five of them, that ever ran under the name of 'Crosville'.

"*No. 1*, the chassis brought from Paris, was an amazing vehicle, four cylinders, and only two speeds, about 50 h.p. and fitted with auxiliary exhaust ports at the bottom of the stroke, after the manner of a two stroke engine, although it was otherwise of ordinary four cycle design.

15

A body, of my father's design, was made at the Helsby Works; it had a short wheelbase, made a terrible noise, and frightened all the horses in Cheshire. It was run for some time and finally the engine cylinder block cracked. It was finally converted into the tyre testing vehicle which ran on a figure eight track at the Helsby Works, driven by an electric motor. Some people may remember it.

"*No. 2* was a long chassis five-seated open car of 20 h.p. with fixed canopy top, the whole made in France. Mr. Catt finally took this car and used it for some years. I never knew its ultimate fate.

"*No. 3* was a car with the same engine as No. 2 and a magnificent 'coupé de ville' body. It had many extraordinary features; one was a double reduction gear and worm drive, a dropped frame at the rear, four speeds forward with a reversing clutch, same as a motor boat; very difficult to handle in traffic as when you came to a stop it proceeded backwards unless you held the clutch pedal in exact neutral. This car was used by my mother for several years; it had patent leather mudguards of graceful design, mother-of-pearl fittings, and always created a sensation wherever it went, particularly by its ability to reverse on all four speeds.

"*No. 4* was constructed at Crane Wharf from parts bought from France, same engine as Nos. 2 and 3, but short chassis, an open body made specially. This was used extensively by myself, and afterwards by my brother, Claude. I never learnt its ultimate fate.

"*No. 5* was the round radiator machine of modern design, parts all made in England. It was finished and delivered to Mr. Catt at Belper, an open car. To the best of my memory it was not a success and I never heard what became of it.

The First Crosville car, a 50hp model, with my brother Claude at the wheel. Note the chains to pick nails from the tyres.

The Second Crosville car, a 20hp model made in France. My father at the wheel.

(Facing) Crane House and the warehouse which my father rented from the Shropshire Union Railway and Canal Company. Crosville began its existence here and expanded by moving into a modern building across the access lane on the left of this illustration.

The Third Crosville car with its exquisite bodywork. Shown at the Paris Exhibition of 1905.

The last Crosville car, with its distinctive radiator, ready for bodying.

"During the years from 1908 to 1911 a general business was also carried on at Crane Wharf as a garage and machine shop. We did all kinds of heavy overhaul work; some motor boat work was done.

"Mr. Catt's nephew, Bertie Catt, was the first Manager; he was followed by Mr. Hellberg from Helsby, a native of Sweden. I went to Sweden with Hellberg and came back with a motor boat hull; this was fitted with a 2-cylinder Darracq engine, taken from a car of my father's, and competed in the Mersey motor boat races which in those days was a matter of great enterprise; probably the year 1909. During our race we broke down in the Crosby Channel and narrowly escaped being run down by an outgoing liner; only the oars saved us; we were swept up the river by the incoming tide, and only saved ourselves from becoming involved with the ferry steamers by grabbing the New Brighton Life Boat with our boat hook as we swept up the river.

"A large motor boat was constructed at Roberts' Yacht Yard, close to the shop, and now defunct, and fitted with the engine taken from the car which was used at the Helsby Works as a tyre tester, No. 1 in my story above. This was sold to a Mr. Brage of Manchester and once got as far as Beaumaris, where the engine cracked up, and I can remember bringing the crankcase back to Chester, in the back of a small car, for repairs.

"The Office Manager of the Crosville was a Mr. Jack Morris. About the spring of 1910 Morris suggested to my father that, to support our

Roberts' Yard built the hull for this 50hp Crosville Motor Boat.

waning finances, we should run a motor passenger service from Chester to Ellesmere Port. It was not possible to get to Ellesmere Port from Chester without changing trains, a roundabout journey. My father agreed, and I went to Swansea in search of a char-a-banc, that I had seen advertised, with which to start a service.

"At Swansea I was more interested in the ships and the docks than in the condition of the HERALD char-a-banc, of French manufacture, that I bought sight unseen, so to speak, in the intervals of looking at ships. I started out to drive this leviathan to Chester, myself alone. After it warmed up water spurted out of the jackets of the separate cylinders from numerous cracks, and I then realised that I had been fooled, but I had accepted it as in good order so I dragged it to the railway station and despatched it to Chester on a railway wagon. No parts could be bought in England for this make of car, but I advertised and found some cylinders on a junked vehicle of the same make, near Huddersfield, which I went and bought.

"This must have been during the summer of 1910, and I went away to the U.S.A. for a visit whilst Morris tried to get the service started to Ellesmere Port. Whatever he did showed results, as although the ancient HERALD broke down on my return and there was no more service, it was decided to scout around for further vehicles. I went to an auction at a garage opposite the Grosvenor Hotel and bought a GERMAINE wagonette for fifty pounds. This peculiar machine with the

The Germaine at Crane Wharf, in front of an advertisement for SWIFT cars.

engine under the driver got *down* the hill to Crane Wharf but was totally incapable of going up again, so I went to Liverpool and bought an ALBION char-a-banc from, I think, Lawton's, and being determined not to be bilked again, took it in front of the Lime Street station and attracted a crowd of loafers whom I offered a shilling each to sit in it whilst I tried it with full load up a hill.

"This ALBION was taken to Chester and put on to run from Chester to Ellesmere Port, and I left for the U.S.A. about that time, January 1911. My brother Claude afterwards came from the Helsby Works to take my place, and I have recollections of dealing with a man who had a Kelsall service just before I left. We either bought his vehicles or his business.

We purchased Lightfoot's Kelsall business in 1911 — our first take-over. His Lacre had come second-best to a tree. It was repaired and ran for a couple of years.

"From that point on the story belongs to my brother Claude, who persevered through all difficulties to the point where he had developed a really large business. In 1929 I came over to the final meeting of the old Crosville Motor Co. Ltd., at the Grosvenor Hotel, and at which meeting we accepted the offer of the railway companies for our concern.

"The average number of men at Crane Wharf in my day was twenty. The pay of a mechanic, or a fitter if you will, was 8½d. an hour, 48 hours a week, with time and a half for overtime. I got myself 30/- a week, as the records, if they exist, will show, and my father nothing at all. We took in boys as apprentices; their families paid us fifty pounds or so for the privilege of having them work in the shop and learn the trade. Three years' apprenticeship was the rule; they were paid small sums after the first year I think.

"I think the greatest interest of all, to me, was the amazing variety of cars that we dealt with, both for repairs and sales. We had an agency for the Swift Motor Company of Coventry, at whose factory I had served two years' apprenticeship. Sometimes we had as many as half-a-dozen Swift cars in stock.

"The Company possessed a 1-cylinder De Dion car at one time which I adopted as my own; no hood or windshield, but I erected a canvas screen in the right hand corner with the words 'Look Out' painted on it. With this car, running on benzol bought from the Queensferry tar works, I scoured much of North Wales in the summers. I ran the Conway and the Anglesey bridges, at night, without stopping to pay toll. When I left Chester in 1911 no one could be found who could run this car and it was sold or scrapped. It had a habit of overheating and pre-firing itself and I found a remedy for this by reaching over the front and opening the compression tap, thereby admitting air and cooling the inside of the cylinder, all of which was done without stopping the car.

"We also possessed at one time a Berliet of some 60 h.p. with an enormous 4-cylinder engine and make-and-break ignition. This car at 60 miles an hour, running down a North Wales limestone road, raised a tail like Halley's Comet for fully a mile behind it. Our foreman, Wally Wright, who followed Tom Carter in that position, always said of this car, 'This is the goods'.

"Tom Carter, mentioned above, was an all-round mechanic, and could make repairs to a car, starting with the patterns themselves, the castings and the subsequent machine work. He built for himself a small car in the shop at Crane Wharf, using discarded parts from other cars. It was, without exception, a meek and lowly machine, having a small 2-cylinder White and Poppe engine, mounted on the frame of the old Darracq, out of which we put the engine in the boat mentioned above; the body was from still another car. On this vehicle he travelled back and forth to his home at Mouldsworth for some years.

" One of the side lines at Crane Wharf was the sale of aluminium sheeting of serrated form, for covering running boards and foot boards of cars; this material was made by the Prescot Works of the B.I. and had quite a vogue for a while.

"We also sold tyres made at Helsby. At one time, after the Helsby Works gave up tyre making, we had a stock of tyres left, none of them in such shape that we could guarantee them. I toured North Wales offering these tyres to garages, in an old Wolseley 2-cylinder horizontal delivery wagon that we inherited from the Neston Laundry. These tyres required two strong men with crow bars to get them on the rims and I never stayed long enough at any of these garages to hear the remarks of those who had to deal with them.

"I have mentioned some of these old cars and their vagaries to point the difference between present times and forty years ago. If we did not get rich, at least we had fun.

"I should mention a few of the personalities that had to do with the early days of the Company. I mentioned Tom Carter, still living at Mouldsworth House, and I mentioned Wally Wright. Wright visited me here for a holiday on one occasion and I must needs drive him up into the mountains and get stuck in a mud wallow, in my Ford, from which we had to be pulled by a pair of strong farm horses. There was Mr. Jones, the Auditor; I believe his son is still employed by the C.M.S. There was Jack Morris, who was a survivor of the siege of Ladysmith in the Boer War; he ran the office. There was a little shorty in the Stores Department, whose name escapes me. There was a fitter of the name of Dronsfield who was one of the early Union men. An apprentice called Marsh who was the son of the chauffeur who worked for Harmood Banner of Liverpool, an M.P. at that time. Another apprentice called Jones I remember too; a dark-haired boy. And still another one, the son of a pub keeper on the Grosvenor Road. At one time we had a cousin of my own from Australia who cut quite a dash in the Flint Boat, next door to Crane House. Likewise Mr. Catt's nephew, who afterwards achieved fame by falling out of an express train at 60 miles per hour and surviving; he afterwards made a record by riding a motor cycle for a week with very few stops; he worked in the office sometimes. Also Mr. Gardner, the Solicitor, now dead; he was a great help to my father when the Company was founded.

"At one time we hired cars out, with driver, to people usually staying at the Grosvenor Hotel. On these occasions I managed to do the driving and became quite a guide to the neighbourhood. The Cheshire

County Council Surveyor, Mr. Bull, hired me many times to take him on his inspection trips; in this way I knew the roads of Cheshire better than most.

"The fascination of motor cars has never left me and I got as much of a kick last April in tooling down the Manchester road in a car lent me by my brother, and without a licence as usual, as I did in 1906, forty years before, down the same road in a 1-cylinder jallopy and also without a licence.

"The future holds the threat of nationalisation of the motor bus business in Britain; possibly some form of nationalisation would work, but no government control can take the place of a man whose livelihood depends on it, sitting at a desk, and making decisions which mean the difference between convenience and inconvenience to the bus-riding public. Imagine the situation on a market day somewhere, if the 'phone should ring from some bus station saying that extras were needed to handle the crowd, and the wretched government manager having to say, 'All right, hold them there whilst I refer the matter to the Minister of Transport; he will be back from his vacation next month!' In the bad old days we would have said, 'All right, Bill, coming right up; Joe will be there with the blasted old Lacre in a jiffy'.

"It has occurred to me to state that the Crosville Motor Company was concerned, in the early days, with several experiments made by my father to market 'dope' for aeroplane wings, this being before the day of all-metal wings. He had the idea that wire mesh, filled with some form of varnish, would be better than fabric for aeroplane wings. Canvas wings were varnished in this manner at the time, but were not so enduring as wire wings would have been. Experiments were also made with a spring wheel, which was patented, and a car equipped with such was run by us for some time. The springs were made down Birmingham way. The mud wore out the working parts and the experiments were a failure for that reason. I travelled many miles in this spring wheel equipped car.

"The engines for the BEND OR and ORMONDE, small steamboats running on the Dee, were rebuilt in the Crosville shops; in fact we turned our hand to anything at all.

"Driving lessons were one of the things we sold. I taught many people, men, girls and coachmen, to drive cars, including the Manager of Summers' Ironworks at that time. Cars from Eaton Hall were brought to us occasionally to repair, usually Mercedes, which at that time were the *ne plus ultra* of automobilism.

The *Royal George* was our first new Lacre, and was purchased in 1912. The open rear platform was standard in the early fleet and may owe something to the French influence in our Company — contemporary Schneider buses operating in Paris had open platforms.

"Crosville Motor Services Ltd., although not the largest concern in its particular line, is big business, and would be so considered even in the U.S.A. where such things as the Greyhound Corporation exist, so people employed by the C.M.S. should consider themselves engaged in a concern which has no apologies to make on account of its small beginnings. The Greyhound Corporation, which is a holding company for a number of concerns with the same trademark, a running greyhound, had its origin in much the same manner as the Crosville, to wit a service between two small mining towns which had no rail service, and the vehicles that it used were just about as bad as ours were, in fact worse in many ways.

"I stood, this last July, on the precise spot in Paris where the agreement was made which eventually resulted in the present C.M.S. which I understand employs some 5,000 people. That development has taken roughly forty years. Who can say what the next forty years will bring forth and what employment your sons and daughters will then have?

"As things get big they lose their individuality, but I never in all these years have lost the thought that the C.M.S., in its present form, is the result of my buying, that day in Swansea, a char-a-banc with cracked water jackets. Who could say I erred?"

EDWARD C. TAYLOR

Behind this story lies the tale of the financial struggle that took place and which had to be won if the Company was to continue to exist. The fact that it *was* won speaks volumes for the Yorkshire tenacity displayed by Crosland, who refused to acknowledge defeat when it was abundantly clear to everybody else that the whole idea was a washout, and money was just going down the drain. His faith may have seemed pathetic at times, but he must have sensed a spark somewhere that could be made to ignite the apparently dead body of the poor old Crosville if only he could blow on it from the right direction.

Appendix I tells the financial story in cold figures and if one examines the capital and loans figures for the first ten years one can get some idea of what happened.

But we can make it a little more interesting than that, and so let us first look a little further back, to an earlier time in the life of Chester, and then follow the story through to the present day.

An all-male party ready for an outing on the *Busy Bee*, a 1913-built Daimler. The side window frames could be removed completely on some of these vehicles but it was a job which had to be done in the depot. This group from the Golden Lion Hotel look confident the weather will hold good.

1911-1919

In the early eighteenth century, Chester was a flourishing port and the Dee had just been diverted from its old meandering course under the Blacon bluff and then along just below Great Saughall village and past Shotwick Church. The new arrangement was a straight cut from the Queen's Ferry up to Saltney, and another straight reach to Cop House, after which the old bed of the river remained right up to the Weir. Just above Cop House, a wharf was built—Crane Wharf, and warehouses were provided for storing corn and anything else that came up by ship. Here also the Shropshire Union Canal joined the river, and there was a great exchange of traffic at the Wharf.

As the new cut got silted up, and Liverpool grew in size, Chester began to lose their sea trade, and in 1906 only an occasional schooner arrived from Ireland with grass seed or some such cargo, but even then they came. Now, forty years later, they do not come at all.

These warehouses, then, at Crane Wharf were empty in 1906 as was also the house adjoining, then known as Crane House, and it was here

The river at Crane Wharf showing Crane House and the slipway. The entrance to the lock leading to the Shropshire Union Canal can be seen to the left.

that Crosland decided to set up his venture into the motor manufacturing business. The Shropshire Union Canal Company were delighted to get a tenant and not much rent was asked, so that both sides were well suited with the arrangement, and the bottom floor of the four-storied building began to take shape as a workshop with pits of an antique design, but then the latest of their sort, benches and some machinery. We do not know what the initial outlay was, but it was soon evident that a limited company was required if things were to go on. The Certificate of Incorporation is dated May 6th, 1906 and hangs in my office at this moment and on Monday, 19th November, 1906, the first Directors' Meeting was held at Crane House.

Present: Mr. Charles William Catt.
             Mr. George Crosland Taylor.
In attendance: Mr E. Gardner, *Solicitor.*

Crosland was made Chairman, and Mr. Arthur Ethelbert Catt Secretary. Messrs. Warmsley Jones & Co. were appointed Auditors, and Parrs (now Westminster) Bank Ltd. were named as bankers. My brother Edward or Mr. A. E. Catt were authorised to draw wages cheques.

The object of the new Company was of course mainly to take over Crosland's lease of Crane House and the warehouse, and to run the business which had been started. The Memorandum and Articles of Association were fairly widely drawn up, and their possible activities covered a pretty wide field.

3,750 shares were allotted as follows:-

George Crosland Taylor and nominees	2,500
Charles William Catt of Duffield	725
Arthur Ethelbert Catt	500
Tom Carter of Manley, near Chester	25
	3,750

Tom Carter, by the way, was sort of foreman in the works, and there was nothing much he could not do. He is still alive, and has let me have a good deal of useful information for this book.

In June 1907, the following additional shares were allotted:-

Arthur Ethelbert Catt	500
Charles William Catt	1,250
Edward Crosland Taylor	500
	2,250

Thus Crosland held 3,000 shares, the Catts 2,975, and Tom Carter the balance of 25. 6,000 shares in all.

The money seemed simply to disappear and the two Directors were already making loans in order to enable the business to be carried on, and on 4th October, 1907, we see dividends in reverse in that it was resolved that the shareholders should be asked to make a present to the Company of 3/- per share!! In point of fact this was not done, but at an Annual Meeting in July, 1908, the loans stood at £2,000 each from the two Directors, interest to be at 5%. Mr. A. E. Catt had resigned early in 1908 and Mr. Gardner had been made Secretary, but this loan business must have been too much for Mr. C. W. Catt, for on 11th January, 1909, he also resigned and assigned his interest and directorship to his son, Charles Bernard Catt.

There was a man named Hellberg as Manager and on 29th January, 1909, he was given three months' notice on grounds of economy. Edward was appointed General Manager on 23rd June, 1909, at a salary of 35/- per week. He had been employed from the beginning at 30/.

Losses were heavy and on 9th September, 1910, Mr. C. B. Catt resigned from the Board. Edward took his place, and Crosland apparently took over the Catt interest both as regards shares and loan, so that now he shouldered the full burden to the extent of nearly £10,000, although 2,500 actual shares were surrendered.

According to all the rules of the game Crosland should have given up when Catt left and put the Company into liquidation, but he hung on. Edward went to America in 1911 to get married and live there. On 24th April, 1911, my brother Claude replaced him on the Board and the struggle continued.

It was now indeed a family affair. In January 1911, it had been decided to buy a bus for the Ellesmere Port service, but even this did not quite stop the losses, although there seemed to be some improvement:-

Year ending April, 1909 ... £2,531 loss.
Year ending April, 1910 ... £1,526 loss.
Year ending April, 1911 ... £432 loss.
Year ending April, 1912 ... £2,094 loss

But in April, 1913 the loss suddenly went down to £21 and next April there was a profit of £1,302.

Crosland celebrated this triumph in characteristic fashion by surrendering outright £2,500 of the loans he had made towards the reduction of the adverse balance. There is no doubt that it was the bus services which had turned the tide.

Namely: Chester—Ellesmere Port, Chester—Kelsall, and Nantwich to Crewe and Sandbach.

The first world war had now arrived and although planned expansion of services was stopped, there was a lot of work at the Queensferry munition factory and a fleet of some twenty or thirty buses was soon got together.

Claude was a hard worker. He had come in at Crosland's request and given up work that he was doing in the motor tyre section of British Insulated Cables. There were a number of things he did not like in this tyre business and he would probably have left in any case, but the Crosville Company had an attraction for him, and especially compelling was the bus service just started by Edward and then left to him to develop. He was reserved and shy almost to rudeness in those early days, and extremely conservative, or perhaps one should call it solid. He did not act impulsively, but only after careful consideration of the facts.

The result of this was a very sure foundation with no gambling which might or might not have come off. Appendix II which sets out the starting dates for each service shows how it all happened. Later on from 1929 onwards, additions were mostly due to purchases of existing businesses, but even after that date we often devised and established completely new services over our own territory.

There is no doubt that from 1911 to 1929 Claude did guide the destinies of the Company, fully backed by his father on the financial side up to 1923 when Crosland died, and was loyally supported by the Staff and shareholders the whole of that time. He came in at the bottom—30/- per week he once told me—the same as Edward—and he went out suddenly after a short week's illness on 31st March, 1935, as Managing Director of the third largest provincial omnibus company in England. Such men seem to arise in this country when occasion demands, and I am sure that he will always be remembered with some affection by those who came into contact with him.

During the 1914/18 war a munitions factory was set up by Lloyd George at Queensferry and labour was obtained from Mold and Flint districts. This led to a series of bus services run by the Company to the factory, and eventually a visit from His late Majesty King George V when the vehicles were drawn up in the factory yard for inspection. Whilst one cannot compare this effort with the Marchwiel organisation in 1942 where 250 vehicles were used, it was big for its time, and maintenance during the winter months was not easy.

Profits were moderate, but steady, while total traffic receipts rose from £6,041 in 1914 to £27,522 in 1918.

Claude lived on the job at Crane House, and was always to be found there early or late.

There was a side line developing—goods haulage—and it is not generally realised that between 1912 and 1919 the Company did a fair amount of this work for people like Frosts Flour Mills. Foden steam wagons and trailers were in favour for this work owing to the petrol shortage, but we also had several Daimler lorries.

There were tractors, too, ploughing at the farms nearby. Many hundreds of acres were cultivated by Crosville tractors towing ploughs.

In 1915 a garage was built at Nantwich, since the service to Crewe seemed to have become a permanency and the conditions in the Cocoa House yard were rather primitive. The building had a span of about 32 ft. and would hold nine buses. There was a Bowser 1-gallon petrol pump and a 1,250-gallon tank. What a luxury after the eternal filling from tins! There was enough land, too, for an extension some day. This additional outlay required some courage since in those days expenditure on anything that did not produce immediate revenue was not thought advisable.

We had started operations in Nantwich because Northwich U.D.C. had refused us licences in favour of a local company. Arrangements were quite simple. We set out the main fares and said that intermediate fares were *pro rata*, thus leaving it to the conductor to charge what he thought best for the latter. Petrol in tins was stored in a 'petrol pit'. The office was part of a stable, but the money came in, including four and five shilling pieces and sovereigns. Claude and I used to go over once a week and collect it in a bag, leaving enough to pay wages. This practice continued until 1920 when we suddenly realised that there was a bank in the town and that wages ought to be paid by cheque. We went in a 42 h.p. Daimler, chain driven, capable of a fairly high speed, but not easy to start when cold. Randal (our Superintendent) used to meet us at the Cocoa House and then we would call in to see old Picken for a cup of cocoa and have a chat with him and Mrs. Picken, who suffered from goitre.

The *Royal George* again, this time posed for a photograph before setting off for Chester. It appears to have lost one of its headlamps.

A retired engine driver named Gregory had set up with a steam bus—he didn't trust petrol. I never rode on it, but those who did were always afraid of it going up in flames. Eventually we bought him out, and also Ward Bros. who ran the horse buses in Crewe town. With them came a rare type of man named Freddie Harrison, who had been with them since 1896 when he was twelve years of age. He still drives double-deckers in Crewe town after fifty years' service, being sixty-two years of age. There are so many of our people who deserve some mention in this history that there is not room to put them all in, but in those days they were more than just employees. They were true friends of a baby industry. Paul Newns, Bill Jones, Dick Davies, Joe Chapman and his brother Ernest, Harry Yeates, Ted Tansley, Jack Fleet, Jack Lea, but there—we can't do justice to them all. They had to do more than merely drive or conduct. They had to find out what was wanted and then do it. Above all they had to coax along their antiquated vehicles in a very personal fashion. The Lacres with sprocket drive keys continually shearing, the Daimlers with outer

A splendid line-up of Daimler and Lacre buses, together with a couple of charabancs. Note the large registration numbers painted on the dash of two Lacre vehicles, including FM 1102. Our first Daimler, shown in Company records as having been a demonstrator owned by that company, stands to the left of the straw-boatered gentleman. Registered DU 2007 it was given the name Flying Fox. The arched doorway on the first three Daimlers was a feature of bodywork by the London coachbuilding concern, Hora. The smart turn out of our drivers suggests this may have been the occasion of the Royal Visit mentioned overleaf.

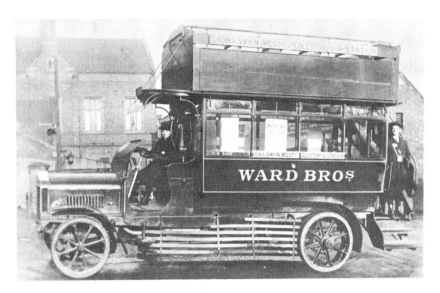

During the Great War the first double-deckers entered service with Crosville. They were Tilling-Stevens TS3 models and came from Ward Bros of Crewe. Their reign was shortlived and both had gone by the end of the war.

sleeves always breaking at the lug, no brakes most of the time, but our fellows were clever and drove mostly on gears—they had to.

At the very beginning in 1911 our buses had names. The "Royal George" was the first Lacre, followed by a Dennis called the "Alma", and another one named "Deva". Then there were CC and CD type Daimlers called the "Flying Fox" and the "Busy Bee". After that we got tired of names and they had numbers, but to those who had to run them they were still very much "individuals"—almost like horses in a stable. Later there were so many that they deteriorated into "machines" and in spite of all the modern improvements they remain just buses.

In the end the war finished and we were free to look around. The view was a good one in all directions if only we could get money and vehicles. Buildings did not matter at the moment. There was going to be a race to establish bus services all over the country. I think Claude saw this—at any rate he set to work to consolidate an area which included North and Central Wales, Cheshire, South Lancashire with bits of other counties. It took until now to do it, and he never saw the end, but he carried out the initial campaign before he died in 1935, leaving the consequential consolidation and development to those who came after him. We could not have had a better foundation for our labours.

The Alma was the first Dennis and was fitted with bodywork built by Henry Eaton in Manchester. It ran for some six years with Crosville.

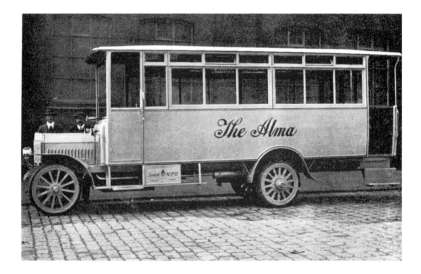

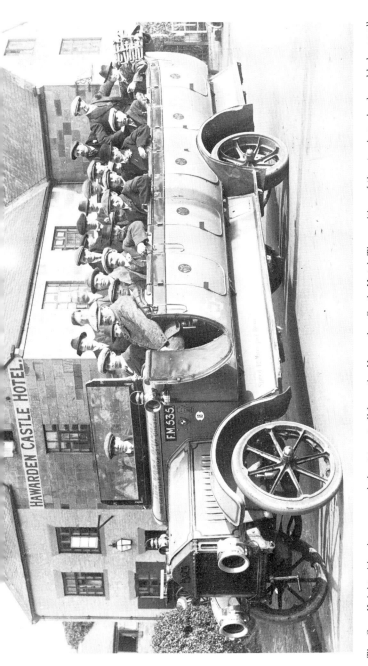

The *Grey Knight* with a happy crowd about to set off from the Hawarden Castle Hotel. The position of the steering wheel enabled a small person to sit to the *right* of the driver on these early machines and there was no legal constraint for some time. The speed would be limited by law to 12 mph but the solid tyres would still raise clouds of dust on the open roads and everyone would probably need a drink and a good brushing down when they got back.

The steady increase in the size of the fleet led to a change away from names for the buses. The *Busy Bee* was the last such, followed by *Number 7* (FM 703) whose identity was spelt out using lettering of a style matching the named vehicles. The Company name was sometimes displayed across the front scuttle. The block lettering with numerals, as seen above, introduced around 1915, continued until 1929 when the oval design was adopted. Number 15 shows evidence of its wartime origins—the Lacre chassis lasted only three years, until the end of the war, and then the body, still numbered 15 and carrying the registration number of the Lacre, FM 1092, was transferred to a new Daimler chassis. Exchanges of this nature were common practice and not illegal at the time.

Sunday morning in the repair shops with cars awaiting attention. The Germaine wagonette can be seen at the right. Doubtless No. 11, a Daimler Y-type, will be paying a visit very shortly, after inspecting the depths of Offa's Dyke!

1919-1929

On Christmas Eve 1918 I was on leave from the Orkney Islands for a few days and was due for demobilisation from the Royal Marines. My father, Claude and I had been talking about various things when Dad suddenly asked me whether I wanted to go ahead with my University training and, if not, what I proposed to do.

In common with all young men at that time and, indeed, after this last war, I felt that it would be best to start doing something for my living straight away and not lose time training—otherwise I should be left behind in the race for jobs. When this was explained to him, Crosland said, "I'm not sure I ought not to insist on your going back to the University, but Claude and I have agreed that if you like you can join the Crosville Company now that there seems to be a chance of expansion. He has seen it through eight difficult years and if you can work with him you can come in and see what you can do."

"All right," I said, "I'll come as soon as ever I am released." Claude looked at me. "Very well, Jim—I'll be in Chester and you can be outside, but you'll have to work. That is understood, isn't it? You can go to Nantwich for a start and the first bus is out at 7.15 a.m. Last bus in 9.45 p.m. week-days and about 11.30 p.m. Saturdays. £3 per week. Will you do it?"

Thus the bargain was made and, I hope, kept, and on 19th January, 1919, I went to Nantwich, finding four buses there, two Lacres and two Daimlers. "Sandbach" was out at 8.30 a.m., "Middlewich" at 9.25 a.m., and the "Two Towns" left at 7.15 a.m. and 7.30 a.m. to work on Crewe Town all day. The Lacres started fairly easily but wouldn't keep going. The Daimlers were more stubborn to start, but seldom gave trouble once they were nice and hot. We used to heat petrol in a tin (God help us!) and pour it into the induction taps whilst somebody was swinging the engine. This ensured a start, but washed the oil off the sleeves, so it was immediately followed by a dose of engine oil and thus all was well. Bill Smith was mechanic, and Mrs. Hughes, who had worked through the war, was in the office. She taught me all there was to know about waybills, which was not much as they were simple affairs—just a card with about eight values down one side and spaces to book in ticket numbers at the end of each trip. No parcels, returns, exchanges, vouchers or any of the modern complications that harass a conductor nowadays. At the end of the day a man was over or short and his punch

In 1919 I went to Nantwich. One of the Daimlers, No. 6, formerly *Busy Bee*, is seen here together with one of the first Leylands, dating this photograph around 1921. The Daimler is working the Crewe-Nantwich service, confirmed by the under-canopy destination board.

was right or it wasn't.

There were very few weekly or other returns, and wage sheet calculations were simple, the rate being 10/4d. per week-day, 12/6d. extra if Saturday was worked, and 15/- if Sunday was worked. No overtime, spreadover or other complications, and it should be noted that Saturdays were paid at well over double time and were popular accordingly. Sundays were paid at about time and a half. Bank Holidays counted as Saturdays. Full week 89/6d.

There was, therefore, plenty of time to get out on to routes and see what was happening, so that before long we were able to start additional vehicles, and in that way the build-up began and went on as fast as Claude could get new buses. For a year at least I kept full hours and learned quite a lot, including what went on in Nantwich at night—especially Saturday night. The first time I heard the heartrending shrieks from Pratchetts Row just round the corner at about 11 p.m. I really thought that there must have been a murder, but apparently the inhabitants of that delectable street were famous for their Saturday evening fights and nobody took any notice except to avoid the place in case one became involved.

The technique of starting a new route was amazingly simple. First of all one travelled over it in a car and decided the places of the fare stages and their mileage. Then we worked out the time table and fare table for one bus, say three or four trips on a week-day and a late one on Saturdays, allowing times for meals for the crew. Handbills were printed announcing the date of starting and details of the service. These were distributed at every house within half a mile of the route, and at the appointed hour the service was launched and was very soon made use of. It was just as easy as that. The bus crew kept the same vehicle as far as possible. They cleaned it, too, and because it was theirs and they were always with it the public got to know the whole outfit. How different times are now!

I soon started going to Mold, Warrington and West Kirby every week to watch similar developments at those places, arriving before breakfast and often staying the night. Claude in the meantime looked after Chester and schemed to get still more vehicles. He had great ideas and Dad backed him up to the hilt. Every year an increase of capital was wanted and obtained and we outside produced the corresponding increase of revenue.

Local authorities licensed vehicles, but not services, so once we got into town we could run anywhere. Some authorities had never adopted the bye-laws and there we simply ran without anybody's permission.

The goods carrying business still went on, but we felt that it ought not to be continued, and that we would do best to sell up and put the money into buses. There were four Foden steam wagons and trailers amongst other vehicles, and it was decided to put them in Edwin Bradshaw's auction in Manchester. They made an average of £1,750 each—about four times what they were worth, and we were duly thrilled.

With part of the money we immediately bought two Rolls Royce cars, and Claude and I each drove one to Manchester and put them in the auction, thinking to be able to do it again, but apparently the market was breaking and we made £25 loss so there were no more adventures of that sort. Incidentally, I sold my 9 h.p. Zenith motor bike there at the same time for £110. I had paid £60 for it four years before.

I felt that I was settling down and, of course, the whole thing was tremendously interesting. On 13th October, 1919, I was made a Director of the Company. Board Minutes consisted almost entirely of allotments of shares to various local people and we easily obtained all the money we wanted.

By 1922 Crosland had spent some sixteen years as Chairman of the Company. Never very strong owing to the weakness of one lung, he spent a lot of time at Valley, near Holyhead, where the sea air seemed to do him good. Winter was always a trying time for him, and for the last few years he had suffered from bad attacks of bronchitis with shortness of breath. He conducted the Annual Meeting in June, 1922, but afterwards found himself too ill to attend subsequent Board Meetings during that year. We were really concerned about him, and not without cause. I remember Christmas 1922, which he spent in bed at 20, Castle Street, Chester. My daughter, Joan, his first granddaughter, had just found her feet at the age of sixteen months and managed to walk across his room from the door to his bedside. He was delighted, after the fashion of all good grandparents, and must have her sit on his bed for a while. But he was very sick. I saw him once again, early in the New Year, sitting on a chair by the fire in his dressing gown. He could not speak much, breathing was too difficult, but he made me sit awhile and tell him how things were. "I'm very ill, this time," he said—and other things too—but I can only remember just those words. He would do no more designing of machines, no more backing of new inventions and new industries, no more strumming on the piano or smoking No. 11 Abdulla cigarettes. He was not yet 65, and he died on 12th January, 1923.

While we had lost our faithful Chairman who had piloted us through the many rocks on which we might easily have been wrecked in the early days, it should not be forgotten that Crosville was not his chief activity. It was really only a sideline, and his executive ability had always been devoted to British Insulated and Helsby Cables (now British Insulated Callenders Cables Ltd.) of which he was the founder. Tom Callender was a friend and a competitor. The two concerns recently joined forces and will find new strength in their amalgamation, but I am sure that they will not forget their past history when the foundations were laid which have put them into a leading position in the world's electrical industry.

I reproduce here an article that appeared in *The Link*, which is or was the official magazine, published by B.I. at that time:

"Mr. George Crosland Taylor was the elder son of the late Henry Dyson Taylor, of Huddersfield, who was one of the pioneers of the Worsted Coating Industry, and it was at his father's works that he received his training, in those early days when the sons of the proprietors were expected to be in the factory, duly clad in their overalls, at 6.30 a.m. and to learn every detail of the business in the most thorough manner.

"He possessed, even in his youth, to an extraordinary degree, a scientific prevision, and when he paid a visit to the Electrical Exhibition held in Paris in 1881 he foresaw some of the great future the electrical industry was to enjoy, and determined to leave the woollen business and enter electrical engineering. Early in 1882 he started, at Neston, a works known as G. C. Taylor & Co., with the intention of making electrical machinery, but during a visit to London he came across a new process for insulating wires with gutta-percha. In those days, when electric light was almost unknown as a commercial proposition, large quantities of gutta-percha insulated wires were used for submarine cables, railway signalling, and Post Office telegraphs.

"It was during this period that he was joined by his brother, Mr. James Taylor, and by Mr. Whiteley, and it was not long before it was found that the geographical position and railway accommodation at Neston were unsuitable, and the works were therefore transferred to Helsby, where the railway facilities were good, and, what is essential in the manufacture of gutta-percha insulated wire, there was a plentiful supply of water at a low temperature.

"Shortly after this, a new private Company was formed known as the Telegraph Manufacturing Co. Ltd., and, in addition to the manufacture of insulated wires, those of telegraph and telephone instruments, batteries, insulators, and many other appliances needed in the electrical trade were started.

"From this it will be seen that Mr. Crosland Taylor was the pioneer of the Helsby Works, and it was in the building-up of the industry here, where initiative and imagination were required, that his valuable qualifications became essential. He planned the buildings and the lay-out of the plant; he designed many of the machines; and in those early days was the sole draughtsman and designer of the Company.

"By the year 1898 the business of the Company had progressed to such an extent that it was necessary to increase the capital, and the Telegraph Manufacturing Co. of 1898 came into existence. The three gentlemen previously named, together with the well-known electrical engineer, Dr. John Hopkinson, forming the Board. The shares were offered to the public, and the issue was largely over-subscribed.

"The firm continued to prosper, and in 1902 negotiations were entered into with a view to amalgamation with the British Insulated Wire Company, of Prescot, who were the introducers of paper insulated cable, now almost universally employed for electrical distribution. These negotations being satisfactorily concluded, the name was altered to the British Insulated and Helsby Cables Ltd., which, though somewhat unwieldy, retains the essentials of the names of the British Insulated Wire Company and of the Helsby Cables, both of which were so well known throughout the world.

"Dr. A. K. Muspratt, of the British Insulated Wire Company, was the Chairman of the new Board, Mr. Crosland Taylor, his brother, Mr. James Taylor, Mr.(now Sir) J. S. Harmood Banner, of the Helsby Company, together with Mr. S. Z. de Ferranti and Mr. J. Carlton Stitt, formed the new Board.

"Mr. Crosland Taylor's activities in the firm subsequent to the amalgamation will be known to all members of the Staff.

"In addition to his work in connection with this firm, he was a Magistrate for the County of Cheshire from 1899, and a member of the Royal Geographical Society. He was also the pioneer of the Crosville Motor Company, which is now one of the largest concerns of its kind in the country, and of which his son, Mr. C. C. Taylor, is now Managing Director.

"All the Staff will feel great sympathy with the family, and great sorrow that Mr. Crosland Taylor was not spared longer to enjoy the results of his pioneer work, and to help them with his advanced ideas, which he was ever pushing forward, to stimulate them to look to the future of the industry, and to keep the B.I. in the forefront of progress in the electrical world; but, in addition to this, there are a number of us who, especially in the past, were in daily contact with him, and knew and loved his kindly, generous, and sympathetic nature, and his readiness to assist anyone who needed his help."

Claude now found himself made Chairman of the Crosville, which was still largely a family concern, and which was growing every year. We held our Board Meetings sometimes at Mr. Gardner's office in Northgate Street where the Odeon Cinema now stands, and later in a room still called the "Old Board Room", Crane Wharf, where the Assistant Traffic Manager now works.

Whilst the vast majority of the money raised was spent on vehicles, we were beginning to consider proper housing for our business, and even bus stations. 1923 and 1924 saw arrangements made for garages at Mold, Warrington and Chester, and in January of 1924 we made a big purchase of Johnny Pye's service between Heswall and Birkenhead. This included all his machines and a fair amount of land right in the centre of Heswall. The loading place in the village was actually off the main road on private property, so here, ready made, was the first condition necessary to the modern terminus. It only required covered platforms and a waiting room and lavatories to make it into the real thing. Thus the station we built in 1924 must have been one of the first in the country.

Appendix No. III shows the dates when depot buildings were bought or put up, and it is interesting to see how they were mostly brought into use during a certain period some time *after* the commencement of the services which operated from them.

Following my father's death it was thought that outside shareholders should be represented on the Board and it was decided to ask an old friend, Mr. E. Gardner, the Company's Secretary and Solicitor, to become a Director, and Mr. Henry Middleton, his chief clerk, to become Secretary. This was on 8th March, 1923, and on 7th June, Mr. John Davies joined us. We then felt that we had a sure basis of representation on which we could safely ask for the new capital which was evidently going to be necessary every year for some time to come.

We were not free from competition during these years. The first serious effort we had to meet was in 1919 from J. M. Hudson who started running between Chester and Ellesmere Port. "Joey" has been a valued member of the Staff for many years now, and his own point of view from the other side of the fence may be interesting to hear. He held the ticket of a Chief Engineer in the Merchant Service but was twice torpedoed in the 1914-1918 war so one can readily imagine that he had great ideas of settling down ashore for a change. This is what he writes:-

"I took my discharge in Liverpool on 23rd August, 1919, after serving both before and during the Great War of 1914-1918 as a sea-going engineer, amd immediately looked round for something to do to earn a living. This did not take long and I commenced running my service from Ellesmere Port to Chester in September, 1919, with two vehicles, a F.I.A.T. and a Studebaker, both ex-Army ambulances which had been re-seated to hold fourteen people.

"At that time the Crosville Motor Company were running a service with Lacre chain-driven buses, from Chester to New Ferry via Ellesmere Port, at approximately a two-hour interval with no service to Ellesmere Port only, this having been taken off as a war measure. The Crosville Chester to Ellesmere Port service was, I believe, the first genuine bus service to be run in Cheshire.

"The service then running seemed to be inadequate, the first bus leaving Ellesmere Port at 10 a.m. and the last from Chester 6 p.m. My idea was to run an hourly service with these small pneumatic-tyred buses from 9 a.m. ex Ellesmere Port to 9 p.m. ex Chester, but this ambitious programme had to be curtailed after the first few days owing to the pneumatic tyre of those days being unable to stand up to the work.

"I was granted a licence by the Ellesmere Port U.D.C. but my first application to Chester Corporation was refused and this caused great indignation in Ellesmere Port.

"It was then found that if I used privately-owned land, or a yard, I could pick up and set down without a licence from the Corporation, and acting on this information I received permission from the then manager of the Coach and Horses Hotel, Market Square, Chester, to use the yard of his hotel for my Chester terminus. The entrance to this yard is almost opposite to the entrance to the Police Station.

"I was still using the hotel as my Chester terminus, and was being carefully watched so that I did not pick up passengers in the open street, but there was no real bad feeling as yet although I knew by now that things would happen. About this time I was instructed to re-apply to the Corporation for licences. I sent in my second application and received a reply telling me to appear before the Watch Committee and state my case on a certain date.

"I arrived in Chester with the late Mr. T. Francis, Clerk to the Ellesmere Port U.D.C., who was to represent me at the meeting, and up to this time I had never even seen the late Mr. C. C. Taylor, the Managing Director of the Crosville Motor Co. Ltd. On arrival at the top of the Town Hall steps I noticed a gentleman standing there alone, and on seeing Mr. Francis he walked over and spoke to him. Mr. Francis then introduced me to Mr. C. C. Taylor, Managing Director of the Crosville Motor Co. Ltd., and walked away. I must say that Mr. Taylor was decent about it — we looked at each other for about a minute, then he merely remarked, 'What the hell did you want to start a bus service for? Why did you not start some other business? You will not get a licence in Chester, and even if you do I intend running you off the road.' I looked at him and I laughed, and so did he, and we walked into the Committee Room together. (This incident I will never forget).

"The Watch Committee, after listening to arguments from both sides, asked us to leave, and a few days later I was informed that my application had been granted. I was given a stand on the Market Square, alongside the Coach and Horses Hotel.

"About this time I was approached by the Vicar of Stoke to run a service from Ellesmere Port to Chester via Stanney, Stoker, Wervin and Upton to Chester, on Tuesdays, Thursdays and Saturdays. I started to run as requested, and worked up a good trade (with no competition as yet). This service coming through Upton village led the Upton people to ask me to run them some trips from the village to Chester and return on Saturdays only, there being no service to the village. They had to walk to the main road and then often enough the main road buses passed them full up. I started this also and received splendid patronage (still no competition).

"Occasionally Mr. Taylor came and spoke to me during my standing time on the Square, on one occasion remaining about one hour, when he got me to talk about my experience as a sea-going engineer—anything but buses. About this time rumours began to circulate that the Crosville were preparing to have a real smack at me, and to make it impossible for me to continue, but how it was to be done was a secret well kept.

"AUGUST 1920. SATURDAY, 14th.

"My driver arrived on the Dock Street stand for the 9 a.m. service, to be told by the few people waiting that *I* had already left with a load. He knew this was not so as I intended to relieve him at 12 noon. He carried on with the service and was told the same thing all along the route. He did not see anything that trip, but on returning told me what people had said on his outward journey.

"At approximately 11 a.m. I was standing opposite the Knott Hotel when a small bus, a stranger, pulled up and the conductor called out 'Chester!' This bus was a Crossley R.A.F. chassis on which had been built a body resembling mine as near as possible, and painted grey the same colour. I realised that real opposition had come and, to make it more convincing, the driver, seeing me standing there, yelled out (I think these were his exact words), 'That you, Hudson? It is our turn now. We will have you off the road before next b————y month.' He was answered by a man in the crowd standing round who shouted back, 'That you will never b————y well do.'

"Only the one Crossley was used at the start, running just in front of my vehicle whenever possible, with orders to follow my service through Stanney, etc. and collect all passengers he could, and so kill

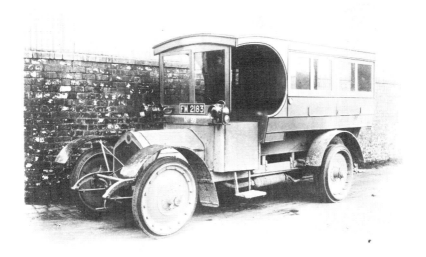

One of the Crossley chasers we obtained from the RFC and which Hudson had cause to remember so well. The lightweight body helped give them a good turn of speed.

that service for me if possible. I am afraid I lost my head a little at this stage and chased round, keeping no time table and losing services. My receipts also suffered a reduction.

"The second Crossley then appeared for a time on Tuesdays, Thursdays, Saturdays and Sundays only, but as time went on and I showed no signs of quitting the two ran daily and a third appeared at week-ends.

"Up to this time the fare from Ellesmere Port to Chester was 8d. single, there being no return fare given, but there had been no suggestion of cutting. Suddenly the Crosville decided to cut the fare to 1s. 2d. return and put the Crossleys on a half-hour service which was for a while strictly kept, hoping, as Mr. Taylor himself told me, to collect all the trade going, but the reverse happened and Ellesmere Port people took advantage of the cheap fare, using the buses as never before, and I found to my astonishment that my receipts began to increase. *There was no doubt about it, the cheap fare and numerous services offered had made the people bus conscious.*

"The peculiar part of it all was that while relations on the road definitely deteriorated, those between Mr. Taylor and myself seemed to become more friendly, and on one (now never to be forgotten)

Our vehicles ended up in the ditch from time to time too.

occasion he came and sat in my bus on the Square and *told me* some of his plans for the future expansion of his Company in Wales and other places. I was so interested that I forgot my service, missed my passengers who all got into the Crossley, and had to return with what few stragglers there were about. I grumbled at him about this, but I never heard him laugh so heartily at any time afterwards as he did at my discomfiture.

"The finish came in rather a peculiar way; some of the Crosville drivers had begun to get quite nasty and started doing dirty tricks on the road, such as cutting in and trying to drive me into the ditch, etc. One day I was coming to Chester with a bus load, one of whom was the wife of the Chairman of the Ellesmere Port Council. The driver of the Crossley following me suddenly shot right in front of me, cutting me so close I had to pull up suddenly. My passengers were much upset and the Chairman's wife, speaking for them all, said she would complain to her husband. The upshot of this incident was a letter received by Mr. Taylor and myself instructing us to meet the Port Council, and try to come to some agreement or they would take steps to stop us both. We duly attended the meeting, each stated his own case (more or less truthfully) and after a discussion the Chairman asked us to come to an agreement about time tables and report back to the Council in one week. I knew Mr. Taylor would never agree to co-operate with me as an equal and was rather downhearted.

"*But* when I left the Council Offices Mr. Taylor was waiting for me. He asked 'Will you come to my office on Monday afternoon to talk this over and write finish to it all?' I, with memories of my last visit, was not inclined to agree, preferring, say, Mr. Francis's office for our talk. Anyhow he smiled and said we would not fall out again, and I agreed to the appointment.

"RESULT.

"Hudson's bus, as it was called in Ellesmere Port, went into liquidation on 27th January, 1922. About three days later I received a message from Mr. Francis *ordering* me to go and see Mr. Taylor at Crane Wharf, so, wondering what it could be this time, I went. My fears that something had gone wrong were dispelled by my reception. Mr. Taylor started by saying that, owing to the increasing number of enquiries being received each day for the private hiring of vehicles, he had decided to open a new department to be called the Private Hire Department, and explained its functions. Then he offered me the position of Manager of this new Department, saying that from the talks we had had and his own observations he thought I could do it and was prepared to back his own judgement. The hard things we had said to each other all came to my mind, and I was speechless, but after a while he went on to say what my duties would be and told me straight out that if I did not make it go he would find someone who would, etc. He gave me two days to make up my mind and let him know. I decided to accept the position, receiving his permission for a few days' holiday first, and so I took up my duties as Hire Department Manager, Crosville Motor Co. Ltd., Crane Wharf, Chester, on 2nd February, 1922.

J. M. HUDSON

In the summer of 1923 a garage proprietor in Crewe named Jim Gibson started running a Ford 14-seater between Crewe and Nantwich just in front of our trips. It was easy to do this, and when he applied to Crewe and Nantwich for licences he got them without question. Our people were wild, and not without reason. It was just as if one had set up a shop and gathered regular customers over a long period, only to have somebody come up and park outside one's shop door with a wheelbarrow full of exactly the same goods as one was selling inside the shop. Generally there was a cut price too and, of course, the public were delighted. If the wheelbarrow was not there on certain days it did not matter because there was always the shop to go to. Our customers were being filched from under our very noses. There was only one

Gibson's White Leyland spent a couple of years in our fleet after the 1923 take-over of his business, though its Benzole days were over.

thing to do and that was to put out a still better and cheaper wheelbarrow and so hoist him with his own petard. It must take the form of a fast bus, and the crew simply had *carte blanche* to stay with Gibson all day. This in turn made Gibson mad and he immediately mobilised certain relatives' money, added it to his own, and bought several more wheelbarrows or rather vehicles, including a Crossley (just as fast as ours) and a Leyland that was much faster. This latter bus puzzled us for some time until we found that it was run on benzole mixture which gave it just that extra turn of speed that was necessary in competition work. All this at a time when we could ill spare anything, especially for such a wasteful purpose, when new services were being established in Wales as fast as we could find machines for them. I was on this work almost day and night, and one day Claude and I went to Leyland and bought a big fire pump engine that would fit in a standard Leyland bus but, of course, was much more powerful. This we put into "No. 72" and introduced it to Gibson's White Leyland. Although we only did four or five miles to the gallon we had an unbeatable acceleration and thus the tables were turned for the moment. This big engine idea was also useful when the hill from Maentwrog to Festiniog gave us such a lot of trouble a little later on.

We bought our last four true charabancs, with side-door entry to each row of seats, in 1924 — so rapidly did motor bus design change that within a few months they were obsolete and by 1928 they had gone. The batch started at No. 12, seen above, but superstition then got the better of us and the next vehicle was designated AC. This practice continued in the Crosville fleet for some years.

Funnily enough there was no cutting of fares, but the hate between us was intense, leading to "incidents", and in one case I saw a deliberate collision between two buses, both of which tried to get out of Prince Albert Street at the same time on a Saturday night.

I used to see Jim Gibson from time to time. He was a stout man of about 50-55, hard as nails, and with a habit of shutting one eye and looking at you out of the other in a fierce sort of way. We didn't seem to be able to come to terms and so it went on for about three years. Eventually he sold us the vehicles and the goodwill in April, 1925, at a reasonable price and we had peace again—at any rate for a time.

It was not until 1929 that once again there was competition on the long-established Nantwich to Crewe route, and when it did come we were up against a much more formidable competitor. In the small village of Willaston between Nantwich and Crewe there was a family named Jackson—father, three sons and a daughter. Sam Jackson senior was getting older, but when a young man he had established a business of running steam traction engines and rollers with all its attendant activities of ploughing, dredging and other things. His three sons, Sam, Hugh and John grew up in the trade and each looked after a particular branch, such as the maintenance of plant, the outside work, etc. The daughter looked after the old man who lived in the farm house which was the nucleus of the considerable business he had worked up. Claude and I went there for lunch one day and afterwards he took us to a big estate near Market Drayton where he was dredging the mud out of a lake in a 3-ton scoop with a traction engine on each side of the water, dragging it to and fro!

Sam Jackson junior told me that he and his brothers had often wanted to change over to petrol, or at least run some petrol vehicles, but the old man wouldn't hear of it. However, now, in 1929, he changed his mind and they started. It was war to the knife and before long the return fare between Nantwich and Crewe was down to 4d. for over ten miles. Private hire rates were cut to pieces and we both lost a lot of money. This went on until February, 1931, when the Road Traffic Act forced us to submit proper time tables and we also agreed that the fares should be put back to a proper figure. I don't know how long the old man would have gone on, but he did well to stick it, as under the Act he was firmly established, and things went on smoothly until 1934.

In June of that year I happened to be talking to him and one of his sons when the subject came up and I asked what his price would really be. He said it would be stiff and named a figure. I think perhaps he was

We were not too happy with the AEC Ys, much preferring the basically similar but for us more reliable Daimler with its sleeve valve engine. Some of the AECs we bought new in 1919 were later transferred to the Colwills fleet in Ilfracombe when we started operations there, but others joined our main fleet as operators were taken over. Busy Bee of Caernarvon ran this 505 model, new to them in 1925, for only a few months before we took over that company and CC 5214 became Crosville 198, and did better, operating until 1931. This photograph was taken at the manufacturers before delivery to Busy Bee and, as I recall, the oval badge, adjacent to the front window pillar, identifies the bodywork as having been built by Strachan & Brown in Acton, west London.

surprised when I asked for time to consider it, but he agreed that a reasonable time should be allowed. The next day I went back to say that we would accept his terms, but to my surprise he did not want to sell. However, he had given his word and I knew that he had always been so straight in his dealings that he would never really go back on it, and of course he didn't.

Of all our competitors I think that S. Jackson & Sons played fairest in every way—I only hope that we did the same by them in spite of the severe struggle we had.

In 1923 also we had to fight Birkenhead Corporation in Parliament over a Bill which would have given them powers to run anywhere outside the Borough with the Ministry of Transport's consent. In 1914 they had obtained omnibus powers in a number of outside areas but were confined to specific routes, and this new attempt to rush the fences was a serious menace to our efforts in the surrounding districts. Claude came over to Nantwich one afternoon and we went off to a footbridge over the L.M.S. main line just on the Crewe side of Madeley station and proceeded to discuss the matter. He had a copy of the Bill with him and in the intervals between watching the trains (a favourite occupation for us) we discussed its implications and decided to oppose in Parliament—an expensive, but not too difficult operation, although there is always a lot of spade work in getting out the information for Counsel.

We had been hearing about similar cases elsewhere and decided to try and engage Lyndon Macassey and Wrottesley as Counsel to take our case; Parliamentary Agents, Rees & Freres.

"To the Honourable the Commons of the United Kingdom of Great Britain and Ireland (in those days) in Parliament assembled.

"The Humble Petition of the Crosville Motor Company Limited under their Common Seal.

"Sheweth as follows..." Then came the main arguments, and finally "Your Petitioners therefore humbly pray, etc., etc." Long live the ancient customs and rights of Parliament! It didn't matter how big Birkenhead Corporation were, or how little we were—our humble prayer would be heard in any case and a fair decision would be given. Such is Parliament, and such we hope it will remain as a safeguard to the rights of all our people.

Birkenhead was thrown out, or rather their Bill was. Our bill (the sort you have to pay) was £658, of which Sir Lyndon Macassey got £194 and Mr. F. Wrottesley £144.

We had both been to London to attend the Committee stage of the Bill, and when it was all over Claude rang up to say he had some sandwiches and was coming over to Nantwich. Of course we went up to Madeley and established ourselves on our favourite bridge. That day we smoked cigars after lunch and watched our trains with a feeling of some satisfaction that for the moment at any rate Birkenhead had been held at arm's length in spite of their size.

"Put not your trust in Councils," Claude suddenly said—this after a silence of some minutes. "Tie them down by agreement if you can, but don't trust them. A different set of men may be in power next year with entirely diferent views—and then what?" We returned via Crewe and called to see old Feltham, the Town Clerk at that time. He seemed pleased that we had won the case, but almost immediately began talking about Gibson who was competing against us in Crewe. "The Council is determined to put a stop to it," he said. We had no answer except to say that we were there first and must protect our interests. He calmed down after a bit but said he was worried because his Councillors were continually pressing him to do something. Finally he showed us the figure of a hare etched on several windows in the Town Hall—it was the name of the architect—Hare. We parted good friends as always.

This fight in Parliament led almost immediately to our first agreement with the Birkenhead Corporation on 26th February, 1924, when we were allowed to extend certain services to Park Station on the Mersey Electric Railway, and so for the first time have access to Liverpool with its three quarters of a million inhabitants.

Developments of this sort were bound to come up, but the old proverb says "God helps those who help themselves," and it was up to us to do the pushing. For years we had seen the teeming mass of people on Merseyside through a glass darkly, and somehow we were determined to get face to face with them. The big Corporations naturally wanted to keep us out, but they were fighting a losing battle.

Two years later, in 1926, Birkenhead against deposited a Bill, this time to enable them to run anywhere within a five-mile radius. Once more we put in a petition and were immediately approached with a view to an agreed Bill. They had bought Arrowe Park and wanted to run out to the place. This seemed reasonable and on 15th March, 1926, we had withdrawn our petition while the Corporation on their part had confined their application to certain agreed routes.

It was a much more sensible way of doing things, and much less expensive. E. W. Tame, the Town Clerk, must have thought so too, and from then onwards there was a different atmosphere in our dealings with them. Mr. Clarke, the Transport Manager, had not forgotten 1924 and remained a little suspicious, I think. He was wise to be cautious but there was really no plot to ruin his transport undertaking, but merely a fight to be allowed to bring our outside people to the centre of the town and, of course, to confine the Corporation to looking after its own people and prevent them trading outside their own area.

In those years we found, too, many examples of local authorities wanting to extend their boundaries and then trying to trade in those extensions. The extension was necessarily at the expense of some other authority, and the trade was obtained from private enterprise. Each case in its way was the lust for power and it still goes on. Government control in war time had developed into grand nationalisation schemes to gather power into the hands of those who are supposed to be our servants, but who will rule us with a rod of iron if they get the chance. Germany did the same thing on a grand scale but the worm turned and they came to grief. Let others take warning.

However, we must return to Birkenhead to complete our story. After

Birkenhead—but not without a struggle! Two of our vehicles stand outside the former Pye premises in Singleton Avenue. The tremendous leap forward in bus design is clearly apparent—both are Leylands but the PLSC1 Lion is much lower and sleeker. Some of these Lions, which later became the 'A' class, gave 22 years' service though the original Leyland bodies were replaced in the mid-thirties.

1926 we dreamed more and more of how nice it would be if, having got to Park Station, we could also get from Chester and Heswall right down to Woodside Ferry. Birkenhead also had a pleasant dream about the extension of their Woodside Ferry to New Ferry tram route to Bromborough and even to Eastham.

We did not know enough about the coming Road Traffic Act, 1930, or I think we would have waited a bit and eventually run through to Woodside for nothing, giving full protection to the Corporation. We could not have been reasonably refused. But as it was we traded in a perfectly good local service between New Ferry and Bromborough in exchange for the Woodside facility, and that was that. We also gave them facilities to come out as far as Heswall, and that was bad. In fact the Corporation was one up on us, and we might as well admit it. Clarke must have been pleased and rubbed his hands. I can see him doing it. The agreement has stood for sixteen years, with a slight variation in 1938, and it might well do so, at any rate from the Corporation point of view. They certainly got a bargain.

There were agreements, too, with other towns — not the spate of such arrangements as control affairs in Lancashire and Yorkshire, but they can be briefly summarised in this chapter.

Wallasey allowed us to come into what is known as Liscard Village in 1926 instead of terminating at Wallasey Village. This was a settlement of our application to run through to the Ferry, and was fair enough, giving the Corporation protection.

Warrington in 1921 imposed a toll of 1½d. per passenger carried over their route or any part of it. This was ruinous and unfair, but it was not until 1931 that the Traffic Commissioners overruled the arrangement and an ordinary picking-up limit was substituted. Later on, in February 1939, when they wanted to buy Pusill's service between Penketh and Warrington, we got our own back by establishing a principle of absolute free trade for us between Penketh and Warrington.

Between Warrington and Liverpool lies Widnes, a martyr to the chemical fumes that used to come from works which never should have been allowed so near the houses. But if the town was not so good, its Council made up for it. We were always well treated in Widnes. The Town Clerk was courtesy itself and the Corporation backed him up. We were given free trade with naturally a toll for their Transport Undertaking. No signed and sealed agreement — simply an exchange of letters, and the thing was done. When one is treated like that one takes more than ordinary care to see that the bargain is strictly honoured. I have many pleasant memories of meetings with Mr. Oppenheim and his Assistant, Mr. McNorton, in their nice warm office in the Town Hall. The two Mr. Woods used to be there too, Transport Manager and Bridge Engineer. For nineteen years—since 1927—there has been no other agreement, so we must have got it right in the first place.

The story of Chester—our home town—is not so smooth. The city is very ancient and rightly jealous of its rights and prerogatives. That is all to the good, but like all other places it derives great benefits from any industries that have made their home within its boundaries. These interests in their turn will be proud of their home, if properly encouraged by the local authority, but there was a period in Chester when there arose some differences between us and the Council. I think it was only the Council, as the people themselves have always supported us right from the beginning. It was the usual tale—private trading versus municipal trading aggravated by the fact that the financial position of the Corporation undertaking was not too strong—indeed a little later on it had to be heavily subsidised from the rates.

I remember the horse tram days when I was a boy, and after them the electric trams from the Station through the centre of the city to Saltney.

In 1929 a Bill was produced according to which trams would be scrapped and Bus Powers were to be obtained for a radius of ten miles. This included Ellesmere Port and many other places to which we had run important services for many years. It was rather a shock, but we had our remedy and proceeded to prepare a Petition against it. Perhaps Clarke of Birkenhead advised Mr. Ellis, the Transport Manager of Chester, that they would never get what they were asking for, but whatever it was, the radius was reduced to three and a half miles, and to this we agreed. Actually buses started running in February, 1930. They had a good bargain and were able to run to Vicar's Cross and other places never touched by the trams in the old days.

As I have said above, Chester Corporation put their first buses on the road in February, 1930, and by June that year it was evident that some sort of agreement must be come to between us if there were not to be long drawn out arguments over every little extension by either side. Accordingly, on 3rd June, 1930, there was a joint meeting in London at which Ashton Davies, Chief Commercial Manager of the L.M.S., was

Chester. The Cross.

An open-top tramcar in Chester, photographed at The Cross around 1903, and just as I remember them rumbling through the narrow streets.

present, and it was decided that we should get out some heads of agreement to try and come to terms.

By October the first proposals were drafted, but the Corporation rather complicated things in June, 1931, by applying to the Traffic Commissioners to run in certain parts of Hoole, having in mind, perhaps, their extension Bill of 1932, but they were refused permission and on 4th January, 1932, the extension Bill was thrown out by a poll of townspeople so that the ground was once again clear to proceed with the agreement. Thus on 1st July, 1932, it was signed and is still in force.

These agreements are common throughout the country, and no two of them are quite the same although they serve the same purpose, which is to provide the best possible service to the public whilst retaining a fair division of traffic as between operators.

But to go back to 1923. I have already explained that we tried to get licences in Northwich in 1912 but we were unsuccessful. That had resulted in a Company being formed called the Mid Cheshire Bus Company which had done fairly well, but they now seemed anxious to sell their undertaking because there were difficulties due to its small size, and the undue proportion of workmen's services which had to be run in that town. On 4th October, 1923, we met them at the Queens Hotel, Chester, and had a long discussion. Claude and I represented our Company and there were about four Directors of the Mid Cheshire. The meeting was cordial, but there was a big difference between us as to the value of their business. I had been there and inspected the schedules beforehand and they seemed to be asking too much, so we left them to think it over. Alas! our skill in these matters was not as good then as it became later, and they simply went elsewhere and got their price—selling to the North Western Road Car Company the next year. We were wild about it, but our wildness was tempered with admiration for our good friend George Cardwell, who had got the better of us on that occasion, and soon after that we met Cardwell at the Abbey Arms and over a friendly glass of beer agreed a pooling arrangement of joint services from Northwich to our territory that has worked well ever since.

Almost at the same time (about November, 1923) I was having lunch

The Mid-Cheshire Company operated some Leyland buses similar to our own, and this one is operating in Urmston, near Manchester. As recorded in the text, Cardwell acquired Mid-Cheshire for the North Western Road Car Company.

with Claude at Crane House on a Thursday as usual when he said "Johnny Pye's in the market." This news was electrifying. For a long time we had looked on his main service from Heswall to Birkenhead with some envy. There it was—bang in the middle of the place where the money came from—and Johnny Pye himself—what a character!—not to speak of the invisible uncle who backed him financially and was pressing him to sell. "How do you know?" I asked. Claude winked an eye. "Never mind about that," he said; "the point is the terms." And then we embarked upon a long discussion as to his cash takings, vehicles, etc. Claude wanted to get him to take some thousands of shares as part payment as we were always short of actual money, and since the Directors' holding was so large we thought it would be quite safe to do this. "Anyway, I'm seeing him to-night, and if I can get him to agree a proper price we'll call a Board Meeting." With that we got up and went our ways.

Sure enough he called the Board Meeting. The price was £25,000 including £7,500 in shares. Date of taking over to be 1st January, 1924. I went down there and stayed at the Victoria Hotel in Heswall, working till midnight every night to get the bus and duty schedules into some sort of order. J. E. Williams came down from Crane Wharf to take charge of the office, and J. F. Burnley joined us a little later as Depot Superintendent. It was difficult to find out exactly what they did, and

A variety of makes and types of bus joined Crosville as a result of takeovers—many had very short lives being non-standard or simply worn out, others were never operated. MA 8259, an Albion new to Pye in 1921, is seen in his colours.

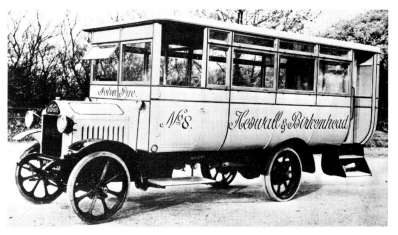

Two of the three Daimlers we acquired in 1916 from the New Brighton Coach Company had interesting lives, being rebodied by Davidsons of Manchester as shown below with replacement charabanc bodies. One was subsequently rebodied for a second time — this time by Leyland, in 1924, after we had rehabilitated it and fitted pneumatic tyres. In this final form it remained in service until 1930.

Wally Wright, our engineer, poses with Claude and our first two Leyland buses in July 1921, just after they were delivered to Chester. Inside No. 61 Harold Jones, a foreman at Chester, watches the proceedings with interest. Jones rose to become our Divisional Manager Wirral after having been at Rhyl. He later became Assistant Traffic Manager under Roberts. These Leylands were G7 models powered by a 36 hp engine and proved extremely reliable — upon the success of these early Leyland vehicles was built a relationship with the Lancashire company which lasted unbroken for 20 years until Leyland's output was diverted entirely to the war effort. This particular body design was known as the Edinburgh type; soon we would have a design of our own and carrying our Company's name.

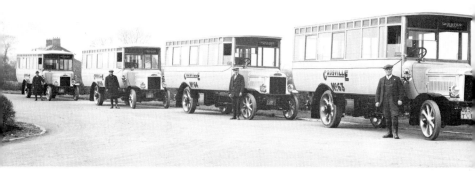

The mixture as before, and a further four vehicles stand with our drivers ready to leave Lancashire for Crane Wharf. By 1930 over 360 more Leylands, representative of almost every model that Company had then built, would make their way to Chester. When production temporarily ceased in 1941 we had purchased over 1300 Leyland chassis and fitted them with bus and coach bodywork of a wide variety of styles, many built by Leyland at its famous South Works.

still more difficult to make the old buses run, but the route was good and more than worth the money—even then. Now it is worth about four times the price.

But there was no Road Traffic Act, and Alfred Harding started in against us. We applied the usual methods and kept him in check, but the whole thing was wasteful and in January, 1925, we bought him out and began to consolidate the route.

H. H. Merchant, in charge of West Kirby, joined Heswall to his district and so became responsible for the Wirral generally, including New Ferry where I used to arrive at 7 a.m. one morning a week and have tea and cake in the office with H. C. Buchanan, our Superintendent there at that time. We discussed the traffic at Planters Works, inspected the Depot and then up into the old "T" model Ford and on to West Kirby to see Merchant.

It was obvious that the Wirral services were to be our foundation and on them would be built the routes extending right out into Wales, both North and Central. Traffic in the summer was grand, and not too bad in winter. We bought New Ferry Depot, and more land at Heswall and West Kirby, and applied for licences at Aberystwyth. The answer was no. That was in November 1923. We promptly placed an order with Leyland for new vehicles to the tune of £32,400 and leased a shed at Barmouth from Sydney Beer who owned a laundry there. 1924 was going to be a good year if we could make it so and in May that year our appeal at Aberystwyth succeeded and we were in, together with the G.W.R. and Corris Railway who were already running, so we agreed our routes with them and there was no undue competition. It will be seen in Appendix No. II that we opened routes all along the Cambrian Coast during that year and we used up all the available buses.

Things at home were not neglected. My mother, Mrs. G. Crosland Taylor, and Dr. J. G. Taylor had joined our Board in April, and Claude must have had so many schemes in his head that he hardly knew which way to turn. He had leased a large plot of land for seventy-five years from the Corporation to provide a Depot for Chester. It was just by Crane Wharf and in the right place, since up to then our Chester service buses had operated from an open yard adjoining the repair shops.

The Welsh extensions began to give us an insight into the Welsh character that is gravely lacking in most English people who live more than a few miles from the border. They also gave us opportunities to explore that wonderful country which we should otherwise never have had. The mountains, the woods in the autumn with their changing colours, and the common or garden weather which is never twice the same in the same place. Even now, after all these years, there are fresh by-roads to explore and new conditions to experience—all in the course of business too. Places to have meals—sites for picnics—the single line railways, and up till fairly recently the narrow gauge railways. Floods and droughts. You may find them all there.

But to come to earth, I must say that the bus services are, with few exceptions, pitifully thin, and the houses in villages of any size are ugly and without imagination. One wonders why that is so when the people are so full of music and poetry, but there it is. Still, one soon gets away from the badly designed houses and into the country again.

The Welsh bus crews are notoriously self-sufficient and reliable. They do not need nursing. They are in fact rather fine people who make the bus service their own even though they are working for others. Their natural suspicion and their independence are due to generations of men having to fend for themselves against the original Saxons who drove them into the west. For the same reason they are reserved and distrustful of the English, but once they open their hearts to you they are very lovable characters and loyal to the core. We have many men of that sort—and some bad ones too—but they make up for the thin receipts.

Thus it was possible to send a vehicle to a place like Barmouth or

The growing Crosville company depended on its ability to move people efficiently, and bigger buses with more seats were part of the strategy. The 1922 purchases included three of these fully-fronted dual-door models — this was the Crosville body type mentioned earlier. Forty seated passengers could be carried and the driver was positioned further forward than in previous models — passengers willing to brave the noise and heat could sit 'up-front' with him though in hot weather it was not to be recommended. Soon the driver would be located in a cab alongside the engine, segregated from the passengers completely — this semi-forward-control model was a sort of half

Aberystwyth and give it to a driver and conductor as a sort of a tool to work with and then go away for six months and forget about it. They seemed to get over all sorts of difficulties and the services were run like clockwork. Many of the men who came in 1924 are still with us—mellowing a little, perhaps, but they remain the backbone on which the rest of the body has been built.

Every Board Meeting we discussed the Cambrian services and were told what was happening.

In 1922 the first Sick Club had been formed at Nantwich, and this was natural in that the Crewe area was very strong in such matters. I don't know who thought of it first—anyway it was started at 6d. per week, benefit being 15/-; and it was found that the amount of sickness experienced made the scheme just right from the financial point of view. An extra 2d. per week was found to cover all ordinary hospital cases, and this led to social activities and one or two concerts and shows at the Town Hall, both at Nantwich and Crewe. A small mess room—the first—was built at Nantwich Depot and lo and behold there was a billiards table of a sort, a canteen or rather a shop for sweets and cigarettes, and other things including many surreptitious card games

More powerful 40hp engines helped overcome the more daunting hills. Numbers 89 and 90 of 1924 were so equipped and the higher bonnet line will be noted. Solid tyres are still the order of the day and hats are optional; most of our men preferred caps.

Llandrindod Wells in 1924, with the three Leylands allocated to the depot there ready to depart for Rhayader, Builth Wells and New Radnor. Notice how the Leyland bodywork has been adapted to fit the three different chassis models.

on a Friday night. However, it was historic from the Crosville point of view in that it was an acknowledgement of the fact that social activities of a community of employment were necessary and we see them very much more developed at the present day.

In February, 1924, Festiniog—Portmadoc route was opened and proved good except that the hill up to Blaenau Festiniog was a thorn in our side. A good thing we had not got the old Herald to start it with—or some of the other old machines either! The prevailing wind was a following one up the hill, and we might have considered runing on our own steam from the boiling water in the radiators, but it paid, nevertheless, and I suppose a serious blow was struck to the light railway which had run so delightfully down the mountain side for so many years. Bob Owen was sent from West Kirby to take charge at Blaenau since he was a native of those parts. The best and most powerful buses were provided and the hill was conquered.

We hoped that year to get going in Aberystwyth after the refusal of licences in 1923, and in May we had appealed successfully against their refusal, so that by July we were able to start at last. Aberystwyth is a town with practically no freehold property except the railway station. It is owned by the Corporation. They are on a good thing because when a lease runs out they renew at an increased ground rent, and improvements are easy to control. The G.W.R. and Corris Railway (now one) ran buses in from south and north respectively. Our first effort, therefore, was from the east—Devil's Bridge, a remarkable place about twelve miles away, but things were thin, except in the high season, when they were uncomfortably thick. Capt. Roberts was Superintendent, and Geoffrey Shiers, whose headquarters were at Barmouth, used to pay visits as he was nominally in charge of Cambrian Coast services.

That whole year was a mad rush to start new services and we were hard put to it to provide vehicles. A glance at Appendix No. II will show what we did, including some very important routes that were opened simply by running a service—no heavy goodwill payments such as take place nowadays, although in December we did pay £900 for D. M. Jenkins' business at Aberayron in order to get on to the route.

The Municipal and General Workers' Union were organising our people at one or two places and we had dealings with them, but not for all Depots. Wage rates in Wales were much lower than in England. This was general in all trades since trade was so thin there that English rates simply could not be paid. At one time we had as many as five grades of wages—now there is only one, but this result could never have been achieved if it had not been for the financial support from the English area. The Welsh services could not have stood by themselves except at cut wage rates and a standard of vehicle maintenance much below that rightly required by modern practice in these things. Anglesey was the worst paid district, although we did not go there until 1930. The Transport and General Workers' Union enrolled some of our men too, but we were paying good rates and we attracted the best men, or so it seemed.

Saturday was the best of days—all bus people know this. As I have said before, we paid 22/10d. for Saturday against 10/4d. for other week-days, and so there was no difficulty in getting extra work done on the one day that really mattered. Bank Holidays were paid as Saturdays, so there again everybody worked themselves to the bone with one eye on any possible rain clouds and the other eye on the people waiting to be carried.

Early in 1925 uniforms were started and there were more cleaners, because in the early days the crew cleaned their own buses at most places. Uniforms, however, had to be kept smart and so bus cleaning became a separate thing, to be studied scientifically and brought to a fine art. We thought that pressure washers were the right thing and much money was spent on equipment. We diligently forced water at 300 lbs. per square inch right into the joints and cracks of our body work and before it could dry out we forced in still more. Muddy buses received the full force of water on their panels, forcing the grit particles into the varnish and doing no end of damage. This precipitated a sudden reversion to dry cleaning with various preparations, but it was too late and a few years later dry rot cost us a great deal of money even though much of it was due to steam-dried timber that was extensively used for body building about that time.

To return to Trade Unions, however. Volumes could be written on this subject. There were the craft unions, membership of which was a man's trade mark—a guarantee that he could do his job. They were and still are jealous of the standard of work done by their members. Not quite as jealous now, perhaps, because of the dilution which was necessary in two world wars, but there was always the feeling of skill connected with them, and that is a fine thing from all points of view. Somewhat different from these were the more politically-minded unions, and it was the Transport and General Workers' Union to which the vast majority of our people eventually belonged. Here membership

A cloud of exhaust fumes drifts across Crewe Square as one of the venerable Daimlers, now equipped with pneumatic tyres as were many of our vehicles from 1925 onwards, and fitted with a new body by Leyland Motors, warms up ready for the off. The boys watch with interest.

denoted the fact that a man was employed doing a certain thing, but it did not mean that he was an expert at his job. Perhaps we ought to have instituted some sort of training course ourselves, but we were in a hurry and actual training was primitive in the extreme. A conductor, for instance, was given tickets and a fare list and told to get on with it. A driver was given a time-table and, provided he could change gear, had to make his way as best he could. It was remarkable how well they did, but neither Union nor Company took the slightest interest in the finer points of their jobs. The Union had a member and the Company had an employee, the man had some work, and that was that.

Whilst there was no provision as yet for teaching men their trade, I think that even then the egg was laid, and although it would take a prodigious time to hatch, it was going to produce some method of training and realisation that driving and conducting buses is a skilled job. Once this point became recognised there was going to be a new interest in life for thousands of busmen all over the country.

Our first trouble occurred over the Union's Political Levy. A good Trade Unionist who was not Labour as regards politics had to pay 1d. per week towards the Labour Party funds. On 25th May, 1925, one such man at Crewe refused to pay the levy. The others refused to work with him. Driver P. Platt (now Inspector Platt) was promptly sacked as a result of his three-hour strike, but just as promptly reinstated and we heard no more about it, but there was unrest in the country generally which was to lead to the General Strike in 1926. We had an agreement with the Transport and General Workers' Union which was then broken in common with all other such agreements, and our relations with Trade Unions were put back a long way. The General Strike itself affected all English and some Welsh Depots, but in the far parts of Wales, where they don't take any notice of what the English do, there was no strike and things went on much as usual.

Crewe was a strange town in April, 1926, whilst the strike was on. Crowds of people gathered on the Square ready to overturn any bus that showed its nose. One did, for some reason or other. They wanted to burn it, and were about to do so when one of our men made a speech from the roof asking them what would become of his job if his bus was burnt. This idea tickled the crowd and the same man drove it back to its Depot without further fuss.

The days passed. We cleaned everything we could clean and mended everything we could mend. We had endless talks at garage doors as to what it was all about and what the outcome would be, and then all of a sudden the end came, and we found ourselves back at work in what seemed to be a sort of anti-climax. Nobody, except perhaps Ernest Bevin, knew exactly how it had happened, but we were thankful to get back and earn money again. For many it had been an anxious time with no wages coming in and mouths to feed.

Once the strike was over we were in the thick of it again. We were pressing to get into the centre of Merseyside, and in May, 1925, we managed to push right into Liverpool by extending services from Garston Tram Terminus to Canning Place—not an ideal centre, but only a few hundred yards from the top of Lord Street. We stood by the old Customs House, and in spite of the bad surroundings trade was brisk, because the people of Liverpool wanted these services and were going to have them.

Riding was going to be more comfortable, too. All new vehicles were on pneumatic tyres, and it was decided in July to convert solid-tyred machines as fast as it could be done.

Pneumatic tyres were fitted to all new vehicles purchased from 1925—many older vehicles were progressively converted. This example carried 32-seat Leyland-built bodywork, with access to a roof luggage pen via the rear-mounted ladder.

Mr. S. E. Garcke had tentatively proposed some sort of amalgamation with the Wrexham Transport and Llandudno Coaching Companies, but we could not agree on terms and the matter was dropped for the time being. It was rightly thought that the only satisfactory way to work the North Wales territory was to have it all under one control. Traffic was so thin in the winter that it looked as if it would have to be done that way, and Mr. Garcke, with his fine experience of these things, was right. I think we would have to come to terms if we had not been so very busy on the development of our own area, and as a matter of fact this result was achieved only a very few years later.

We became established at Caernarvon by the purchase of the Busy Bee Service in November, 1925, and Capt. Edward Roberts joined us at the same time and went to Aberystwyth, where we had opened services, and began to prepare for the next season.

Early the following year (1926) we invested more money in premises as well as looking after an ambitious new vehicle programme. There was extra land at Heswall, a Depot at Blaenau Festiniog, and then the old Roller Skating Rink in Upper Northgate Street, Chester. Finally, Claude and I went to an auction sale in Mold and spent £1,600 in buying a portion of the Loggerheads Estate which was being sold in lots by Mr. Poole of Marbury, near Whitchurch. Loggerheads was a favourite beauty spot, some three miles from Mold on the Ruthin Road, and we had developed a good bus service there from Birkenhead, especially in the summer, but the tiny public house known as "We Three Loggerheads" was quite unable to provide teas, etc. for these people, nor did they show any inclination to do so. We had discussed the possibility of providing some sort of tea house ourselves, if it could be done without spoiling the place. "Anyway, let's go to the sale," Claude said to me when we had talked it over from all angles. So we went and sat on hard chairs in a dingy room in Mold. There was the pub above mentioned—there were various odd fields—two or three cottages and the woods—yes, the woods were the thing. We would like to have the woods and the rock and the old lead mine shafts, not to speak of part of the ancient Leete walk. It was all rather fascinating to think about as we sat on those very hard chairs. Even the pub had possibilities, but it went for £5,000, a price out of all proportion to its turn-over in beer, and no land with it, so we left it alone. However, we bought two fields and the woods and came out £1,600 poorer. What was to be done with them? We toyed with the idea of forming a syndicate to run the place. We should need two or three thousand

The way it used to be—independent buses in Castle Square.

pounds extra to build what we wanted in the way of a tea house, but we might be accused of trying to make money out of our own Company, so in the end the Directors took it over and the syndicate idea was dropped.

Although the three pieces of ground we bought were complicated by numerous peculiar rights of way, we managed to sort it all out and build a tea house which was later extended and could easily accommodate parties of 100 people or more. The woods were thrown open to the public, and we had bands and free entertainments in the summer. On the other hand, we never made any money out of it because of the short season, and the place had to close in the winter. The bus service from Birkenhead was doubled, however, and that was what we really wanted.

Sick Clubs had started in 1922. These had led to social clubs of various sorts, and there seemed to be a general desire to play football and billiard matches — also to have entertainments. This always meant hiring rooms outside. We certainly had no facilities ourselves. Some depots had a "men's room" — usually a dingy and quite unsuitable place for recreation. To tell the bare truth, our education in this respect was sadly lacking and we did not realise that to get the best work out of people they must be given not only an interest in what they do, but they must have some social contact with those with whom they work. This cannot possibly be done without the goodwill and practical support of the management, and money so spent will bring a very adequate return to the standard of work. Thus in March, 1927, premises were rented above Burtons' shop in Foregate Street, Chester, and occupied by a Crosville Club, fully licensed and equipped with billiards tables, etc. This club ran for a number of years, but it was gradually killed by its position away from the centre of our work. There was a high rent to pay too, although I think it could have been paid if the location had been right. Anyway, we learned our lesson, and after that clubrooms were always placed right close to the places where we worked — but that was not until 1937.

In June, 1927, the Cheshire Lines suddenly found that some of their main road bridges were not strong enough for heavy vehicles to cross. Other railways found the same thing and we were faced with perhaps having to stop or divert all services over Helsby, Hartford and Meols bridges. The latter was most important since there was no possible diversion and it was on the route from West Kirby to Birkenhead. We thought that perhaps it was a policy move by the railway who were

Although the charabanc was becoming outdated by the mid-1920s, convertible bodies were still popular. The new style of bodywork was dubbed 'all-weather' and naturally we purchased examples for the new long-distance coach tours. This 1927-built PLSC Lion carries dual-doorway bodywork with a folding hood. The driver is now firmly in his place — only a few more 'normal-control' examples will be bought where he will be able to sit with the customers.

preparing their 1928 Bill for road powers, but experts declared that the bridges were truly weak, and so something had to be done about it. At Helsby and Hartford we made diversions, and so handed the baby to the local authorities, but at Meols Claude took the bull by the horns and asked how much it would cost to strengthen the bridge. We paid £1,140 and that was that. Earlier in 1921 we had paid £3,000 to widen the road between Upton and Moreton in the Wirral, and only a few years ago we paid £700 to lower a road under a bridge to take double-deckers on an important route. Perhaps these payments should not have been made, but on the whole it was best to say good-bye to the money and get on with our job rather than wait and lose revenue in the meantime.

1927 too saw land bought in Liverpool for a Depot and the buying-out of what we thought was the last opposition in Crewe—Messrs. D. Taylor, and Harry Peach of Haslington.

There was an undercurrent of nerves in the industry gradually creeping in with the approach of the new Railway Road Powers Bill. In 1924 they had been thrown out, but this time it was feared that they would get their powers and, if so, what then? They could hardly be refused licences by all local authorities. They had unlimited finance for competition in any chosen area, and there was no doubt that during the last eight years they had been hard hit and were buzzing about like angry wasps in a nest when one had put one's foot over the entrance. It looked as if in 1928 we should have to take our foot off, and then we should certainly get stung, and badly. During the first months of that year we held on hard, but the tide was running strongly against us and I think all operators must have known in their hearts that the end was near, and there would have to be a show-down.

On 3rd August, 1928, the Bill received the Royal Assent and for a time there was silence. The great ones were evidently thinking it over. Perhaps they were even numbed by their tremendous success. We on our part were afraid that we might not get the new capital that we still required to develop our area. Claude and I went to the Liverpool Stock Exchange and were told that we had every chance of getting our shares quoted, so the matter was put in the hands of Gamon & Stacey, brokers, and early in 1929 we went on the list at 26/- per pound share. This was encouraging as we had only been getting 23/- for new shares issued. We had also accepted a 5% reduction in wages and salaries in August, 1928—a sort of tightening of the belt ready for the coming fight with the railways.

The Lion was one of Leyland's great successes, and was available in two versions, both of which entered the Crosville fleet in quantity. This is the Long Lion or, to give it its correct title, PLSC3. The new livery of red, lined out with gold leaf, made these vehicles very distinctive. Although many fleets operated similar buses for well over a decade we disposed of some of ours after only five or six years and had the rest fitted with new bodies in a vast rebodying programme organised with Eastern Counties at Lowestoft. We also rebuilt some of the normal control Lioness models to PLSC3 specification to allow them to be similarly rebodied. This rebodying created considerable standardisation at a time when the fleet had also included a somewhat motley assortment of vehicles taken over from other operators. In the 1935 reclassification of vehicles, where different types were allocated different letters of the alphabet, the Long Lions became the 'B' class. many outlasting the second war.

It took them four months to think it over and then at the beginning of 1929 we were approached by the L.M.S., probably because we were one of the largest independent omnibus companies in existence at that time. On 5th February, 1929, I joined Claude at Crewe Station on an early train and we travelled to London—first class, and *free* for the first time in our lives. We had two free tickets to go for an interview with the L.M.S. at Euston Hotel. It was quite unforgettable. We were shown to a private room on the ground floor where there was a large table. Ashton Davies was in the chair as Chief Commercial Manager, and Mr. W. P. Bradbury as his Roads Assistant, Ernest Taylor, Chief Accountant, and representing the G.W.R. that memorable character, Mr. R. H. Nicholls, Superintendent of the Line. There were others, too, whose names I do not remember.

The subject was the proposed offer to be made to all Crosville shareholders by the L.M.S. in order to buy the concern right out and enable them to see what it felt like to become an operator on a fair scale. We argued it all ways. We nearly walked out when Ernest Taylor made certain disparaging remarks, but it was all in the game. We had a magnificent lunch served on the same table, then talked still more.

We came home that night with a offer in our pockets of 27/6d. per share. In the meantime we were to proceed with ordinary development as if nothing had happened. There were other offers by speculators, but these were all turned down and the Board decided to recommend the shareholders to accept. Claude and I were to continue in the employment of the L.M.S. and the rest of the Staff would be taken over *en bloc.* Were we right in doing this or not? It is easy to be wise after the event. The alternative might have been unlimited competition. The Road Traffic Act was still more than a year away. It would have protected us, but we didn't know that at the time. I think we played for safety under the circumstances, but the L.M.S. drove a hard bargain and have done well out of their investment. Even they did not know what the future held in store for them any more than we did, but they were wise enough to leave the management to the experts and immediately to foster co-ordination between the two forms of transport. How that was done is related in the next period of our history. Suffice it to say that the name "CROSVILLE" remained, and the spirit of Crosville, too, for that matter. There is value in a name. It costs nothing, but people swarm round it like bees round their queen. And so we remained Crosville and embarked on a new era of our existence that brought great developments.

In 1927 we took over A & R Motors which gave us the opportunity to link Portmadoc and Pwllheli. A & R Motors originated in Liverpool, and Gustav Roberts, who was also connected with Bangor Blue, had been precluded from operating coaches in the Liverpool area through his connections with Lancashire United. He extended his activities to be outside the agreement area. As well as the service the local staff (but not the vehicles) were retained and continued in our employ for many years, as seen in these two illustrations, before and after the take-over.

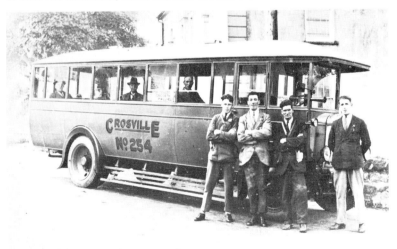

Six magnificent six-cylinder normal-control Lioness models were added to the coaching fleet in 1929. They carried either 24 or 27 passengers in the dual-doorway bodies which had been built by United Automobile's coach building factory at Lowestoft. The ownership of this factory later passed to Eastern Counties and remains, Eastern Coach Works Ltd. Many of our buses and coaches would be built in that factory over the years. Crosville tradition was maintained with this batch of vehicles, for although they were numbered from 12 to 17 the letters AC graced the second vehicle.

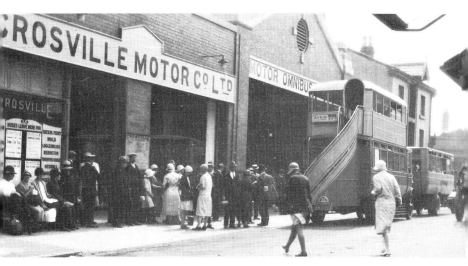

The early bus fleet was almost entirely single-decked and over the sixteen years we had been running our services great strides had taken place in design, performance and reliability. Not until 1928 did double-deck design catch up. The Leviathans of 1926—our first new double-deckers—were ungainly vehicles, and unable to take advantage of the pneumatic tyre because it had not reached the stage where it was available for the weights imposed by a double-decker bus. One is seen above at New Ferry. In 1927 a brilliant engineer at Leyland designed a new bus with sunken side gangway which reduced the body height sufficient to allow passage below the main railway bridges which abound on our routes. It was mounted on the new lower-frame Titan chassis—with pneumatic tyres—and overnight revolutionised the bus industry.

1929-1935

Yes, there was no doubt about it. From 1st May, 1929, the Crosville belonged to the L.M.S. We had taken the decisive step and there was no going back. "A bird in the hand is worth two in the bush," Claude had said one day on Madeley railway bridge when we had discussed whether it was best to sell or stick. "We might be perfectly all right," he went on, "but on the other hand we might not, and we can't risk other people's jobs or the shareholder's money." This seemed a sound argument from one noted for his conservative outlook on life. It was like backing a horse for a place instead of a win. One got a better chance of obtaining something out of the deal even if the odds had to be sacrificed to do so.

I was inclined to risk more and remain independent, and as things turned out we should have been all right, but then it is easy to talk after the event. On balance, therefore, Claude was correct in his judgement of the facts as they stood, although even he had doubts every now and then—I could tell that by the way he talked about it. The point was that we had no right to risk other people's money, and we didn't. The shareholders came out with a good profit and there were no complaints.

"He who pays the piper calls the tune." The L.M.S. had paid up straight away, although the money was not shared out until the end of the year, since voluntary liquidation takes time. First of all then, they decided to keep the goodwill attached to the name, and we were known as L.M.S. (Crosville). A few vehicles had the actual L.M.S. crest put on them but that was rather elaborate and in any case did not convey our real name to the public. So an oval design was adopted with the words L.M.S. (Crosville) and we were still known by the old name "Crosville"—praised and reviled in turn according to circumstances. This was a good thing because I think that the vast majority of employees had some pride in the name.

Whilst we carried on, the Railway Company negotiated direct with Brookes Bros. of Rhyl, U.N.U. (You Need Us!) of Llangefni and Mona Maroon of Holyhead. They bought all three concerns at prices which were out of all proportion to their value and which hung rather a deadload of capital on to us in the form of goodwill, but they were ours and we were told to work the whole thing into one concern. Thus we

From late 1929, our Titans had a re-designed rear, with enclosed staircase. There was general concern in the industry about how passengers would escape should such a vehicle overturn onto its nearside and the cut away doorway was designed with this in mind. This 1929 Show vehicle incorporated a folding ladder which could be lowered from the upper-deck in emergency—the hinged rear emergency exit window was introduced shortly afterwards as a more reliable alternative. The new oval fleetname design replaced the previous block style in use since 1914.

floundered through 1929 and the early part of 1930 trying to straighten up these adjustments and waiting for we knew not what.

Negotiations must have started at more or less the same time between the various railway companies and the Tilling and British Electric Traction groups in London. It was quite evident that some agreement would have to be made between them. As we all know now, it was finally arranged that the omnibus groups would sell to the railways a number of shares in each omnibus company equal to that held by the largest shareholder—in many cases that meant half, but in no case did it mean control. Tilling and B.E.T. were to be responsible for the operating because of their experience, and the railways would have suitable representation on the Boards of Directors. The Chairman in each case would be appointed by the omnibus groups. Thus the L.M.S. would put Crosville into the pool and sell half their interest to Tilling and British Automobile Traction Ltd. A new company would be formed called Crosville Motor Services Ltd. of which half the shares were to be held by L.M.S. and the other half by Tilling and British, the Chairman to be found by the latter. Claude was to be Managing Director, appointed as an L.M.S. nomination.

And so on 1st May, 1930, the period of uncertainty came to an end, and the new Company was launched, the first Directors being W. S. Wreathall, Chairman, G. Cardwell, C. D. Stanley, Ashton Davies, O. Glynne Roberts and Claude, the last three representing the L.M.S.

I record this rather dry information because it must be recorded to show how the new set-up came into being—how Crosville Motor Co. Ltd. became Crosville Motor Services Ltd. after an L.M.S. *interregnum* period of just one year from 1st May, 1929, to 30th April, 1930. It was as if we had been in a train passing over a rather uneven bit of track with a slow speed limit, and then had come out on to the good permanent way where we could make up for lost time.

Old Man Wreathall, as we called him, was a remarkable person with an extraordinarily agile brain. A man of few words—his letters rarely ran to more than four or five lines. He never used adjectives—said they were unnecessary. Claude was uneasy at first, but they soon understood each other, and things went ahead rapidly. I did not know him well until several years later.

W. S. Wreathall,
Chairman from 1930-1939.

One of the results of the LMS take-over was the transfer of some Albion coaches to our fleet. Although we had by then standardised on Leylands the Albions performed well and remained in service until 1937. A new style of lettering for the coach fleet had been adopted, as seen here, and complemented the smart green and grey livery also recently adopted.

I have mentioned the three L.M.S. purchases made during their year of tenure, and it would be as well to describe these a little more fully but they were made at prices which were high and we in turn felt their weight financially for a number of years. They had to be bought and we thought that they could have been obtained very much cheaper if our advice had been sought in the first place.

On 4th November, 1929, Sir Robert Thomas, Chairman of the Seaside Resorts and Development Co. Ltd., sold the Mona Maroon omnibus services to the L.M.S. for a figure about five times its value. It consisted of some eighteen buses of various vintages and £8,400 annual takings at 5.1d. per mile with alleged costs of 4d. per mile without depreciation. Conductors got 12/6d. per week—a scandalous state of affairs. We were given this information and told to take over the management. Anglesey bus services were and are notoriously thin. The Mona Maroon assets were even thinner since we found most of the vehicles entirely unsuitable or unserviceable. The stocks of spares were obsolete. Tyres were bad and the whole concern was on its last legs unless a lot of money was spent on it at once. However, there it was and we had to make the best of it. Capt. Roberts took charge and this is what he says about it:-

"On 4th November, 1929, I proceeded to Holyhead to take over the concern known as Mona Maroons which operated services principally on the north end of the island.

"I took over six Albions, two fabric-bodied Chevrolets, two Dennis, one G.M.C., two taxis (Chevrolet and Minerva), also three garages, one which was used for parking private cars, another used as a repair and sales depot for the light car business, and the third was the bus depot which consisted of two galvanised sheds placed in a garden with an old house in the centre of the garden as an office.

"The concern did a great deal of light car work, most of this being obtained from travellers proceeding to Ireland who left their cars at the garage for repairs, overhaul, etc. which they collected on their return, sometimes days, and sometimes weeks or even months after. In fact, one or two cars were left there from time to time and the owners never returned. The whole concern was run in a very slip-shod manner. On the bus side they had very little experience in bus operation and the services were run very haphazardly.

"Some concern had been caused by the entry to the island of the 'U.N.U.' (You Need Us) Motor Services, who had established a depot at

Leyland followed their PLSC Lions with a new range of single-deckers to complement the all-pervading Titan. The Tiger was a six-cylinder model which we used for express or long-distance work, and No. 370 carried a 25-seat dual-purpose Leyland-built body with comfortable seating as befitted its role. Luggage was still carried on the roof. The matching four-cylinder model was a new Lion, and No. 389 was clearly destined for lesser things. Thirty-five seats, a single recessed doorway and simpler livery mark the difference between the two versions.

Llangefni and were running in competition with the Royal Blue Motors between Llangefni and Holyhead on the main road. The Mona Maroons were operating on the old road via Trevor and it was feared that they were very shortly to be subjected to severe competition.

"The buses were, of course, in a dreadful state, except for the Albions, and in order to re-organise and carry on the services an odd assortment of vehicles was sent from Brookes' fleet at Rhyl, which was of a variety of makes and colours. The services were very soon tidied up and the light car business repairs, etc. more or less disposed of, and the huge stocks of unsaleable stores scrapped. The garages were cleared, including Rhos-y-gaer, the old house was taken down and a proper bus Depot built. The car hire business was retained.

"There was nothing outside the normal procedure that took place except that I can recall an incident which occurred when a large yacht arrived in the harbour with lighting trouble. I believe the yacht was owned by Mr. Scott, the Editor of the *Manchester Guardian*. We were asked if we could instal a new lighting plant, and as it happened to be over a week-end it was not possible to get in touch with Chester. We took on the job and obtained a complete new plant from a firm in Manchester. This was collected on the Saturday and as we had a marine fitter the whole thing was installed on the yacht over the week-end and she was able to sail on the Monday. The job we undertook cost somewhere in the region of £120. Needless to say, the owner of the yacht was delighted with the service given."

E. ROBERTS

Next came the U.N.U. Motors of Llangefni, bought from W. Webster of Wigan on 1st January, 1930. Mr. Webster had stepped in at the right time as far as he and his two sons were concerned. They had all worked like the very devil to gain a foothold, and then sold to a buyer who was somewhat inexperienced in the value of such businesses, but was determined to have them at any cost. I shall not mention the figure but it was worth perhaps half of what was paid. Here we found things not quite so bad, but Llangefni garage had been bought without full possession since the first thing we found was the existence of a lease of part of it to somebody else. Luckily nothing came of this, but the railway's buying fever took no notice of such details.

Finally there were negotiations with Brookes Bros. of Rhyl. On 29th December, 1929, they met the L.M.S. at Colwyn Bay and discussed prices. They had started a small business in 1912 and gradually worked things up in a very enterprising manner. Buildings were put up by direct labour in a rather unorthodox way, but takings were good and wages small. There was a fine disregard for any regulations—for instance many double-deckers were 8 feet wide, and there was war to the death between Brookes Bros. and Red Dragon of Denbigh.

It was to be based on assets plus goodwill. There were over 80 vehicles and a figure approaching a quarter of a million was put forward. Ashton Davies was very patient and finally came up to a sum that was, of course, much too much, but Brookes was adamant and the meeting broke up with nothing achieved.

In February, 1930, the matter was again discussed and it was agreed that there should be a valuation of assets. It must have dawned on the L.M.S. that they were throwing money away, because as a result of the valuation their price came down. Brookes Bros. must also have seen that they were losing their market, but they had held on too long and had to accept a price 22% less than the L.M.S. December offer that they had originally refused point blank.

There were all sorts of complications. No arrangements had been made to take over booking offices on the Promenade. These were essential to the trade and they had to be arranged for at the last minute. Naturally the Brookes family wanted a rent that was much too high and we had no alternative but to look pleasant and pay it. We found that their wages had been increased just before the agreement came into force. This had not been provided for, and so we had no remedy. Vehicles had been let go as regards maintenance. It appeared that we would have to spend £3,000 at once on tyres alone. Machinery was over-valued and there were all the usual things wrong that could have been avoided if we had been consulted in the first place.

The summer of 1930 was spent trying to deal with the traffic on the one hand and clearing up the innumerable snags connected with these expensive purchases on the other.

The new Crosville Motor Services Ltd. had a capital of £800,000 as compared with £290,000 when we had sold it one year previously. Where was the odd half-million pounds? Well, it was accounted for by the L.M.S. purchases outlined above, together with a substantial loan they had had to provide to enable us to get them into working order.

As soon as the new Company was formed the Silver Motor Company was bought out and provision was also made for the transfer to Crosville of the Llandudno Coaching and Carriage Company by means of a share exchange.

The White Rose fleet of Brookes Bros. contained a wide selection of makes and types. Some, like this PLSC Lion, needed only a coat of paint to transform them to Crosville vehicles though the sharp eyed would notice the DM registrations — we registered our vehicles in Chester and they carried FM markings. As for the rest of the White Rose fleet, suffice to say that out of the 87 vehicles we acquired nearly 50 had been disposed of within two years, and without any regrets. We were heartily glad to see the back of them. The modern Leylands, including DM 5259 shown here, we retained and some were rebodied at the same time as our 'own' vehicles. In this rebuilt form they gave good service, as would be expected, and lasted until around 1950.

Imitation is ... Brookes Bros bequeathed some 'Crosville' type Leylands which had been operating in and around Rhyl. DM 2842 was one of a pair which we kept for only a few months, and is seen here at Dyserth Waterfalls before we acquired it. Although pneumatic tyres have been fitted to the front, solids are still in evidence to the rear. Birds of a very different feather were the basically similar pair which also had seats on top—64 passengers could be carried, making them quite useful vehicles. They survived until 1934, and I believe they were unique.

Perhaps the most unusual, and yet amongst the longest-lived in our fleet, were the ex-Brookes Bros. S & D toastracks. Shelvoke & Drewry specialised in building refuse collection vehicles and the small wheels made for a low platform body which assisted the men emptying the bins into the special bodywork. They were geared for slow running speeds, ideal for seaside work with frequent stops and no need for hurrying whilst the conductor struggled to get the fares in. We purchased some similar vehicles, new, a year or two later and they ran in Rhyl and Prestatyn taking visitors to the Botanical Gardens and Winkups Camp as late as 1952. DM 6234 was quite new on take-over and is seen with White Rose emblem but Crosville fleet number 491.

We had just seen off our own charabancs when we were landed with some more. This 1920-built veteran from Brookes was amongst the first to go although not the oldest model we acquired—that dubious honour fell to a pair of 1916-built open-toppers. Rather more to our liking were the six Lionesses with Burlingham bodywork—they were similar to the six we had just purchased. The twelve became K1-12 in the 1935 renumbering but there never was a KAC, Tiger 171 broke with tradition to become K13. The Lionesses lasted until the end of the 1936 season and some, at least, were resold for further service in Jersey.

The open-topped Thornycroft bus and the horse-drawn wagonettes impart an air of tranquility to this picture of Llandudno in the 1920s. In reality cut throat competition between the local operators was more the order of things, as recorded in the text.

One can quite see that if the railway wanted their pound of flesh in the way of shares for the money they had spent, then Tilling and British would take the same view as regards their contribution of the Llandudno organisation. The result was that five Crosville shares were exchanged for every four Llandudno shares. Our old 10 per cent. dividend basis disappeared into the future with the rapidity of an express train. In fact, when it was all boiled down we found ourselves just, and only just, able to pay 4 per cent.

One can imagine that this amalgamation meant many changes. New depots were wanted, especially at the larger places such as Bangor and Caernarvon, not to speak of fresh arrangements at Birkenhead and Liverpool, where a traffic agreement was now imminent with the Corporation.

We first approached Liverpool in 1920 from the direction of Widnes and Speke, but we only got as far as Garston on the city boundary, and from there people had to continue by tram. There, dangling just out of reach, were nearly a million people—just think of it—a million people with twopences in their pockets, and we couldn't get amongst them! Trade was good, even as far as Garston, but it was going to be better, and after a time we got down into the city to a stand by the old Customs House. Not a pretentious place, and we more or less used the back streets to get there. What a cold and desolate spot it was! All one could see was an endless procession of heavy horse drays, lorries, and the trains on the Overhead Railway. There was no shelter of any sort—just an open space laid in greasy granite sets. But we were in at last and traffic increased. Heavy protection was given to the Corporation and there were many complaints when the trams were full. We had empty seats which made people's mouths water, and public opinion is very strong.

The 1930 Road Traffic Act came into force in February, 1931, and this hastened the necessity for some agreement with the Corporation. Others to be considered were the Ribble Company and the Railways. Let us go back, therefore, to 7th December, 1929, when Claude heard from Ashton Davies that there was to be a meeting with the Corporation at the Exchange Station Hotel to discuss these matters. At that time we had the service from Warrington and Widnes to Canning Place, and there were other routes from Widnes terminating at our garage in Edge Lane, together with one from Warrington via Prescot which came down as far as Mount Pleasant, and finally the London express service which ran from Pier Head.

Company letterhead, post 1930.

There was a 6d. single or return minimum protective fare into Liverpool with absolute protection in the city. The Watch Committee's policy was wavering and uncertain, and anything that would clarify the position was obviously going to be helpful. Claude suggested that the Pier Head was the logical terminus for all country services. There was plenty of room and it seemed to be the focal point. As usual, nothing much was done, but the L.M.S. said they would do their best. On 3rd July, 1930, another meeting was held, attended by the Corporation, L.M.S. and L.N.E. Railways and Ribble, but not Crosville. It was then proposed on broad lines that the Corporation should operate city services exclusively, and should share other services to points up to three miles outside the city area. Routes from beyond this limit to be operated by the Companies concerned.

There were further meetings to discuss details, such as protection either by minimum fares or otherwise, but the main principles agreed in July were adhered to, and we ended up on 2nd July, 1931, with a general terminus at the Pier Head and permission to pick up all local passengers in the city at a minimum fare of 4d. of which 30 per cent. was payable to the Corporation. There were five parties, namely, Ribble, Crosville, L.M.S. and L.N.E. Railways, and the Corporation. The period of operation was five years.

Mr. Priestly, the Corporation Transport General Manager, was in difficulties with his buses and had asked us to run one of the city services to Brodie Avenue, paying him a toll of 20 per cent., so we enjoyed this extra facility for five years, after which it was handed back to the Corporation when the new agreement was made in 1936.

The new licensing scheme came into force on 9th February, 1931, and some of us went to Manchester Town Hall to attend the first public sitting of the North Western Traffic Commissioners. It was just a matter of curiosity really because we had no cases, but everybody of note turned up to see how it was done, and at 11 a.m. Mr. Chamberlain walked in, accompanied by two other Commissioners. We all stood whilst they took their seats. Sir Walter Greaves Lord was taking an opposition for the Railways, and we heard the usual cut-and-dried speech that we were to hear so many times during the next eight years. Chamberlain looked the part all right and if he had had wig and robe might easily have been a High Court judge. We thought that he would be a good man for the job, and events proved that we were right. Always fair to everybody—a firm and kindly guide for the other part-time Commissioners—he held the balance in a difficult and complicated area.

I was to have considerable experience in Traffic Courts during the next few years and I think we felt more confidence when dealing with Chamberlain than with any of the others. He had been an operator, and that made a lot of difference. From 1938 to the time of his death I was privileged to be a member of his War Advisory Committee and it was at those meetings that he unburdened his heart of all the things that worried him during those difficult years—and he had worries, not the least of which was his health although he never spared himself. All the time it was getting worse and it was sad to think that he never lived to see the end of the long war effort to which he gave so generously of his personal energy.

When the Road Traffic Act became law in 1930 we had arranged a series of lectures on its provisions. They were given by Mr. J. P. Elsden, a Chester barrister who subsequently took many of our more important cases in the Traffic Courts. Then we had an examination at which Mills (later Divisional Manager, Bangor) won a money prize offered by the Company. After that we got down to the more serious business of starting the Licensing Department.

I undertook to do this with the assistance of S. M. Johnson, and the first thing we did was to get a van load of forms to fill up. I say a van load—perhaps it was two—in any case there was a prodigious number of them. Our other equipment consisted of scissors, paste and ever so many time tables to cut up with the scissors. Every route, including shorts, had to have a licence. This was a tall order since each form had a page of questions to be answered and they were wanted in quadruplicate. The time table and fare list had also to be submitted. Vehicles too wanted licences and certificates of fitness.

When "the appointed day" arrived we sent them all to Manchester in a lorry and had an evening off. For three weeks we had worked till 8 p.m. or 9 p.m. every night.

After that every alteration in timing or fares had to be applied for, published for everybody to see, and, if objected to, fought in the Traffic Courts. It was a lengthy process, but it was on a sound basis and we welcomed it. Never again would we wake up in the morning to be told that so-and-so had got a bus and was pirating one of our best routes. No, he must apply first, and we could oppose him with every chance of success, always provided that we ourselves were behaving properly.

I remember going to London one day to appear before Mr. Gleeson Robinson for a backing to our Liverpool-London services. He wanted all sorts of details. I had not got them and was nearly thrown out. He did order two men out for talking during that hearing.

Col. Redman of the West Midland area was fiery, but very quick in assessing the cases that came before him.

A. T. James was quite different from everybody else. His area was South Wales and he was really an eminent barrister but, being very deaf, he took up an appointment as Traffic Commissioner. His local knowledge of obscure places was astounding and his memory quite faultless. I don't think he heard a word at the sittings, but had studied each case the night before, knew his man, and had his decision ready before each applicant came forward. He used to speak very quickly and size up a situation like lightning. Arthur Bevan, a Nantwich solicitor, came with me to many of these cases, and if we were staying in the same hotel with James he would have a chat with him the evening before. "Why, hullo, Bevan!" he would say. "Are you people coming before me tomorrow? Well, I see the case like this." And he would immediately outline the whole thing and tell us what he was going to do before we could get a word in. "Don't tell anyone you have seen me," he would say, and then we would have an interesting talk about all sorts of other things, for A.T. was a great talker. There were many mutual acquaintances for him and Bevan and conversation flowed easily.

The next morning we would walk into the court as complete strangers. Nearly always he granted our reasonable requests, and we saw to it that they were reasonable, so that in the course of years a kind of trust grew up between us and, in fact, with all the Commissioners, and a goodwill was established which said in effect "If Crosville want it they have good reason for asking."

Whilst visits to Manchester courts were dull, there were sittings at many places in North Wales, the Midlands, and Central Wales. These visits meant journeys through fascinating country. Such journeys, if in company with Arthur Bevan, became romances and adventures in themselves. We always chose special routes—not just the main road—and then we would stop and look at churches and old buildings, and all the time the talk flowed easily about people and the things we were seeing. A night or two at Llandrindod, Aberystwyth, Swansea, and perhaps a trip to Fishguard, and on one memorable occasion in 1939 to Tenby with an exploration of the Pembroke coast. Walks after dinner, picnics. We worked all these things in, and, I hope, conducted our cases none the worse for having done so. We knew our Commissioners and they knew us. The British are conservative in these matters and like the old familiar faces. But we must come back to earth.

One of the terms of the arrangement under which the Railways had become interested in Passenger Road Transport was that each of the Companies concerned should set up a Standing Joint Committeee with the Railway or Railways interested. Thus we formed one of the earliest of these bodies and set to work to devise the ways and means of

A peaceful scene in Llanwrst in 1927 as Royal Blue Leyland C7 No. 32 stands in the Market Square. Like so many other buses in the area this one—CA 8709—became part of the Crosville fleet, albeit briefly. I don't believe we ever ran it.

Vehicles taken over ranged from the very large to the very small. Typical of the latter was this 1928 GMC with locally-built bodywork acquired from Red Dragon of Denbigh which operated with us for a couple of years. UNU (You Need Us) had eight Dukes and two Duchesses amongst their 22 vehicles, and six of the former are seen below. They were Vulcans, yet another new make to us, but needless to say their departure was swift and unlamented. Some of their Leyland brethren followed the well-defined route back to Lowestoft and, suitably rebodied, survived until 1949.

co-ordination with our new shareholders. The first members were, I think, W. P. Bradbury, F. H. Cowell, Claude and myself. We met at Crane Wharf and lunched at the Grosvenor. This happened three times a year but it wasn't all festivities. Appendix No. IV gives a few details of the Committee's general activities. Later on, the G.W.R. came in, and our summer meeting included a visit to some part of the Crosville area to see for ourselves what things were like.

Some Standing Joint Committees in other parts of the country were famous for the difficulties they had to see eye to eye with each other, but in the case of Crosville it was never like that. The whole time during Claude's four-year chairmanship, and ever since I followed him in that position, we have got on well and liked each other. Various railway people have come and gone and when one goes I ask him to have a word with his successor and tell him that we are not so bad after all. It works.

Joe Morris, well known all over the G.W.R., was a member from 1933 until his retirement about 1938. We had been warned that he was difficult to get on with and that he didn't like buses anyway, but Joe liked a good lunch and Joe liked snooker. He got both. As a matter of fact he was never difficult. Nobody could have been more reasonable, and we got on famously. At the Grosvenor we used to have a long table. Joe sat on my left and an L.M.S. member on my right. The waiter would come round with a large selection of hors d'oeuvres. "Any prawns?" Joe would say, and he would eat a whole glass jar full as well as everything else, and the Grosvenor lunch was a lunch in those days. Afterwards we used to go the the club to play snooker.

When he retired we gave him a pair of silver hair brushes with his name on them. He didn't know about it, and was much touched. Old David Roberts of the Snowdon Mountain Railway had invited us to lunch at the Victoria Hotel, Llanberis, and when we had finished and made the presentation, we had a special train up the mountain, but couldn't get all the way because the high wind made it dangerous. Good old Joe! He only lived a very short time after he had retired, although he managed to come on one more trip into Wales with us as our guest.

By the summer of 1931 North Wales was consolidated, except for Wrexham which was to come later, and a number of smaller operators who were now pinned down to regular work under the Road Traffic Act.

The Llandudno Blues and the Silver Company had been the last to be taken over, and they both had interesting histories.

On 18th December, 1866, George Woodyatt was born—I don't know where, but in 1876 he came to Llandudno. "This is the place for me," is what he probably said, and so it was, because he went into the coaching business when about twenty years of age and sixty years later on his eightieth birthday, 18th December, 1946, he could have been seen gaily mounting his bicycle after a day's work in the parcels and enquiry office in Clonmel Street. Needless to say, he always wore a black bowler hat and I'm sure he will forgive me for mentioning this. A bowler is not often seen now outside the big cities but when worn by a man like Woodyatt it is a mark of proper respect for one's life work, a proof of years of devoted service to one's employers, and a sure sign that the wearer is one of that rare group of men who value all these things at their true worth.

Talking about bowlers, I cannot resist mentioning a famous case, also in Wales, of a green bowler. It was worn for many years by Mr. Davies, Manager of Moelferna Slate Quarries, near Corwen. There again it was the trade mark of years of faithful service, but when I met him he had changed it for a black one. The quarry was three miles up on the mountain, and Col. Wynne-Edwards of Nantglyn, near Denbigh, had taken Roberts and myself up to have a talk about their transport problems. We went up and up—a typical mountain road—and at 1,700 feet we reached the quarry. "Just a minute," said Wynne-Edwards, "I'll go and fetch Mr. Davies." And there he was, complete with bowler. I was told about the green one afterwards. Apparently Rosemary Wynne-Edwards, the Colonel's daughter, had pulled his leg about it, hence the change, but as it was he put the kettle on and brewed us some tea and we shared out our sandwiches whilst we talked things over. The day was perfect and the air at that height made one feel very much alive, but it must have been pretty wild there at times. The men all walked that three miles to work, to the roof of the world it seemed, and then back at night. They were wiry fellows and some were sixty years of age. Wynne-Edwards had a cheery word for everybody and they were genuinely glad to see him. I felt that the bowler hat was just right, but was sorry that the green one had gone. Up there there was much of the charm of the old-fashioned Wales, and I hope it will continue like that. We walked down along an old tramway, right back to the main road, and discussed the possibility of having an engine to take the men up in trucks, but eventually it seemed better to improve the road and take them up by lorry. Everybody else rode to work, and now they wanted to do the same.

Well, George Woodyatt came at a time when the pier was not built, and the railway station was a very small affair. There were horse-drawn vehicles called basket carriages, indeed, some were drawn by donkeys, followed by brakes which ran round the Orme for 1/- Then came the first four-in-hand driven by Evan Jones that took three hours

The Llandudno and Colwyn Bay Electric Railway operated a 3ft. 6in. gauge tramway between Colwyn Bay and West Shore, Llandudno, much of it on private right of way. During the early 'thirties second-hand trams were purchased to replace some of the original 1907 stock. This 1909 example, supplied new to LCBER, was of an unusual type, known as semi-convertible—incorporating full-drop or detachable windows like our earlier buses—and was operated until 1936. It is believed that these were the only such trams to operate in this country, though many were built for service overseas in hotter climates, where the facility would be appreciated.

The 1930 take-overs in North Wales continued to introduce more new vehicle makes to our ranks. Silver Motors of Llandudno contributed some bonnetted Guys. Although CC 7462 spent only two years in Crosville ownership it was, like most acquired vehicles, quickly repainted into full maroon livery. It was photographed by the youthful Deacon in Clonmel Street, Llandudno, in 1931.

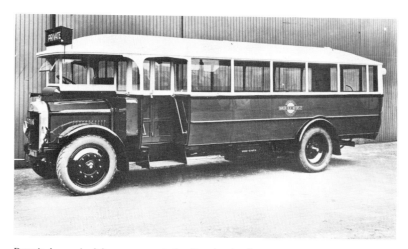

Dennis buses had been amongst the first in the fledgling Crosville fleet and the operators in and around Llandudno also favoured the make. The Blues and Silvers between them added 36 to our 1930 fleet though none lasted beyond 1934. This Dennis E, seen in original Bangor Blue livery and with Ransomes body, received short shrift, being amongst the first to go in 1931.

to go to Bettws-y-Coed where they had lunch and visited the sights, arriving back at 6 p.m.

This led to a Mr. Hartley starting in a big way at what is now our Oxford Road Depot, having as many as 150 horses in the summer season and selling them off again in the autumn. He eventually formed a company called the Llandudno Coaching and Carriage Co. Ltd. They began stage work with a two horse bus from Gogarth Abbey Hotel and then along the Promenade to the Little Orme. All the way for 2d., and in 1912 they ran from the Pier to Penrhynside, but the motor vehicle had now appeared and in 1918 they sold all the horses and other equipment and concentrated on the motor side of the business. By 1912 Woodyatt and his partner, Jarvis, had worked up a considerable independent trade including the ownership of two motor coaches. It was agreed that they should join up with the Llandudno Coaching Company and become Managers of that Company.

In 1923 the British Automobile Traction Co. Ltd. acquired the major holding in the Llandudno concern, and Mr. W. S. Wreathall became Chairman. He put in D. Bowen from the Wrexham Company, as Secretary, but was himself struck down by a serious illness which kept him away for two years, and Mr. R. J. Howley carried on in his absence.

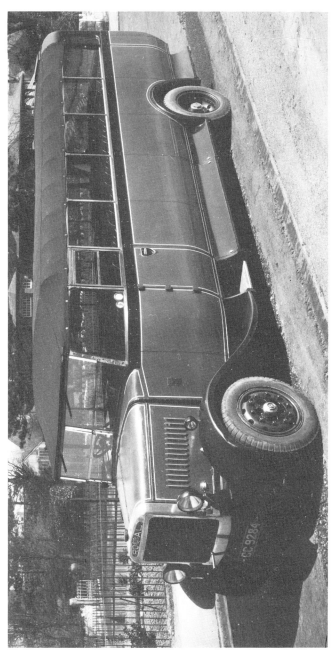

The Blues were among the handful of companies in the BET/BAT empire to obtain part of their rolling-stock from Midland Red, which built its own chassis under the SOS name and we inherited no less than 44 of them, of assorted shapes and sizes. Four bonnetted QLC models carried all-weather bodywork by Short Bros, famous for building sea planes, and although two of these were disposed of with our Lionesses at the end of 1936 the other two actually survived the war. Deacon at least was not sorry since in 1947 they constituted the whole of his coaching allocation for tours at Llandudno.

In 1925 A. C. Clifford became General Manager, but only stayed a year, his place being taken by C. R. Taylor who remained in that position until the amalgamation with Crosville in 1931. As the years went on increasing difficulty was encountered from competition—Silver Motors founded in 1911—the electric trams—and later on the New Blues and U.N.U. at the Bangor end. In 1928 they had bought up the Bangor Blue Company and so set foot in Anglesey where U.N.U. immediately started fierce competition on all their routes.

For many years they had paid a 10 per cent. dividend but it had to be missed for the last year before the amalgamation, and yet shareholders got five Crosville shares for every four Llandudno ones.

The North Wales Silver Motors Ltd. was promoted by local people in 1911 as the Llandudno Automobile Touring Co. Ltd. with a capital of £18,000—a formidable competitor to the Coaching Company, one would say. In 1913 they ran to Penmaenmawr and later on to Llanfairfechan. They became the "Silvers" in 1914 and managed to

All shapes and sizes ... The SOS buses had one thing in common—their old-fashioned appearance. Nevertheless they put in a few years' useful work, including CC 7743 which, seen here in 1931 at the Old Colwyn (Penmaen Head) terminus with its new livery, worked until the end of the 1934 season. The roof-mounted destination boards were in sharp contrast to the usual Crosville 'Wid' cards in the saloon windows.

More Vulcans came our way in 1933, this time from Bethesda Grey who handed over eleven out of a fleet total of thirteen—no superstition there apparently. The other two vehicles were Chevrolets but none of their fleet remained with us for more than a few months. Above is a 20-seat VSD model, new in 1926, and below a VWB4, with 30-seat dual-doorway bodywork, new in 1927. It is seen operating in Darwen, Lancashire, after we sold it. Many of the vehicles we acquired had plenty of life left in them but the enormous variety of makes would have made maintenance and spares a nightmare.

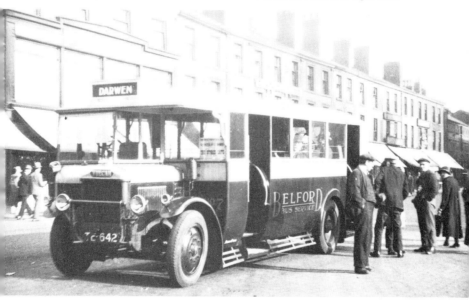

open up to Llanrwst in 1916, also serving Kinmel Camp during the war. At their Broadway Depot they sold cars and petrol, and in 1930 they had thirty-one vehicles, but were heavily committed at the Bank and in other directions, so they had either to find new capital or sell out. They chose the latter and in August 1930, the Crosville took over the business.

This was followed closely by the take-over of the Llandudno Coaching Company on 18th February, 1931, and, of course, U.N.U. had already come over, so it looked as if the principal North Wales interests had now been consolidated. What a busy time that must have been and indeed was for Claude! The files are full of arrangements for endless meetings and still more meetings, but it all came out right in the end. In the middle of it all Colwyn Bay objected to the licensing of double-deck buses. They said that the passengers on the top deck would spend their time looking in at the upstairs windows of indignant rate-payers. This might have been argued twenty years earlier, but the Traffic Commissioners gave them no change, and as far as we could tell Colwyn Bay morals remained at their usual high level in spite of the novel temptation that might have caused them to suffer a slight lapse.

1930 and 1931 had other worries. They were slump years and we were desperately put to it to find means of effecting economies in running costs. The possibility of getting a bit by means of increased traffic either in volume or by cutting out bad mileage seemed to escape us. We had not enough imagination, perhaps, and the general lack of money made us think that there was no more to be had out of our public. There again it is easy to speak after the event and it was not until 1936 that we really began to try and increase the slender margin between receipts and expenses by endeavouring to increase the former instead of cheese-paring, for that was what much of it amounted to.

At the same time in 1930 and 1931 there was a grand field for re-organisation and a golden opportunity to take advantage of the savings that were dangling under our noses because of the North Wales amalgamations.

It was still my job to look after the outside places, and I had an interesting time gathering all sorts of data and trying the find the best methods of working.

One of the principal items of expenditure is the wages of the platform crews. For every 100 hours paid the wheels were only turning for about 70 hours. This was disastrous. For some depots the figure was 60 hours and even less. It was not a question of the rate paid per hour

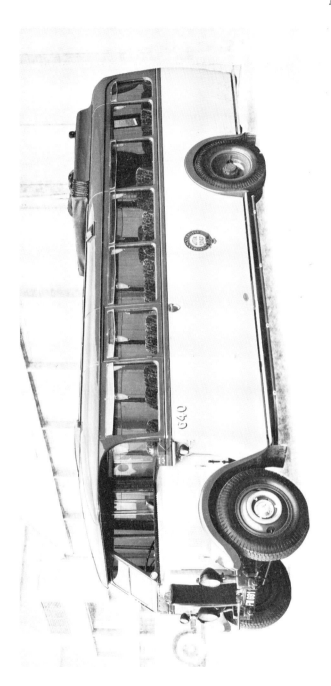

This 1932 Leyland Tiger TS4 coach still carried passengers' luggage on the roof — a folding head gave plenty of fresh air but retained the modern appearance above window level. Not until drop-frame extensions were added to the rear of the chassis would we be able to put luggage in the sensible place, a luggage boot. The garter emblem and gold numerals gave a dignified appearance in keeping with contemporary tastes. Although No. 640 was built in Lowestoft, as many of our previous vehicles had been, the new owners of the factory were the Eastern Counties Omnibus Company Ltd, whose emblem is displayed just to the rear of the outward opening door of the coach.

113

though that was low enough in all conscience at some of the Welsh depots. Let there be a reasonable rate for each hour worked, but our people did not really want to be paid for doing nothing.

Running speeds were all over the place, some too fast, many more too slow. Buses had to stop at intermediate points to avoid running early. Others went hell for leather because they had not sufficient time. The speed, of course, depends on the route and can vary quite a lot. Time-tables had been planned with no regard to waiting time, and duties were set out in different ways at every depot. There were no reliable statistics and I found the whole problem a fascinating study for many months.

Needless to say, the Divisional Managers were enthusiastic and most helpful. The early pioneering days seemed to have returned and we eventually got out methods of making bus and duty schedules that have stood the test of time because they are very little different to-day after sixteen years of use.

Every month the figures improved until the average running speed was 15 m.p.h. (including intermediate stops) and out of every 100 hours paid the wheels turned for nearly 80 instead of 70.

We couldn't hold this high efficiency during the recent war, but no doubt we shall get back to it in time.

We fought for every hundredth of a penny a mile—and why?—because it meant a saving of £1,250 per annum.

In the meantime the receipts per mile also declined, as will be seen in Appendix No. 1. Was it best to increase mileage in order to decrease costs per mile, or should we cut out some bad mileage which might increase our costs a little but increase our receipts per mile a little more and so give us a better margin? It was indeed a problem.

Nearly all the vehicles we had taken over were on their last legs, and big renewal programmes must be carried out.

The British Electrical Federation helped a lot in buying stores at the cheapest rates, although we were free to buy elsewhere if we could do better, and we often could.

In 1931 too came the first Compression Ignition engine which was to sweep the board during the next ten or fifteen years. Diesel oil was much cheaper than petrol, and owing to its increased efficiency a heavy oil engine did nearly twice as many miles to the gallon. We had one "on trial" for six months. Nothing like caution in trying new things, but we need not have worried—they had come to stay. I remember one they had in Liverpool University Engineering workshops in 1912. We

We still used Lions for bus work but this was the first we bought with bodywork from the Lowestoft factory, dating from 1932. It must have been satisfactory because not long afterwards we started negotiations for a major programme for the rebodying of older vehicles in the fleet and ECOC got the work—albeit at a very competitive price.

used to test it and work out the horsepower and efficiency. It had just one large cylinder with a huge flywheel and started by compressed air.

In 1931 the first mileage contract was signed with Dunlop and they bought all our tyres, afterwards hiring them back to us at a fixed rate per mile. This was a good idea and we probably saved on it because the secret of making your tyres last is maintenance, and a company like Dunlop had unique experience which they could use to the full since they organised their own tyre service in each Depot.

We had had a full-time Accountant since Mr. Eckersley had come to us from the L.M.S. in September, 1930, but the Secretarial Department was still kept separate. Our Head Offices at Crane Wharf left much to be desired, but we simply could not afford anything better although I think at the back of everybody's mind there was always the hope that one day there would be an improvement. Claude had moved out of Crane House to Upton, and the whole house and adjoining warehouse had been made into offices. The warehouse was old—200 years old at least. It was difficult to heat, and badly ventilated. Corn kept oozing out of crevices, and that meant mice, but it was cheap. The whole building was let to us by the L.M.S. for £140 per annum.

My home was in Nantwich, and Claude and I still visited the little footbridge over the railway at Madeley where we had so often talked over our affairs and prospects. We had settled down to the feel of the new ownership, and developments had come so thick and fast that there was no time for regrets, even if there were any, which was doubtful. There may have been some small difference with Kingsway from time to time, but it was not lasting, and our sandwiches and beer tasted just as good as ever.

One day Claude produced a bottle of Contréxeville water. "What have you got that for?" I asked him. "Well, I've been told to drink a bottle a day," he replied, and went on to explain that he had not been very well for some time, and his doctor had told him to try a course of that particular brand of mineral water and see if it would do him any good. I think he would rather have had beer, but it was a large bottle, and there was no room for both. We went on that day to explore Heli Castle near Madeley and I left him after a drink at the Star at Acton, near Nantwich.

Thus the 1931 Summer season was rather a rush, but we got through it somehow and then immediately started to lay plans for 1932. In February, 1932, the Board agreed in principle that the Western Transport Company of Wrexham should be amalgamated with us, thus

By 1931 we were firmly committed — and happily so — to Leyland for chassis and bodies, but were always on the look out for developments from other manufacturers. This Daimler CH6 was purchased in 1931 and fitted with United-built bodywork — I think the main idea was to try out the new fluid flywheel transmission, but we were happier with the normal clutch and gear lever, so it did well to last until 1938. Contemporary Leylands are still in service at the time of writing.

completing the solid block of services for the area. This would take time and meanwhile we were busy negotiating a new hourly wages agreement after paying by the week ever since 1910. There had been various Unions concerned before the General Strike in 1926, but the strike itself had cancelled all previous agreements although we had simply gone on paying the same rate since that time. Now, with the revision and organisation of schedules, it became increasingly apparent that payment must be by the hour. It was the only fair way, and the only possible way to fit in with our plans.

Running buses was becoming an exact science at last.

One day in July, 1932, Claude and several of us went at 9 a.m. to the Queen Hotel, Chester, where we had booked a room, and there we met Ernest Bevin and Tom McLean from the Transport and General Workers' Union, together with about twelve representatives from the various Depots. We had lunch in the room. We had tea in the room. We had supper in the room, and at 10.30 p.m. we all walked out, having made our first hourly agreement which, except for the rates and a few other things, remains in force to-day. There were occasions when Ernest Bevin got up to walk out, but didn't, and there were times when Claude did likewise. We had gone there to build an agreement, and we built one, although it took twelve hours. Perhaps that is why it has lasted so long.

Many years later, in 1941, I met Ernest Bevin, then Minister of Labour and National Service, in the Strand in London—just outside the Strand Palace Hotel. I didn't think he would remember me, but he did, and he well recollected the twelve-hour sitting at the Queen Hotel.

The agreement came into force on 14th July, 1932, and from then onwards we could fit hours with duties and vice versa.

Summer of 1932 was easier to work, and we did quite well.

In the meantime preparations were being made to take over the Wrexham Company on 1st May, 1933. At this point we must go back about sixty years or even longer.

The Western Transport Co. Ltd. was successor to one of the oldest tramway companies in the country which ran from Wrexham to Johnstown (3½ miles). The first street horse tramway was opened in Birkenhead in August, 1860, and, of course, there were no electric trams until 1883, although there were steam ones at various places.

The earliest authentic record I can find of the Wrexham undertaking is in June, 1884, when Wrexham District Tramways Company, which had been in existence since the 70's, sold six horses, two trams, one

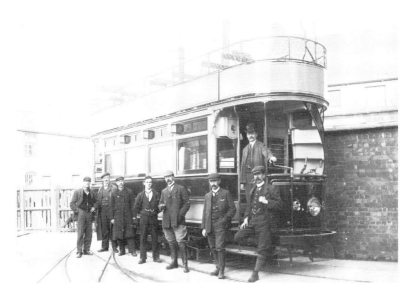

March 1903, and a proud group stand with what was reputedly the first tram, outside Johnstown depot, near Wrexham. Mr. King, the Manager, stands on the platform; in front of him is depot foreman A. G. Grundy who later became Manager of the Stalybridge Joint Board undertaking after having left Wrexham under somewhat of a cloud according to his recently published memoirs. On Grundy's right stand driver Dobbins; G. Malpas, Traffic Inspector; D. Bowen who was Secretary of Wrexham Transport at the time of the 1933 take-over; W. J. Gale, Permanent Way Engineer; and two men from the electrical contractors.

The very formal group below were photographed in 1914 'on parade' with A. A. Hawkins who had taken over as Manager in 1906 and Inspector G. Steen, later Crosville's first depot superintendent at Wrexham.

whip, two French horns and some lamp snippers, to Mr. Fred Jones for £100. £50 was paid on account on 24.8.85 and the remainder not until 3.6.90 in spite of one or two stiff letters from Mr. Bevan, Secretary of the Tramways Company.

Fred Jones leased the tramway at that time, but I believe it was authorised in 1873 under an Act of Parliament (Victoria 36 and 37, Cap. 76). In any case it was opened for traffic in October, 1876. No doubt there were special reasons for going to Parliament, because the Tramways Act of 1870 allowed for such things to be done by application to the Board of Trade.

The original company was the Wrexham Tramways Ltd., and there is an agreement between them and Wrexham District Tramways Company on the one part and Frederick Llewelyn Jones (Coal Merchant) on the other part whereby the line and its equipment were leased to the latter at £3 per week from about 1880 until 25.4.96 and thereafter the agreement was renewed every year at £200 per annum until Mr. Fred Ll. Jones made his last trip from Johnstown to Wrexham and back on 26th April, 1901. The fare from Wrexham to Johnstown was 5d. at that time.

In the meantime Wrexham Tramways Ltd. had sold to the Drake and Gorham Electric Power and Traction Co. Ltd., who on 10.12.98 gave notice under the Tramways Act, 1870, that they proposed to introduce electricity and do away with the horses.

What happened in 1900 is difficult to say, but in 1901 the Wrexham and District Traction Co. Ltd. was formed by the British Electric Traction Co. Ltd., and the electrification was carried out by Dick, Kerr Ltd. (now the English Electric Co. Ltd.). A proper tram shed was built at Johnstown on the original site and Mr. G. W. King came over from the Potteries Electric Traction Co. Ltd. as the first General Manager, and finally the new service started on 4th April, 1903. There was the usual celebration and much joy riding. In 1906 Mr. King went to Scotland, and his place was taken by Mr. A. A. Hawkins, who remained at Wrexham until 1933 when the Company became part of the Crosville organisation.

1913 saw the first buses which were to "feed" the trams, and the next year they started to feel their way outwards, especially in the Chester direction, but the 1914-1918 war froze all development. After the war competition began to creep in from all sides. The Company blindly stuck to the main roads, but astute competitors used smaller roads to get right into the centres of housing and thus give a door-to-door

This rather splendid line of Tilling-Stevens B10A2 models was photographed for the Brush company of Loughborough — builders of the Federation style bodywork — before delivery to Western Transport. Some of these vehicles operated in our fleet until 1938, whilst others, like many vehicles needed for the war effort, survived until quite recently.

service. We suffered from the same complaint in the Crosville. Our policy had been "The service is along the main road. If you live a mile or more up a side road you must walk down to our bus." Luckily we woke up before it was too late, but Wrexham didn't, with the result that everybody bought buses and there was chaos. Even the G.W. Railway started direct competition and that was very serious.

The first part to go under was the tramway, and the track was abandoned on 31st March, 1927. 1930 saw a temporary respite when the G.W.R. services were amalgamated with the Transport services and a new company was formed called Western Transport Co. Ltd.

But the small proprietors were still there and it was impossible to make any money even when the Road Traffic Act came into force and stopped any further chaos developing. Mr. Hawkins could now keep out any new competition, but the Company was small, and the price paid for building the main Maesgwyn Garage was a heavy burden on their finances. No dividend was in sight and something had to be done about it. W. S. Wreathall could see all this and that is why he arranged for the Company to be amalgamated with Crosville on 1st May, 1933. There was to be a clean sweep of everything, and yet it was only a paper transaction, 155,000 Wrexham shares were to be exchanged for 155,000 Crosville shares—a bargain for the Wrexham shareholders.

This was the largest take-over we had made and the detailed arrangements were complicated. Capt. E. Roberts came from Bangor to take charge of what was to be known as the Wrexham Division, and Mr. Hawkins was to stay for a few months to hand over. This is what he says:-

"I was summoned to Headquarters on 11th May, 1933, and on arriving I found gathered together all the local operators from Wrexham who had apparently lodged objections to the various services which had been published in Notices and Proceedings for transfer to Crosville. I was not, at the time, aware why my presence was required at this meeting. However, it continued all day and an agreement was reached somewhere about midnight when I was handed many sheets of notes made by the late Managing Director to shape into an agreement form. Mr. Tooth who had formed an Association of local operators at Wrexham came to my rescue and typed out a number of copies to my dictation from the notes handed to me. It was a memorable meeting, with the Company giving away quite a lot on the recommendation of the General Manager of the Western Transport, Mr. A. A. Hawkins.

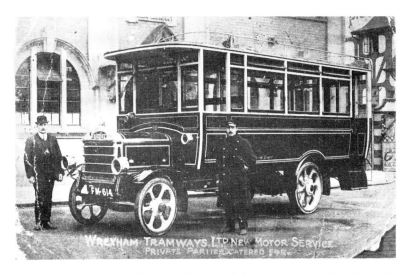

Mr Hawkins with an early Wrexham Tramways Daimler motor bus and its driver. By 1933, the year of the take-over, the motor bus fleet consisted of 133 machines.

Ten of these ADC 423s — a 1928 product of Daimler in conjunction with AEC — were included in the Western Transport fleet. They carried Brush bodywork to an earlier Federation style. One received a Leyland four-cylinder oil engine and lasted long enough to receive a J-prefix fleet number in the 1935 renumbering, this class being otherwise composed of Lion models with similar engines.

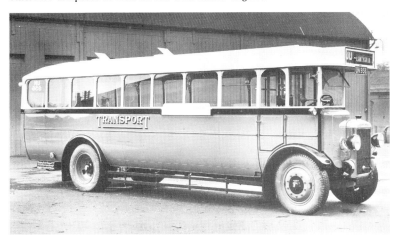

"Some time after, I was told that I was to take over the Western Transport Company on 1st June, 1933. At that time I was extremely busy, as I was in the course of re-organising the Aberystwyth services, where I had been staying two nights, and arrived at Wrexham late on the 1st June. On the 2nd June I spent the day with Mr. Hawkins, and at once I knew that the position was going to be somewhat difficult, as he very much resented handing over.

"In view of the agreement reached to overcome the various objections, there was a great deal of licensing work to be done and adjustment of time-tables. The Licensing Office under Wrexham Transport was kept very much secluded, almost under lock and key, and no one except the General Manager was permitted to examine the Notices and Proceedings. He carefully went through these and made all sorts of remarks for the attention of the Licensing Clerk who was then working in the office which is now the Divisional Manager's.

"Before things settled down it was necessary for a conference to be held when Mr. Hawkins was definitely told to hand over. He had a peculiar habit of turning over everything face downwards on his office desk when anyone appeared in the office. Matters were finally settled when, on Tuesday, 13th June, Mr. Wreathall and the late Managing Director turned up at Wrexham for a general inspection. After this we got down to work and the whole of the offices were re-organised and all correspondence, licensing files, stationery, etc., sent by lorry to Chester.

"For the rest of the month, the late Managing Director frequently visited Wrexham and along with Mr. Hawkins we toured various routes. Many times we got lost, particularly in the Oswestry area, because he didn't know the way.

"On 30th June I finally took over and Mr. Hawkins left for a month's holiday in Scotland.

"Unfortunately the Western Transport had allowed a local printer to do their time tables, and this led them into difficulties in the Traffic Courts. A very big feature had been made of the new Licensing Act, but on examining the licences there was hardly one that conformed with the actual route or the bus workings and this revealed a very serious position. Many diversions had taken place which had not been authorised and were not included on the licences, but we were successful in getting the whole position corrected without a single objection.

"All times had to be co-ordinated with the other operators and finally the time table was prepared, licences corrected and renewed, duties arranged and the system changed over completely to that as operated by Crosville. A number of clerks were working many hours overtime until this re-organisation was completed.

"When Mr. Hawkins returned from his holidays prior to retirement the Managing Director came down and after lunch at the Wynnstay they walked round to see the improvements and the new lay-out, but he declined to take any interest or real notice of any change. In fact, when he had completed his tour he remarked that he had seen nothing.

"Very shortly after this, negotiations commenced with a view to taking over a number of smaller operators, and when this was finally achieved it made a very great change in the whole of the Wrexham position.

"The last connection we had with the Western Transport was when the late Mr. Hawkins attended the Staff Dinner at Chester on 26th October. Unfortunately after going into retirement he never enjoyed very good health and he died early in 1934.

"There was very little organisation amongst the staff. In fact the late Mr. Baynham, who was there as Assistant to Mr. Hawkins, was never allowed to take part in any of the administration but merely spent his time preparing blue prints of routes and maps for the Traffic Courts."

E. ROBERTS

With the Western Transport Staff were G.W.R men known as "loaned staff," and they belonged to the National Union of Railwaymen. They were all sorts of grades who had been employed by the G.W.R. prior to the amalgamation of their omnibus interests with the old Wrexham Transport Company. They had railway rates of pay and railway privileges as regards coal, free travel, and other things. They were scattered over the whole system — Wrexham, Johnstown, Corwen, Oswestry, Pwllheli, Aberystwyth, Machynlleth, Dolgelley. All these places had special railway wage sheets and there was endless bickering between them and the Wrexham Company's staff who were members of the Transport and General Workers' Union. The whole thing was most difficult and we felt that while this state of affairs existed we should get nowhere. Claude used to be wild about it, and eventually he persuaded Mr. Wreathall to agree with him, and negotiations took place whereby a cash compensation would be paid to these N.U.R. men in return for which they would renounce their rights and become members of the T. & G.W. Union working under the same terms as everybody else. A special Board Meeting was held to consider the point and although there was some doubt about the repercussions the arrangement might have elsewhere it was decided to pay them out and end the matter.

Thus on 1st August, 1933, I set out at about 5 a.m. and picked up Capt. Roberts at Wrexham. It was August Bank Holiday Sunday, the only day when we could get the men together at the various Depots. We had to travel considerably over 300 miles, call at every depot and pay everybody and get their receipts with a signed statement that they relinquished all their rights and became part of the Crosville Staff. It was a lovely day and we only had one anxious moment — at Pwllheli, where Driver Griffiths would sign nothing. Roberts spoke to him in Welsh and told him that so-and-so had signed at Johnstown — in fact we showed him the signature. "Good enough," he said, "If . . . . has signed it must be all right." We got back to the Wynnstay Arms at Oswestry at about 6 p.m. where we treated ourselves to a magnificent tea — well-earned, I hope — sitting outside by the Bowling Green in a perfect evening with an attaché case full of a complete set of signatures which had removed one of our major difficulties in re-organising the Western Transport.

Did I say all? Almost! There was one Inspector — Brooker at

Inspector Brooker, left, immaculate as always, seen with his Western Welsh opposite number. In wet weather out came Brooker's umbrella. Amongst his jealously-guarded railway privileges was his uniform issue, considerably more generous than our own, and a better cut than Western Welsh by the look of it.

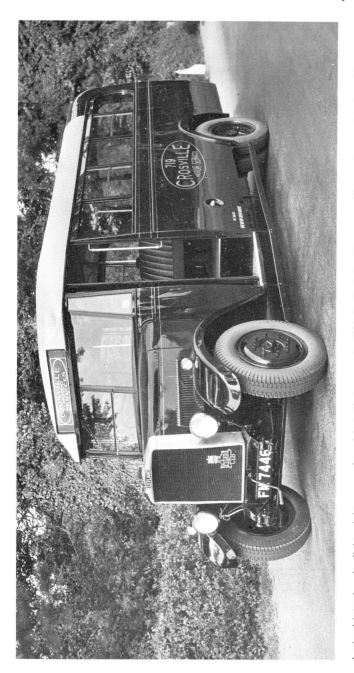

Leyland introduced a lightweight range of models to their range in 1931. Built at the Kingston-on-Thames factory the Cubs filled a gap in many fleets, ours included. We quickly built up a large fleet of these very useful small-capacity vehicles, mainly normal-control models in the 20 or 26-seat range. By 1937 over 150 were in service. This Brush-bodied example was the first of the longer KP3 models, delivered to us in 1932 and still in use at the time of writing.

Aberystwyth—who elected to remain in the N.U.R. He was in the supervisory grade and due to retire a few years later. He was an excellent stand inspector and did good work for us, but would never go outside the regulations as to hours, etc., at a period when we all had to do it from time to time. Perhaps he was wise. At any rate he is now enjoying a well-earned retirement.

Claude was pleased and could see that at last the way was clear to go ahead and buy smaller businesses wherever they offered. In fact that was the next step and a glance at Appendix No. V will show what happened during 1934.

There were also Depots to be built at a number of places, and arrangements were quickly made at Amlwch, Aberystwyth, Corwen, Machynlleth and Pwllheli. Building was cheap, and Cowmeadow, our Architect, had valuable experience. He had been with us since 1927 and knew exactly what was required. Also his estimates were astonishingly accurate. We had to build cheaply using asbestos or Robertsons patent metal rather than brickwork. There was so much to do and we were not a rich company. It might have been better to spend a bit more on land in the right places to avoid light mileage in the future but, as I say, we had a lot to do, and all our money was wanted for vehicles. We got garages, clean, simple and eminently workable places, and that was the main thing.

Claude kept taking various waters. I think a long holiday would have done him more good, but in between times he kept well enough. At any rate he was thoroughly enjoying himself fitting all the pieces together, and so was I. The excursions into Wales were always a joy. It was never quite the same twice running, and I was getting to know all sorts of delightful roads off the beaten track. Some funny place names, too—I don't mean the ones that are difficult to spell or pronounce, but places like New Invention, Cann Office, Evenjobb. How on earth did they come by such names? Devil's Bridge, too, where, if there is time, I always try and walk down to the bottom of the gorge and come up again by the hotel—2,500 ft. climb—just to prove it is easy. Old abbeys and churches. It may be a thin country to run buses in, but there are few more beautiful parts of the world.

Where one has mountains one also gets peculiar weather, by which I mean not just ordinary rain, sunshine, wind and calm, but whirlwinds, floods, cloudbursts, snow and coastal gales of extraordinary intensity. The pier at Aberystwyth has been washed away by stages—each time by a super gale, until there is only a stump left. Many times we have

The New Blues fleet consisted of eight vehicles—all Dennis models. Such standardisation was rare in firms we took over. This EV, registered JC 46, had been new in 1931 and carried bodywork by Jackson. The signwriting confirms its route as Conway - Deganwy - West Shore - Llandudno.

Edwards of Denbigh had ordered three GMC 20-seat models which were delivered direct to Crosville after the take-over. We were looking for a suitable replacement for some of our early, small-capacity Leylands, and in 1930 had purchased some Albions because Leyland at that time had no suitable equivalent. The GMCs provided a useful comparison but we decided against purchasing any more of either make in the light of the introduction of the new lightweight Leyland model, the Cub.

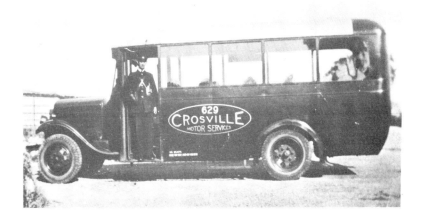

been called in to help out the railways whose lines have become impassable for one reason or another. Sometimes they have helped us when a road bridge has been involved, although usually we can plan a detour. There are strange whirlwinds in the deep valleys. I remember my friend, Edmund Vale, who lives in the Nant Ffrancon Valley, telling me how he was sitting alone in the house one night when he heard a weird noise approaching and a few minutes later half the slates were whipped off the roof and then this strange wind went whirling away up the valley. Sometimes we have had buses marooned in floods, but more often snow has been our trouble. The Welsh bus crew is very resourceful on these occasions. He has it in his bones to do the right thing and look after his passengers, himself, and his vehicle. Thus there have been times when vehicles have been completely missing and cut off for several days, and eventually the people involved have been found quite comfortable in a farm or inn. Certain roads such as the one from Machynlleth to Corris are regularly flooded several times a year, and there seems to be no remedy that is not much too expensive to carry out.

There was not much time for social functions during these years, but we kept our Annual Staff Dinner which had started in 1929 and took place in Chester every October. A special effort was made to get outside officials in to Headquarters, many of them having to stay the night. They were enjoyable affairs up to a point, but somewhat unwieldy towards the end. The atmosphere got pretty thick and one always felt it a bit the next morning. There were speeches, toasts and entertainment, the latter of a very mediocre brand. I always felt that something better ought to have been provided, or else why have them at all?

In 1934 Claude went for a short holiday to Anglesey. I believe he stayed at the Holyhead Station Hotel and explored the island a bit from there. It was always so difficult to get him to forget business for a period. He really ought to have gone right outside the Company's area. Even that brief change did him no end of good, but there was still something wrong, and he didn't seem able to find out what it really was.

In September that year we had the first Directors' Tour. The Board consisted of the following gentlemen: W. S. Wreathall (Chairman), C. D. Stanley, G. Cardwell, J. S. Wills, F. P. Arnold, all representing Tilling and B.A.T., Ashton Davies, O. Glynne Roberts and Claude for the L.M.S., and Sir James Milne and F. C. A. Coventry for the G.W.R. The

This revolutionary double-decker, with its engine mounted at the side of the chassis, *behind* the driver, joined the fleet in 1933. Built by AEC, the model was known as the Q type. We numbered it 1000 and it is seen here in Liverpool operating the Brodie Avenue service.

G.W.R. members had been appointed the previous year following the take-over of the Western Transport. Seven of them came and, after a night at the Grosvenor and an inspection of the Chester premises, went round by motor coach via the Mersey Tunnel to Liverpool, Warrington, Crewe, and so back to Chester where there was a dinner in a private room. The next day we took them to Llandudno, coming back via Corwen and Wrexham. I remember we stopped for a moment at Gresford Colliery where the terrible disaster had occurred only a few days previously whereby more than 350 lives were lost.

This was the forerunner of a number of such tours until the war put an end to them in 1939. It was never possible to cover every district, but by going in a different direction each time we contrived to show the Directors pretty well all there was to see.

And so the winter of 1934 came and went, and it was spring, 1935 — Tuesday, 26th March, to be exact. On that day I had arranged one of my periodic early starts and was booked to turn up at Bangor at 6.30 a.m., followed by visits to a number of Depots throughout the day, getting home quite late that night to be told that they had been trying to find me all day as Claude had been taken ill on Monday night on his return from London, and had been operated on for appendicitis on the Tuesday. He was apparently all right, and would I go and see him the next day at the Westminster Nursing Home? So that was what he had been sickening for during the last few years. I was glad it was nothing worse, having had visions of other more serious ailments such as cancer. On Wednesday morning, then, I went to the Nursing Home and found him slightly propped up in bed looking pale and tired as might be expected. His voice was weak but quite clear, and he still retained that fighting look that I knew so well. I sat down by the bed. "I've had a bad time," he said, "it burst, but they have cleaned me up. There's a Board on 9th April. I don't think I shall be able to go by then, so I want you to go up to town tomorrow and ask the old man to put it off for a week. I shall be all right by that time." I put the date in my diary, and said he need not worry. "Give me a glass of water, Jim," was the next thing he said, and while I was getting it for him he went on, "I'm so damned thirsty. They don't give me enough to drink. Be sure and explain to Wreathall—" I told him not to worry and not to talk so much after a serious operation. "I'm all right," he insisted, "but I'm weak. Look after things for me, Jim. Come in to Chester every day while I'm bad, I'll see you when you get back." It was obvious that he was very tired, and so I got away as soon as I could.

Wreathall told me the whole story. Claude had been to London on Monday and felt bad, saying he would get away by an earlier train, which he had done, but by the time he had got to Chester he was really ill and much valuable time had been lost. He should have been operated on that afternoon in London, but it was left until the next day. "If I'd have even guessed," Wreathall told me, "I'd have put him in a car and taken him to Charing Cross Hospital that very afternoon, but he made out it was nothing. As for the Board Meeting, you can tell him from me that I won't postpone it. We shall manage perfectly well, and you'd better attend yourself in case I want to ask any questions."

On Friday he was not well, so I did not go in. Saturday the same, and on Sunday morning at 8 a.m. I was called up and advised to go to the Nursing Home at once. We were there at 9 a.m. The surgeon came down for a minute. "Hopeless," he said, and rushed back again. Ten minutes later he came down again. "No good—he's gone." They had tried everything, but peritonitis and general poisoning had set in, and poor Claude was just overwhelmed and died. I was stunned. As little boys we had slept in the same room for years, even creeping into the same bed when it was cold and nobody was looking. He was four years older than I, which was quite a lot at that age, but the gap narrowed as we grew older, and now I had been associated with him for sixteen years, and this was the end of it. There would be no more meetings on the railway bridge or anything like that. He had guided the Crosville for twenty-four years and now he had suddenly stopped doing so. I looked out into the Liverpool Road. A bus went by—a Crosville bus. Yes, the wheels he had set going would continue to turn whoever lived or died, and Claude need not worry on that score.

Those twenty-four years had covered a development period for the bus industry that was both unique and interesting, and I'm sure that Claude's name will be remembered for the part he took in consolidating the Crosville services. He was young, only 45 when he died, but that sort of thing happens in the world. The following Wednesday we had a service in the Cathedral and buried him next to his father and mother in Delamere churchyard near the forest where he had so often got a rabbit with his old friend, Dan Dunbabin, of Helsby, one of my father's first employees at the Helsby Cable Works. I should have to tell Dan myself. He was old now and would miss him—so would his wife, and three little daughters—so would I.

May he rest in peace!

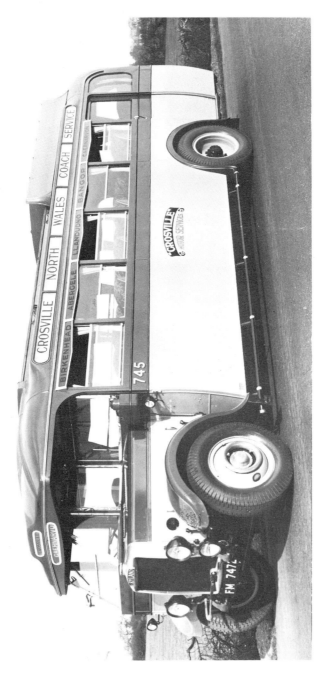

Leyland must have been very conscious of the amount of bodybuilding business they were losing from the TBAT companies, not least ourselves—there was a steady flow of chassis going from Lancashire to Lowestoft. In 1933 they produced some superb coaches, having been concerned principally with bus bodywork up to that date. We took five, one of which is seen above, and a further five from ECOC. The splendidly-appointed interior of one of the Leyland examples is seen opposite. Notice the North Wales Coach Service lettering and banner fleetname.

In 1933 we purchased three double-deck bodies from Eastern Counties — previously we had bought from Leyland. The body design was much more pleasing, with a smoother profile, and the new Leyland TD3 chassis with its deeper radiator put the finishing touch to an attractive trio of vehicles. We had been trying out the Leyland 8.1-litre diesel engine in an earlier chassis and in the light of its satisfactory performance were now introducing these more economical and potentially safer power units into the fleet.

In 1935 we decided to introduce a new system of numbering the fleet, using prefix letters to differentiate between the various model types. A complete list of the old and new numbers will be found in the relevant Appendix. The 'L' class were petrol-engined double-deckers and L3, a 1931 Titan, had previously been numbered 20. Notice the reversion to the original style of lettering for the company name.

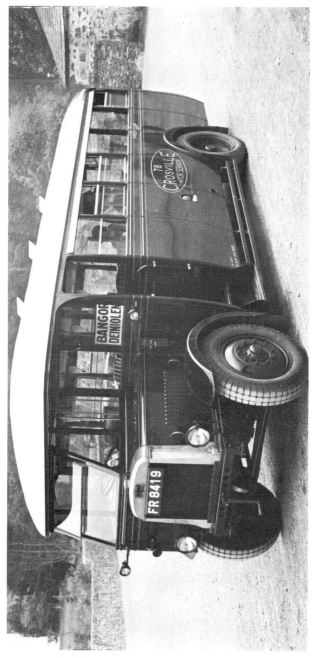

This long Lion, a PLSC3, looked just like all the rest of its rebodied brethren when it was photographed at Llanberis in July 1933 by a Mr G. F. Atkins who apparently travelled many miles in search of interesting transport subjects. He would have found FR 8419 more interesting than most—it was one of Websters (UNU) of Llangefni which the LMSR had been so keen we should acquire. It had not long been back from Lowestoft, where it had been rebodied with a similar, though longer, body to that shown on page 159. In 1935 it became B39, operating a further three years before withdrawal in 1938. Others of the batch are still in service. Fred Webster joined our Birkenhead office working under Merchant—subsequently he returned to Wigan, to form a holiday travel firm, I believe.

The change of livery, and classification of different models using letters of the alphabet as a prefix, did not quite coincide and these views of 1935 and 1936 Brush-bodied Leyland Cubs show the before and after effect. The company name transfer was later reduced in size. Notice the small plinth on the rear of the bodywork, above the rear offside window, where we mount the coloured dome to indicate the vehicle's depot allocation. This system was 'borrowed' from Midland Red when G. K. Palmer joined us from that company. The later vehicle illustrates the flared body skirt which was becoming fashionable at the time.

MacDonald and Company, trading as Maxways, operated from Birkenhead to Caernarvon. We took over their organisation at the end of 1934, together with ten AEC Regals which we later had rebodied by Eastern Coach Works. An earlier vehicle is seen here—its driver appears to be looking in the Echo to see if he has picked a winner. Harry MacDonald joined us and worked in our Woodside Chart Room—just a stone's throw from his old offices.

1935-1939

We found ourselves on 1st April, 1935, in the middle of important developments in the way of consolidation, a number of purchases of businesses were still awaiting completion, and there were the usual preparations for the summer to be made.

By arrangement with Mr. Wreathall, I carried on as Acting Manager and went into Chester every day. This régime worked smoothly, as I knew exactly what had been going on and what our policy was. I made W. Meachin Divisional Manager at Crewe and we formed English and Welsh groups of Divisions so that the work I had done could be carried on by Merchant and Roberts in the English and Welsh areas respectively. Thus I was freed of the detail of my previous work. The original understanding I had had with Claude sixteen years before was invaluable. We had agreed to work together in a certain way and he had always kept me in touch with what was going on. The result was that everything worked smoothly, though I felt that a big effort would have to be made if we were to carry on as he would have wished.

To begin with there were a number of businesses in the process of being taken over, including several large ones such as Pearsons of Liverpool and New Blue of Llandudno. In fact 1935 was a peak year in that respect, twenty-two businesses being purchased as against sixteen in 1934 and ten in 1936. Pearson had sold out to Ribble and ourselves and we were to take the Llandudno to London service as our portion, thus finally consolidating that route on which so many people had tried their luck. There were two schools of thought about it. One said that people wanted to get there by the shortest and quickest road, ignoring intermediate traffic, and the other side held that an hour longer would not matter in what was a full day's run anyway. So why not visit Kenilworth, Warwick and Stratford-on-Avon, not to speak of Oxford? There would then be intermediate traffic—a more interesting road, too, instead of miles of straight highway with nothing to be seen but a succession of motor lorries. Also, even the fastest road could not enable us to compete with the railway in point of speed.

On the night service it was no use arriving at either end before 7 a.m. the next morning, so although we had licences over all the routes it eventually boiled down to the well-tried one touching Birmingham, Stratford-on-Avon and Oxford—212 miles. Day and night, week in, week out. The drivers were picked men and became experts. It was rarely that weather conditions stopped them getting through—and on time too. They worked two days or nights, there and back, and rested the third day or night. We had an Inspector in London at Victoria Coach Station, and the service became just another wheel in our organisation.

By reason of our close relationship with other operators we had the advantage of their service anywhere on the run if there was any trouble, so that we never even carried a spare wheel. When they came into our area they enjoyed the same facilities.

There was another speciality that we arranged every summer, and that was a series of extended tours for anything between four and seventeen days to all parts of the British Isles. They had started in 1927 with seven-day visits to Devon and Scotland, and in 1939, which was, of course, the last year they ran, there were 125 tours and the thing had been worked up to a fine art. Joe Hudson used to go round in his car during the winter and visit all the hotels, the idea being that we would pay full prices in return for proper individual accommodation. A week's tour cost £10, of which £6 10s. 0d. was paid to the hotels. Thus we got 10s. per day per passenger, and as the coach got back on

Pearsons operated this well-appointed Leyland Tiger coach—with its high-backed seats—on the Liverpool-London service in 1931. The livery was a smart red and light yellow scheme with a leaping tiger emblem. I recall other operators using vehicles with similar emblems, one at least in South Africa. There was no toilet on these coaches, the frequent stops en route obviating the need. In 1939 five former Pearsons' vehicles, including this one, were rebodied, and are still in service.

What AEC thought about one of 'their' vehicles carrying the Leyland Tiger emblem isn't recorded — significantly, perhaps, the animal has been turned to face the rear. This Duple-bodied coach, seen in Pearson's original livery, also joined our fleet. It was mounted on the 'Q' side-engined chassis. We had purchased a double-decker of the same type in 1933 and although the two vehicles were definitely odd-men-out, both lasted until post-war days.

Sunday night and left again the next morning, it appeared to be good business. On the other hand, a lot of money was spent on each passenger in time and telephone calls, not to speak of agents' commissions, and we didn't really make much out of it except propaganda value which was excellent. There were many nice letters from all sorts of people who had discovered an easy way of seeing the country. They didn't even handle their suitcases once they had joined the coach. On arrival at a hotel they were given a room number, and lo and behold! there was their luggage. In just the same way it found its way back into the coach the next morning. All tips were paid on a proper scale. It took two men to manage each tour—both could drive—and both helped to organise reception and departure at each hotel.

Leyland continued to introduce new and improved models throughout the 'thirties and the nine double-deckers we purchased in 1935 were of the TD4 type. They were fitted with oil engines and three, including M20, had a form of semi-automatic transmission incorporating a torque converter. The cost of the latter in fuel consumption was simply too great, especially as our profit margin was falling, and we bought no more. Conventional gearboxes were fitted after the war. The bodywork was metal-framed and we were assured that our problems of body rot would be a thing of the past with these bodies. They were—corrosion took over instead and Leyland had to do some quick remedial work soon after we took delivery. The distinctive 'V' front replaced the former 'piano front' design.

Our buses have to conform to the many regulations intended to ensure the safety of passengers. Here another Titan is being subjected to the tilt test which confirms that it complies with the requirement on stability. In the case of a double-decker, weights equivalent to the passenger load are placed on the seats in the upper deck only and the vehicle must then be capable of standing on a platform tilted to 28 degrees from the horizontal without overbalancing. Inevitably, the springs allow the indicator mounted on the vehicle to show a greater angle, but the test is searching enough to ensure that buses rarely overturn. Limits on overall length, width, height and the gross laden weight complete with passengers, are among other numerous requirements.

We seriously thought of running continental tours in 1938 and I went up to London to see if Thos. Cook would organise our hotels for us. I saw their General Manager in Berkeley Street but he was not enthusiastic. Where did we want to go? Well, France, Italy, Germany, in fact anywhere within reason. I wanted to hire couriers from their organisation and had already fixed up for tyre service, fuel and breakdowns. He thought the German State Railways would not like the competition, nor would the French ones. I left it at that and went straight round to the German State Railway office in St. James's Street. The Manager's name was Seydl and I told him what we wanted and that it would be in direct competition with the railways. He smiled. "You needn't worry," he said, "we want visitors to spend money in Germany, and you would bring us new people who would otherwise never come. Our organisation will fix the hotels and give you every help. That is our government's policy." Thos. Cook's gloomy outlook seemed to be at a discount, and I went into more details. The coach would go to Cologne and work different tours from there each week right through the season. We would get our people from London to Cologne by air or boat and rail, whichever they preferred. The advice and help would cost us nothing. I came back to Chester ready to get everything ready, but the storm clouds were looming up and in the end we did not consider it prudent to risk losing a perfectly good coach in Germany, which we certainly should do if Hitler landed us in a war during the summer of 1938. As for Seydl, he sent us a lot of suggestions for tours, as promised, but that was as far as it got.

Sheffield United Tours had organised some continental trips and so we became their agents for the 1939 season, but never booked a single passenger. Our public seemed to prefer to stay in these islands — at any rate that year. We had a number of other express services to Blackpool and North Wales from various places. The latter ran entirely through our own territory and had become all-the-year-round affairs. After running steadily all the week there would be a tremendous Saturday peak which was difficult to meet, in fact we usually had to stop booking, and then there was difficulty at the Caernarvon end since hundreds of people turned up at the last minute wanting to go back to Liverpool without having definitely booked their seats, but we managed somehow, using any vehicles which were to hand.

For the extended tours each year we prepared a brochure. The first one for 1928 was a modest folder offering thirty-six days of travel in all. Amongst other things it said that "each passenger is *automatically*

The six-cylinder Tigers purchased in the 'twenties were still comfortable vehicles for express duties, despite now being down graded from their previous top link work. Number 178 of 1929 carries the long roof boards which appear to have been lengthened to take the extra wording 'and Anglesey'. They must have been awkward things to handle.

provided with the requisite space for his or her comfort." The italics are mine, and one cannot attempt to explain exactly what it meant, but it sounded luxurious which was the main thing. The next year the word "automatically" was left out and perhaps passengers were then required to shift for themselves to find space for their comfort. But the numbers rose as the years went on (see Appendix No. VI.) and from a modest 36 we attained 995 touring days in 1939, when activities of this sort abruptly ceased.

I cannot leave this subject without a word of admiration for Joe Hudson who organised the whole thing to the smallest detail. I am sure that the very sight of his liquid brown eyes was sufficient to calm any irate passenger who had a grievance, imaginary or otherwise, and he saw them nearly all personally either going or returning. Anyway few, if any, complaints reached Head Office.

An altogether different type of tour was the Directors' tour of inspection which, as I have said earlier, started in 1934 and ran for five successive years. It took place in the autumn, and I used to make the arrangements. There were ten Directors, but always one or two could not come, so the party usually consisted of about eight. They arrived by train one evening and spent the next two days on a carefully worked out time table, seeing as much as possible and getting back to London the third night. We used one of our latest coaches and after a hard day of inspection spent the evening very comfortably at one place or another. I remember one time they came from Euston direct to Holyhead, arriving on a wild October night at 11.30 p.m. We had a sitting room ready with a nice fire and plenty of sandwiches and drinks. The wind roared away outside, and they were getting warm and comfortable when Ashton Davies looked at his watch. It was time for the mail boat to arrive. "Come out and let's see the boat in," he said, but at first there was some reluctance to leave the fireside. Wreathall was frankly sceptical. "My dear man, it won't arrive for hours. Can't you hear the wind? No boat could get in to time on a night like this." Ashton Davies jumped up from his chair. "The mail boat is never late," he said, "and I bet you half a crown it's coming in this very minute. Anybody take me?" Old Wreathall stirred from his place by the fire. "All right then," he replied, "we'll go and see." We got our coats and turned up our collars before going out on to the quay which is only twenty yards from the hotel door. Sure enough, there she was, just closing in to the side with the mooring ropes already fast. Wreathall felt in his pocket for the half-crown and handed it over in silence. We

The H class Leyland Lions were the last full-sized petrol-engined vehicles we purchased and were delivered in 1935. They too have metal-framed bodywork and Leyland seem to have it right this time. H2 is seen at Leyland before delivery, whilst H1 was obviously posed in connection with our parcels service. The use of the destination aperture to display the fleet number was short-lived.

stood there waiting for the passengers, but none came down the gangways. W.S.W. grunted. He couldn't resist it. "A fine piece of seamanship," he said, "but it would have been better if you had booked a few passengers." Just then the first one appeared, looking nearly dead. They had had a pretty rough passage. Then we all became interested and finished by seeing them into the train before we went back into our warm room.

The Station Hotel is, of course, an L.M.S. Hotel of the solid comfortable variety—not like the Euston which many people call "Plywood Hall" for reasons which become apparent immediately you go inside. No, it has an air of its own, redolent of the very admirable Miss Thompson who has run it for so many years. I think it is in the right place too—within a few yards of the mail boats that run so exactly to time. All sorts of people pass through, some just for a meal on their way back to the boat, and others—elderly ladies for the most part—use it as a haven of refuge to stay a day or two if they think the crossing will be rough, or perhaps to recover if it has been just such a night as I have described above. The rooms are big and plain and the beds superb. The dining room looks on to the harbour and the same waitresses have been there for years. One feels that one is at a jumping-off point. Sometimes I have arrived by car at 7 a.m. and had a bath before breakfast. There again, the baths are large and generous, and the hot water never fails.

And so that stormy night we were comfortable and the breakfast was good, but the Cub 20-seater on which we had to ride to Menai Bridge was not so good except that we looked on it as a sort of liver tonic. However, once across the bridge and back on the mainland we got into our more comfortable coach and set out for Aberystwyth. The bridge had a weight limit in those days and the big coach was not allowed across it.

F. C. A. Coventry was with us and when we passed into G.W.R. territory he began to perk up and tell us stories of various varieties. We got there about tea time and put up at the Queen's Hotel on the front, where they gave us an excellent dinner, followed by a game of cards and then bed. The next morning we visited the Depot which is built on G.W.R. land. Old Coventry was thrilled. He hadn't been there for six years, but he wanted to see if they had mended the lock on the door of one of the station buildings—and there was a loose slate on the goods warehouse roof. He was indeed a man of many memories. I put them on the train at Crewe that evening and hoped they had had

That's how it was done—although many vehicles had roof-mounted luggage carriers not all of them had the external ladders seen in earlier photographs. These hinged plates folded down to provide footholds for access. This 1931-built Tiger was virtually identical to our own vehicles, being acquired in 1934. It became K88 in the 1935 renumbering and was rebodied by Eastern Coach Works some twelve months later.

a pleasant time. Anyway, they came again each year until the 1939 trip had to be cancelled.

Holyhead is on a separate island of its own—in other words Anglesey consists of two islands separated by a sort of lake and there are two causeways to Holy Island, the main one carrying the railway and A5 road from London. Half-way across there is a bridge over the water with a span of 18 feet. When the tide is high water runs from the sea into the lake and when it is low it runs out again, but the lake never gets time to fill or empty more that a few feet because the opening is so narrow. I once stood there at half-tide and watched the water stop running out under the bridge. When it was quite still I dropped a match stalk on it. In thirty seconds it started running the other way.

Hundreds of horse-power pouring to waste. What a pity it could not be harnessed, and how it used to annoy my father whose cottage at Valley was close by. "If I owned it," he would say, — "but there, — what's the use?"

Traffic in Anglesey is thin and difficult to cater for. The island could never stand by itself as regards bus services. The operator would just go bankrupt and there would be no buses. But we take the thin with the thick and they are, therefore, well served.

Holyhead, too, depends on trade with Ireland. Once upon a time the G.W.R. had plans to set up an opposition port near Nevin, but luckily they went to Fishguard instead. Such competition would have been quite senseless.

For several years before the war there were cheap day excursions to Dublin from Chester and North Wales at 10s. return. We fed the main stations twice a week and boats were well loaded. Mr. Brittlebank of the L.M.S., whom we knew as "Brit," used to get up a private party on the opening date of the excursion, and take us all over to Dublin for the day. The special train left Chester about half past seven in the morning and when we got to Dublin there was a coach tour to Bray followed always by a social call on Alfie Byrne who had been Lord Mayor for a number of years. He would receive us in his parlour and sherry was served all round. Then a visit to see the big Irish Sweepstake Drum and a really good tea at one of the hotels. Suppper on the boat and we were back in Chester before midnight.

These interludes from work are always good fun. They have nothing to do with holidays as such, but all work and no play makes Jack a dull boy. On the other hand, all play and no work soon lands Jack in Queer Street and in 1935, although we had record receipts and did record mileage, it was disquieting to note that the thing that mattered, namely, pence earned for every mile run, was not in very good shape. In fact it had declined a little each year right from 1920. The cost of running one mile had also gone down, but the margin between the two figures had become very narrow, and it was quite evident that it would not be long before we began to lose money. During the bad winter months we always had an adverse balance, but the summer peak used to tip the scales the right way. By increasing the mileage run we had kept up our profits on the principle that it is better to sell a lot of miles at a low profit than only a few at a better rate. But our area was now fixed and there did not seem to be many more good miles to run.

For some years we had been what I called cheese-paring the various costs of running—some of them by force as it were. Maintenance of vehicles, for instance, was cut to three farthings a mile, and no money was allowed for anything more. Much essential work was left undone and we were obviously living on our hump. Sooner or later there would be a show-down. I thought over this and decided that it must be sooner. Wreathall was helpful over the maintenance costs and we decided then and there to abandon the fixed cost idea. We would buy a hundred new bodies and get things up to date whatever the cost. He was a little sceptical, though, about my other idea of improving our vanishing profit margin by increasing the receipts per mile. "I doubt if you can do it," he said, "the other companies are just the same and they can't do it." "Well, do you mind if I try?" I replied. "I don't say it can be done, but we haven't really looked at it that way." "And why haven't you looked at it that way?" The old man was always direct, and if an awkward question was possible he could be depended on to ask it. "We just haven't, and that is why I want to do it now." "Oh, well," he said, "have a try—but I don't suppose you'll be able to do anything."

We tried. In 1935 we had dropped 14 points on 1934. In 1936 the drop was another 9 points. In 1937 it was only one more point, and in 1938 we went up 22 points followed by 7 more in 1939.

All this was before the war and although during the last year unemployment had been much lower, previous trade booms had never succeeded in achieving similar results. The tremendous bulk of mileage that our vehicles were running and the whole organisation of services and the habits of the public too, were like a juggernaut with a terrific momentum. They were akin to a gigantic gyroscope top that once it is set spinning refuses to change the direction of its axis of spin.

The nine Divisional Managers met and I explained the idea to them. We were to attack the revenue side of the business at last. Any reasonable cost of doing it would be allowed. There would be the maximum of new vehicles and the standard of maintenance of all assets would be improved. Publicity was to be completely overhauled, and on top of that all services were to be reviewed twice a year—after winter and summer working—so that we could become more elastic and open up the good traffic and clamp down on the bad.

That in brief was the essence of what we had decided. The Divisional Managers were keen on this new idea. They were tired of continually squeezing the orange that really had no more juice to squeeze. They wanted a new one that by careful cultivation would grow bigger and in the end give us a much bigger yield. As I have said above, it took us two years to stop the rot which had been going on for fifteen years.

Part of this very universal plan was to pay some attention to the social activities of employees. That may have seemed rather a long shot in the dark, but the argument was that a happy employee would do more to increase goodwill with the public than a man who was simply engaged by an organisation without a soul to do so many hours of work and then disappear till the next day.

There were sick clubs in existence at nearly every Depot, but nothing more. What could we do to improve this? Once again Wreathall backed me up. I wanted Club buildings at Wrexham and Crewe. We would have these places on the premises, so to speak, and would let them to employees' clubs at a rent of 5 per cent. on the money invested. The Company would pay the rates as its contribution, in addition to financing the building. They would be licensed clubs, the idea being that our people were not teetotallers and that being the case it was better for them to have their beer where they could be seen. A man who was on duty would not be served. For the rest there would be billiards and other games, and of course social evenings of all sorts. Men could exchange ideas—in fact there were all sorts of possibilities.

Being new to the game we made one or two mistakes such as regulation as to outside members, but the advantages heavily outweighed the disadvantages. The Chairman thought that the idea was sound—so did the Board—and in June, 1935, we obtained sanction for the first two clubs. I went to the opening nights, unlocked the doors, and there we were at our first social evenings on our own premises. Everybody was enthusiastic, the beer flowed, and I hope a good time was had by all.

Thus the summer of 1935 passed and at the end of it we had our first post mortem on each individual service. Each division took about an hour and a half, so that in thirteen hours we had found out our mistakes of 1935, and planned our programme for 1936. It was as simple as that. We had the whole winter to get out the details, fix the vehicles and licences, and everybody knew what was expected of them.

Winter—that is always a bad time for bus companies. Not only is revenue at its lowest ebb, but there are many difficulties of working. The problem of starting a large cold petrol engine has never really been tackled, let alone solved. "Those who make 'em don't have to run 'em." If they did, things might have been different. The same principle applied at that time to drivers' seats, which were hard, badly shaped and quite unadjustable. And as for our offices—"Those who built 'em certainly did not have to work in 'em"—otherwise they would have provided some proper heating. They were, almost without exception, cold inhospitable places where the Staff shivered throughout the

The suspension bridge across the Menai Straits was designed by Thomas Telford and, like the bridge at Conway, was part of the 19th century scheme to improve communication between Ireland and London via the A5—the Roman *Watling Street*. Telford, the son of a Scottish shepherd, was born in 1787 and rose to eminence in British engineering circles. He was appointed by HM Government to investigate and improve public works, and was responsible for the construction of the Caledonian canal. The Menai Bridge, opened in 1826, was one of over 1,000 bridges he designed. The tremendous height above the water—120ft. I believe—was insisted upon by the Admiralty to allow sailing vessels to pass beneath the structure. Two of our Leyland Cubs look suitably diminutive as they cross—weight restrictions prevented full-sized buses operating until the bridge was strengthened during the second war.

winter with perhaps a miserable one-bar electric radiator that was spirited away on 1st May and did not reappear until October. This, of course, was economy carried to a fine art, but we did not realise that cold people cannot do sedentary work—they do it, but only just. They become ill, which means that others must be paid to help out. It is better to spend a little extra money on keeping the place warm.

Very well then, we arranged in September, 1935, to instal central heating for the offices of Rock Ferry and Wrexham, our two largest Depots. Electric fires are expensive to run and the money saved would easily pay the interest on the capital cost of installation. I don't know why we had not done it before and can only ascribe our neglect to the craze for reducing costs without thinking about the possibility of spending in order to save.

At about this time we were thinking about new offices, seriously I mean, for it was a matter that had been in the air for some years. I had sounded the L.M.S. about selling us the Crane Wharf site, except the Old Flint Boat Inn which belonged to the Northgate Brewery. The L.M.S. would sell but the Brewery were not prepared to do so. The site was big enough but there would be no spare land and that was bad. We looked at our Sealand Road premises where we had our new Body Shop and where it was hoped that all our repair works would be situated one day. Which was it to be? I decided to recommend buying more land at Sealand Road as a long term policy, and Wreathall agreed, but we could not afford £25,000 to build just then. In a few years, perhaps, but in the meantime by all means buy the land which was on offer at a very reasonable figure. We bought it, but the war came just one year too soon, so we still go to work in a rabbit warren consisting of Crane House, the big corn warehouse, and an assortment of odd buildings close by. Tucked away, however, are plans and one day
....

Mention of the Flint Boat reminds me of my cousin, Frank Bates, who came from Australia to work with the old Company in 1906. He lived at Crane House during the week and came home to Helsby at weekends. He swore Crane House was haunted, and that somebody came up the stairs at night with chains rattling after he had gone to bed. It was quite true—they did. Old Griffiths and his wife who ran Crane House for Edward and Frank were at their wits' end because Frank spent a lot of time at the Flint Boat and came in most nights a little the worse for wear. They hit on the idea of dragging chains up and down the stairs to frighten him, but it didn't do much good, and poor

The four Shelvoke toast-racks purchased in 1935, U18-21, differed from the earlier versions acquired from Brookes Brothers in one very fundamental way. Whereas on the early examples there was external access to each row of cross-bench seats, (see page 96) these vehicles had a conventional centre gangway and a central entrance or exit. No side glazing was fitted but celluloid screens could be lowered in wet weather. These post-war views show the vehicles back in service after a period of storage 'for the duration'. Both had been renumbered in 1936 — U11 is seen above in Prestatyn, U10, below, stands on the promenade at Rhyl, against the traffic and with passengers loading in the middle of the road, prior to setting off for the Botanical Gardens.

157

Frank had to go back to Australia. Somebody saw him on the ship at Tilbury Dock and remained by the gangway until she sailed to make quite sure that he really did go back.

During 1935 the maintenance of body work had become a serious problem and very many buses were suffering from dry rot, or at any rate rot of some sort, usually in the side pillars at the joints, and of course, over the wheel arches. The Ministry of Transport vehicle examiners would come along with a sharp pointed bradawl and poke it into the bad places. At first we used to reinforce the joints with iron plates, but that did not last long and the plates soon broke away owing to more rot. There were a number of reasons for this. One was that steam-dried timber had been used on many vehicles. Pressure water washing had not helped, and of course there was the old enemy "anno domini". After ten years most timber bodies want a rebuild or even a new body altogether.

We had decided in June to have new bodies for 105 vehicles of one type. I put the contract to tender and in the end Eastern Counties took on the work at a price which would make operators pretty envious nowadays. We also obtained a Body Shop Manager and some extra men and set to work on as many as we could rebuild ourselves. In three months we began to gain, but it took two years to put things right. Later on teak waist rails were used which was a great improvement.

Wally Wright, our Chief Engineer from about 1911 onwards until 1939, had done his best; but had been handicapped by the forcible cutting of expenditure in his department between 1930 and 1935.

Engines were rebuilt by Leyland Motors at a rate per mile, and we had very little machinery in our repair shops. Some day, I thought, we will do our own engines, and have the finest repair shops in the country. To do that we must have a big mileage which in turn depended on getting up the receipts per mile. All the more reason for the scientific review of services.

1936 saw the decision to build a Depot at Flint, half-way between Rhyl and Chester. Garages should not be more than fifteen to twenty miles apart or one gets a lot of light mileage. There was some L.M.S. land at Flint near the station, and we ought to have had it, but they thought it might be wanted for sidings in the dim and distant future. As it was we had to go half a mile out where we were able to build a model place on the most up-to-date lines. More room was wanted at Caernarvon and we bought some land adjoining the Depot. A house on the Square was leased with the option to purchase, and there we

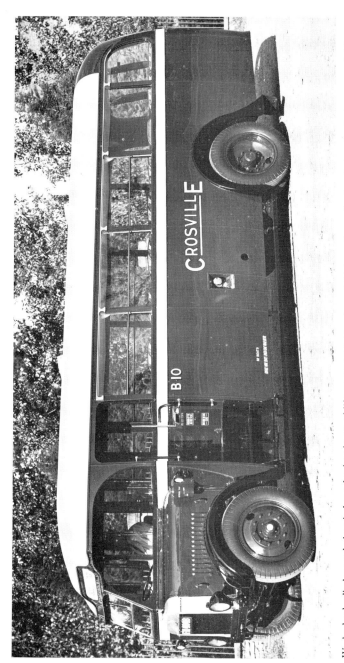

We had rebodied sound chassis for a further lease of life on several occasions right from the early days but embarked on a much bigger exercise in 1935. This resulted in 104 Leyland PLSC Lions and one Tilling-Stevens receiving new bodies built for us by Eastern Counties who won the contract largely on cost—they were by then becoming established as our regular bodybuilders for full-sized buses. The new bodies were intended to cut costly body maintenance and greatly modernised the fleet's appearance. They were among the first buses to carry the new class letters, the B series being used for the long PLSC3-type Lions; 84 of these were involved.

set up a cafe and the Divisional Headquarters.

We had gone on buying businesses and these extensions were a natural outcome of that policy. D. M. Prichard had a good service between Llanberis and Caernarvon. Word had come that he was ready to sell. I went up to Llanrug Post Office, which was run by the old man, and we went through to the house and sat in the tiny parlour, feeling dwarfed by the large piano that took up the whole of one side of the room. There was also a ticket cupboard, conductors' bags and other things, showing that it was from that very room that the whole affair was being run. Stanley Hughes and I talked and talked to old Prichard and his son, and after several hours we came to a price that seemed to me very high, but he knew the value of things and in the end we came out with an option on the business and vehicles together with a promise to rent us the garage at Llanrug. I sent up the particulars to Wreathall, and he consented by return of post in a letter of the usual three lines. What would Prichard do with the money? Well, buy property of course, at least that is what he told me later. I don't know whether he did as he said he would, because he died not long afterwards.

Prichard was based at Llanrug, between Caernarvon and Llanberis, and his fleet of ten vehicles included nine Leylands, six with Leyland bodywork. This investment in 'top of the range' machines reflected the solid nature of the business. JC 606 was a TS4 machine, new in 1932, and in 1939 it was one of the many vehicles rebodied for us by Eastern Coach Works; by then it carried the number K42.

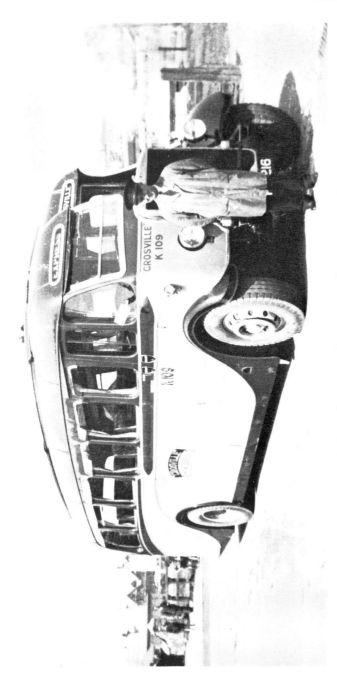

I mentioned earlier that we register our vehicles in Chester, usually reserving substantial blocks of consecutive numbers. An isolated number usually conveys to those who look for these things that the vehicle in question is in some way 'odd': AFM 216, seen here in green and grey, is a Leyland TS7 with Burlingham coachwork—built in Blackpool—which had been ordered by D. M. Prichard of Llanrug. It was delivered direct to us after the take-over of that company in March 1936. Our senior driver at Aberystwyth—W. H. Jenkins—stands in front of it outside Aberystwyth Depot later that year.

The Western Transport fleet had included a large number of Tilling-Stevens machines and some of these were sent to Brush in 1934 for what was euphemistically described as remodelling. Whether this was a new body or a major reconstruction of the old one seems uncertain now. The records show FM 7058 (above) as being of chassis type B10A2, whilst UN 1916 was merely a B10A. The driving position appears to be higher on the latter; both vehicles were photographed by Brush at Loughborough. Number 841 became R9 and was another of the many vehicles sold in 1938.

At Flint, the level of service operated in a mainly industrial area justified a solidly built depot which we completed in 1937. It also split the distance between Rhyl and Chester, thereby reducing dead mileage.

163

The new Caernarvon extensions were to include a first-class club room and offices, and we thought we should have a Depot with lots of room. One always thinks that, but somehow or other more vehicles come in and there is never quite enough space for them. Central heating was installed at Rhyl and Bangor and we started to make a club room at Llandudno Town.

All these developments cost money and it was decided to increase the capital from £955,000 to £1,100,000 in order to repay a loan and wipe off the overdraft we were running on at that time. Our dividend had reached 8 per cent. and it looked as if we would be able to keep that figure without difficulty.

There was one place which gave some anxiety, and that had nothing to do with buses. It was the Loggerheads Tea House, near Mold — unimportant in a way, but at a time when such an effort was being made to put the Company on a sound basis any weak part of the business stood out a mile. I have already mentioned how we came to buy the place in 1927, and of course its natural beauty was a tremendous asset. For nearly ten years now the tea house had been there, open in the summer and shut in the winter. It had cost between six and seven thousand pounds to build, and that was the first stumbling-block. How to make an adequate profit on such a large outlay. It might be and had been argued in the past that the profit came from the increase of passengers who went there on our vehicles, but I was worried in that the shortness of the season and the high expense of running such a large place always made the accounts show a loss.

It is true that the catering department as a whole was very flourishing under the able direction of Faichney, who ran our various shops and cafés with a master hand, and therefore the loss on the tea house was swallowed up quite satisfactorily. The kitchen was large and provided with any amount of boiling water, heated by steam, but there were no cooking facilities except a paraffin stove, the idea being that the sales were mostly cakes and bread and butter, so we got a large Aga cooker and started to make home-made cakes and provide a hot lunch. Surely there was a greater sale for home-made things, and a greater profit too. We engaged a manageress — Miss Jenkins — young, enthusiastic and with some appreciation of colour and art, hoping that she would make the tables and general lay-out look a little less wooden. The main tea room had a lovely oak-block floor and a fine big fireplace for burning logs, but the table china was of cafeteria quality. We went to the Copeland Spode works and ordered a full set

Caernarvon depot and offices form an impressive complex.

of things of more pleasing design, including a generous allowance for breakages, and after the fashion of the times we called the place "Loggerheads Road House". Tucked away in the Clwyd Valley, in a spot that shall be nameless, Faichney found a whole ton of honey stored in 7-lb. tins which he bought at a very low price. It was good local honey, too, and we packed it into 1-lb. jars and put it on the counter. Flowers were for sale, grown on the premises by Leonard Corfield who had come to my mother's service as garden boy many years ago. His rich Herefordshire accent was irresistible when it came to persuading people to buy his flowers. When Mother died he looked after Claude's garden, and now he was head groundsman for the Loggerheads estate.

Loggerheads Tea House near Mold, on the Company's 70 acre Estate.

To get on to the grounds from the main road one had to cross the river Alyn by a rustic bridge which was rather narrow, so we built a new one with more direct access and hung an oak sign over it with two swans and the name of the place.

It only remained to produce enough customers to partake of all these good things and that was where we had difficulty. Cars called and their occupants were pleased with what they found, but the tea house was big and the volume of car trade was relatively small. There would be plenty at week-ends, but it was pitifully thin during the week. People from the buses were a little shy and, of course, there were some objectionable folk who came in when we would rather have done without them. Then there was the "Can we have some hot water?" brigade who asked for just that and nothing more. One would have thought that they would at least have had the decency to get their teapots filled and then retire to some spot in the grounds in order to leave their trail of waste paper and empty tins. But no, they often sat down brazenly at a table inside the room and produced all kinds of food from fibre cases. Miss Jenkins did her best, but she was young and her presence was not sufficiently forbidding to warn them off. Faichney had to do it. We did not want to appear inhospitable but we couldn't put up with that sort of thing.

We tried to run dances, but the place was so isolated that the usual trouble occurred and when we put a stop to it the people would not come.

All this activity brought us lost of extra revenue, but at the end of the season we still found that the size of the place and the heavy capital outlay had once again defeated us—only by a small margin—but it seemed that we just couldn't make it pay. Stories of this sort are supposed to end happily, but right up to 1939 we still showed a small loss on the Road House each year, although it was money well spent for the bus traffic that it brought us.

When the war came it paid at last, because we shut down the tea part and let it as a store house for food—tinned pilchards to be exact. I ought to have reserved this for the next chapter, but perhaps it would be better to finish the story here. The pilchards remained with us for a long time and the place was damp. At certain intervals men appeared with lots of emery paper and Shinio and some new labels. They spent several days shining up the rusty tins and putting new labels on where necessary. I think it must have been an emergency store that was never used. However, when the food regulations come off we shall have another try at the almost hopeless task of making the Road House show a profit.

As for the Loggerheads Estate, it has amply justified the outlay we made that day at Mold auction rooms, and to many thousands of people it is a favourite place where they can wander in the woods to their hearts' content without fear of trespassing. There are trout, too, in the river, but the rocks are limestone, and in the summer the water has a curious habit of disappearing at one place and coming up in another.

Not many bus companies do catering, but a bus station needs

something of the sort and there is a good profit to be made. We have done it for a long time ourselves rather than let it to an outside contractor. One would think poorly of a big railway station that had no refreshment room, and the same principle applies to the large bus termini.

Early in 1937 our Parliamentary Agents wrote to say that the city of Stoke-on-Trent was promoting a new Act called the North Staffordshire Road Transport Bill under which all the operators in the Potteries — and they were legion — would be combined into a Transport Board. The Omnibus Owners' Association, of which we were members, was stirred by righteous indignation and undertook to oppose the Bill. Every M.P. in the country was canvassed by operators and the dangers pointed out to them, with the result that it was thrown right out at the second reading. We were not much affected, except in principle, but the example of the North of Ireland Board was fresh in everybody's mind and opposition was too heavy for it. I think it gave the Potteries operators a salutary shock and since then many of them have combined into one company, but in the old days Stoke-on-Trent simply licensed anybody who came along.

As for us, we were still very active. Extra land was bought in Liverpool in June, 1937, and a new agreement was made with Liverpool Corporation much on the lines of the old one except that it was simpler, and the percentage payment on local passengers was reduced. Also, we gave up the Brodie Avenue service as we were bound to do sooner or later.

Towards the end of the year a number of things happened.

We decided to double the Mold Road Depot at Wrexham, and enlarge the social club. There had been a number of take-overs in that area, and things were crowded. Also Llandudno Junction wanted a club. They got it. In two years we had provided premises at Crewe, Wrexham, Oswestry, Llandudno Town, Caernarvon and Llandudno Junction. In 1938 we added Rhyl and Chester, and several minor premises such as Flint where it was said that one could get the best breakfast in the county.

All these places were run by employees' committees, and well run too — at any rate as regards finance, although there was a tendency to try and make more money by inviting custom from outside. If we had known what was going to happen we would have made certain conditions in the lease. At some places, too, there was a tendency to exclude the management from the Club Committee. This was wrong

Telford's Conway Bridge has created problems for us of a different kind to his crossing at Menai. This view clearly shows the narrow roadway; single line traffic is controlled by lights. The low speed limit and payment of the necessary toll further delays vehicles. Traffic jams in the summer season play havoc with our schedules and the only solution seems to be a completely new bridge. One day perhaps? Meanwhile we shall struggle on and the faithful KAs will continue to slowly and majestically make their way in and out of Conway across this outdated monument to a fine engineer.

169

as they were built for all Crosville employees from top to bottom, and every section should have representation in managing their affairs.

Then again, as soon as any reserve balance of cash was saved up certain short-sighted members wanted a share-out. It is very easy to suggest in a general meeting that all members should now receive £2 bonus. They are all for it. Who wouldn't be? Human beings in the mass are like that. The agitator has only to say "We ought to ask for another five bob a week" and the others are with him to the last ditch without pausing to think of the why's and wherefore's. There were and will be many legitimate share-outs, although I contend that too much profit is a sign of high prices, and those who buy should get the benefit—not those who are members but never spend any money there. Or else the club should buy more and better equipment.

Whilst looking round for more revenue we suddenly thought of parcels. £9,000 a year was coming in without any effort. In fact we often discouraged them as being a nuisance. In 1937, however, things were different. If we could rope in a few more parcels to increase our receipts then we must do it. So there was a campaign and we got up to a level of about £12,000 per annum, and suddenly thought of luggage in advance on the Liverpool to North Wales services. This was perhaps meant more as an additional refinement for passengers than a source of revenue. In fact we would get very little out of it. Ribble came in with us on the idea and we went to Sutton & Co. (Manchester) Ltd., and Karriers Parcels Delivery Ltd. They were to carry and deliver this luggage almost anywhere in North Wales. The joint agreement was complicated, but it seemed possible that the passengers' part would be easy enough, and so we got ready for 1938. It was a flop. Luckily the carriers had not put in extra trips, and the existing parcels service was to be used, but people only send heavy luggage in advance and our type of passenger never has any. He only has a suitcase and prefers to carry it rather than see it depart into the unknown, and on top of that pay extra. I don't think it will come back. We wanted the railways to let us use their established service, but they wouldn't.

Early in 1938 Crewe Corporation promoted a Bill which amongst other things would provide a bus station in a situation not far from the Square. In other words, it looked as if we would have to pay heavily for what we were then getting for nothing. And so we lodged a petition. There is a lot of work in doing that. One must have all the facts and no fancies, because if the Bill gets its second reading it goes to a committee who ask every question under the sun, and a doubtful

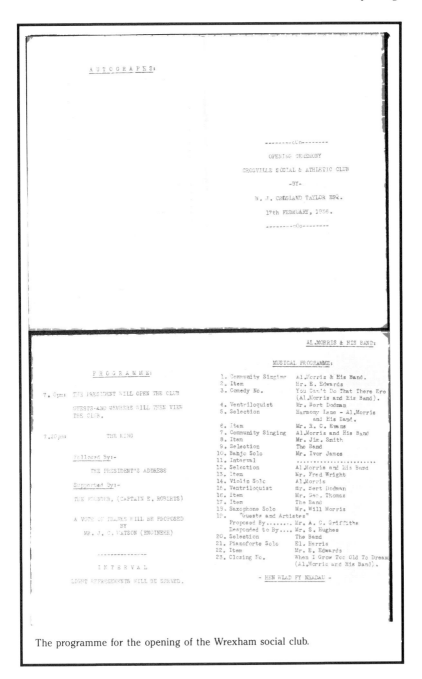

A U T O G R A P H S :

OPENING CEREMONY

CROSVILLE SOCIAL & ATHLETIC CLUB

-BY-

W. J. CROSLAND TAYLOR ESQ.

17th FEBRUARY, 1936.

AL.MORRIS & HIS BAND:

MUSICAL PROGRAMME:

1. Community Singing	Al.Morris & His Band.
2. Item	Mr. E. Edwards
3. Comedy No.	You Can't Do That There Ere (Al.Morris and His Band).
4. Ventriloquist	Mr. Bert Dodman
5. Selection	Harmony Lane - Al.Morris and His Band.
6. Item	Mr. R. C. Evans
7. Community Singing	Al.Morris and His Band
8. Item	Mr. Jim. Smith
9. Selection	The Band
10. Banjo Solo	Mr. Ivor James
11. Interval	....
12. Selection	Al.Morris and His Band
13. Item	Mr. Fred Wright
14. Violin Solo	Al.Morris
15. Ventriloquist	Mr. Bert Dodman
16. Item	Mr. Geo. Thomas
17. Item	The Band
18. Saxophone Solo	Mr. Will Morris
19. "Guests and Artistes"	
Proposed By........	Mr. A. G. Griffiths
Responded to By....	Mr. S. Hughes
20. Selection	The Band
21. Pianoforte Solo	El. Harris
22. Item	Mr. E. Edwards
23. Closing No.	When I Grow Too Old To Dream (Al.Morris and His Band).

- HEN WLAD FY NHADAU -

P R O G R A M M E :

7. 0pm: THE PRESIDENT WILL OPEN THE CLUB

GUESTS AND MEMBERS WILL THEN VIEW THE CLUB.

7.30pm: THE KING

Followed By:-

THE PRESIDENT'S ADDRESS

Supported By:-

THE FOUNDER, (CAPTAIN E. ROBERTS)

A VOTE OF THANKS WILL BE PROPOSED BY
MR. J. C. WATSON (ENGINEER)

I N T E R V A L

LIGHT REFRESHMENTS WILL BE SERVED.

The programme for the opening of the Wrexham social club.

fact is soon discovered under such a cross-examination. It never went that far. The Corporation withdrew the bus station clause altogether in order to get an unopposed Bill.

June, 1938, saw six open-top double-deckers working at Rhyl. They actually had ordinary tops which came off in one piece and could be put back in the winter. People came there for the fresh air. We could let them have it, and we would also be able to use those machines in the winter. Bramham at Eastern Coach Works showed great ingenuity in the design.

During that summer Ashton Davies and D. C. K. McCulloch left the Board of Directors. H. G. N. Read and H. V. Mosley took their places. Ashton Davies was one of the original Directors in 1930, but he was now acting Vice-President of the L.M.S. and could not really spare the time to come on our Boards. His name was magic on the L.M.S. and in Lancashire in particular he was thought of very highly. He must have spent a good many hours of his life travelling by train.

The coach building factory at Lowestoft had been set up as an independent company in 1936 and W. Bramham, who had previously been in charge at the Roe coachworks in Leeds, took command. He quickly grasped what we wanted, and, in addition to supplying normal double-deckers as shown below, created the vehicles shown opposite to our special requirement. The complete roof assembly, windows, pillars *et al*, lifted off quite easily in one piece.

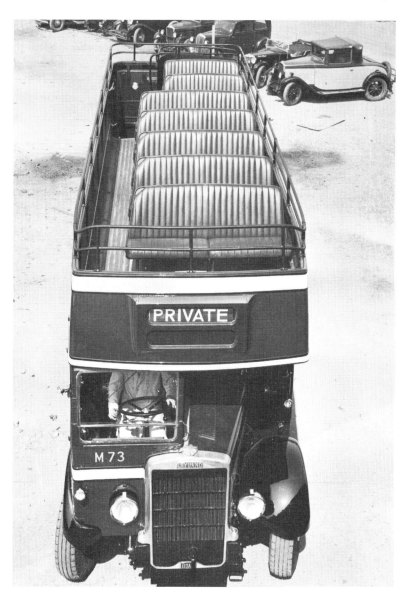

Bramham arranged for his photographer to show a detachable top vehicle without its roof—in doing so he produced the best picture one could possibly want to illustrate how the lowbridge double-decker principle works. The side gangway projects into the lower saloon, of course, as every passenger who has ever cracked his or her head when rising from their seat knows only too well.

We sent the open-top buses to Rhyl and they regularly operated the Llandudno service, competing between Colwyn Bay and West Shore with the open-top tramcars which the LCBER Company had purchased from Bournemouth in 1936. Our driver experiences another novelty here—setting the destination blinds. Use of the 'Wid' displays in saloon windows continued, of course, but we fell into line with accepted practice and started fitting linen blinds to most vehicles.

The various letters of the alphabet were quickly being used up. The LT7 was the final development of the Lions we had been buying since 1926. The H class, illustrated on page 49, were petrol-engined but the J class of LT7 Lions were oil-engined, with a Leyland 4-cylinder unit. We have it in mind to have these vehicles rebodied as soon as we catch up on our wartime arrears. Eastern Counties built the body on J27, seen in Great Orme Road, Llandudno.

The success of the big rebodying programme of 1935/6 encouraged us to take similar steps to modernise further batches of elderly vehicles. This time we concentrated on Leyland Tigers and AEC Regals, but once again the 71 bodies concerned were built at Lowestoft. A new design had been evolved, with a 'half-canopy', and the result was quite distinctive. Official records show these bodies as 'semi-coach'. This particular example can be seen in original condition on page 160. The deeper radiator — a CovRad conversion — will be noted as will the rear entrance. The K class were petrol-engined vehicles, KAs were, and still are, of course, oil-engined.

The early KA class saloons were painted in a slightly different style, with almost the full length of the roof finished in a silver grey. These vehicles had the entrance at the front and I always felt this was the best-looking version of the several variants we operated. Undoubtedly the modern chassis with its substantial radiator was a great improvement. KA17 waits to get back to sunny Rhyl—the grey windswept terminus at Llandudno looks rather inhospitable and definitely not open-top weather.

The shadow of war was approaching and it became a race against time to get as many improvements completed as possible before it started. During the August and September crisis months Sir William Chamberlain, Chairman of North Western Traffic Commissioners, rang me up at home early one morning. He had to form an Advisory Committee at once. Would I serve as representing bus interests in his No. 10 Region? Yes, certainly I would, and that was that. We didn't do much until 1939 when the war started, after which we met regularly in Manchester in the room of the Regional Transport Commissioner as he had then become.

We breathed again after the Prime Minister had staved off the break with Germany for another year, and I got Wreathall to agree to getting the Rhyl Bus Station improvements carried out at once while there was yet time. There had once been a public house in the bus station—the White Lion—but we had pulled it down in 1931. Now we pulled down a house at the back, and started one-way traffic through from back to front. I enquired about some more land next to the station, but the price was £24 per square yard. In any case proximity to some traffic lights made enlargement undesirable.

The standard KA single-deckers were instantly recognisable as **Crosville** buses. By working closely with Eastern Coach Works we had produced a design with our own 'stamp' of individuality, and yet it was practical, without frills, and based on a combination of Lowestoft standard features. Minor differences were apparent in successive batches — the paint scheme for the roof, position of destination displays and so on. Although we had no way of knowing, these were to be the last buses to our exclusive design. The exigencies of the likely post-war demand, coupled to Tilling group policy of rigid standardisation, meant that even while ECW were unable to build more than a few buses during the war, having had to evacuate their Lowestoft premises on 28th May, 1940, new designs were being prepared. After the war, when construction was resumed, there was one design of body for single-deckers, and another for double-deckers. For everyone. And that was it. Henry Ford would have been proud of ECW and Tillings — we were not so sure, though it made good sense at the time. This 1939 example shows the new serif-style lettering then recently adopted and still our standard in 1948.

Rhyl bus station, looking from the rear entrance, and showing the great improvement over the earlier layout (opposite).

Trade had been good in 1938, and promised to be still better in 1939. We prepared for a record number of extended tours, and generally laid our plans as we had always done during the winter. The Chairman had spent a day or two with me in July, 1938. He was Yorkshire, and passionately fond of fishing. One day we had lunch in Llandudno and he was casting longing eyes on the little boats in the bay. As we walked along the promenade afterwards we stopped and talked to the old fishermen, but there was not time to charter a boat and go out. "Some other day," he said, but he never did. Fifteen months later he was dead.

The usual Directors' inspection took place in September, 1938, and when passing Cerrig-y-Druidion I remember Wreathall telling the others that he had arranged with me that if war came Crosville would move their Head Office there to be out of the way. I forget whether it was in 1938 or 1939 that he visited Germany with the British Road Federation to see the new autobahns that had been built there. Straight double-track roads with no crossings and suitable for high average speeds between towns. He had a good time, but was greatly impressed by the strength of Germany, so that he thought we would have a bad time if war broke out.

The way it used to be — a Titan double-decker on the Dyserth Circular eases out into Rhyl High Street in 1931. The timetables and clock are prominent on the wall of the public house.

There was to have been a Commercial Motor Show in November, 1939, but, of course, it was cancelled. It was held every two years at Olympia, and later at Earls Court, and it was an event much looked forward to by the senior Crosville Staff. They were given their expenses to spend a full day and night there and it was much appreciated. Wally Wright had to be there a bit longer, but we used to meet for lunch and have a really good meal, and of course we all had our own friends on certain stands, especially the Leyland one, and there were plenty of free drinks all round. Some firms carried this a bit too far and the evening parties were not altogether a credit to the industry, but then it only happened every two years and one could get up a lot of steam in that time. If we knew nobody else we all knew Colin Percy of Leyland and it must have cost him or his Company quite a lot to entertain the Crosville staff that called on him during the show. Then there was Cadwalader with his gargantuan laugh, and many other characters too numerous to name.

If there is another show in 1948 it will be the first for eleven years. War takes a big slice out of normal life, and many of us have seen it done twice. Man individually is a good fellow but in the mass we are mugs and always will be. We must be ignorant, too. We don't seem able to learn by experience and our memory is short.

I went to our house in France as usual for the last three weeks of August, 1939, determined to enjoy my holiday, come what may. Everybody was at Veules les Roses as usual, and we all did the usual things although there was much talk amongst our French friends. Old Veyrat showed us a secret wall safe in his house where he would hide his money if the Germans came. Madame Lamy of the Hotel des Bains confided in my wife that she had changed her money to English banknotes as she did not trust the franc. Marchand, the painter, went up and down in his nautical cap, often taking apéritifs on the Casino terrace with his wife and the man she was living with. Madame Remy, the washerwoman, washed and ironed in her little cottage till eleven o'clock every night, her gold tooth shining when she smiled at you. Our butter woman from Sotteville still called with dairy produce twice a week. We asked her what she would do if there was war. "Ah," she said, "during the last war I have worked hard for the soldiers. I would do the same again." "And what if the Germans came?" The reply was prompt. "I would not want to work for them, but one must live, and to live one must work, and the Germans would have the work."

I say all this to show that all was normal up to the last moment. One

In 1938 we took delivery of a further three toastracks for Rhyl. They reverted to the old charabanc style with separate entry to each row of seats—loading and unloading was too slow on the previous batch of enclosed models. The continuous running board makes the conductor's job easier but spare a thought for the men who brought these machines over from Lowestoft where the bodies had been built—they had been designed neither for speed nor distance work!

day about the end of August, Jeanne Collet, our woman who came every morning to get breakfast, came up in tears to our bedroom and said "I can't do anything today. I have no heart in me." "Any why not, Jeanne?" "The Russians are no longer with us," she sobbed, "they are with the Germans." They were, too. It had just come through on the wireless, and there were many more French people besides Jeanne who "had no heart in them" on that day.

I stayed a few days longer and then with some difficulty telephoned to Merchant at Chester to ask him what was happening. His voice was faint but clear. He said that the military were making all sorts of arrangements for mobilisation and we might have many vehicles involved. On the whole we agreed that I ought to go back in case of accident. It was decided that I should take the car and try to get it across, so that night I left the family saying that I would let them know if it became necessary for them to come, and would meet them in Newhaven when they eventually arrived. I had to leave the car on the quay in charge of the R.A.C. man. The place was packed with vehicles waiting for a passage. He said it was all right and he would do his best. Merchant was going to send a car down to meet me in Newhaven in any case, so I went on board with no luggage at all. There was no room anywhere except under one of the boats, so I sat down on the deck with my back to one of the engine room hatches. The night was warm and pitch black — also dead calm. There were no lights on deck, so there we were, an invisible cluster of humanity gliding across the channel to our proper country. Towards early morning it became cold, and there was a heavy dew. I was thankful to lean over the open hatch and get the warmth of the hot air coming up from below. All nights end, and it was nearly dawn when we arrived at Newhaven. It was quite light by the time I got through the customs. The car had not arrived, so I walked into the Newhaven Harbour Hotel and went to sleep in a chair. I had breakfast — still no car, but at about 9 a.m. young Eric Edge appeared with it. He had driven the previous day to Hull and back with Goodhall, our new Chief Engineer, who had been called up, and then all night to Newhaven — a truly prodigious feat. I made him get in the back and try to go to sleep, but he wouldn't — said he wanted to see the country.

When I got back there were all sorts of activities going on. Friday, 1st September, was Z-day, which meant that the evacuation of children was to start from the big towns. We had prepared our part ages before. I went up to Northgate Station and watched the first trains arrive.

There was a small crowd, but it went smoothly there like it did elsewhere and the ordinary services were not dislocated. There was nothing I could do, so I went down to Crane Wharf again and we carried on.

On Saturday, 2nd September, I slipped down to Brighton by car to pick up the family who had suddenly decided to cross the previous evening. Saturday was the first night of official black-out, so I got a brush and some black enamel and painted over the lights, leaving what I thought was a small strip of light to see by. The last twenty miles in the dark from Whitchurch were most difficult. Neither I nor anybody else could see a thing, but we got home and went to bed by candle light, having no black-out curtains.

Sunday was to be the fatal day. We went to church at St. Werburgh's at 10.30 a.m. In the middle of the sermon somebody went across to Canon Hayes and whispered in his ear. He told us immediately, and when we came out there were policemen and volunteer helpers building sandbag barricades round the County Police Station. A lot of useless things were done at that time, but people wanted to be active, so they just did whatever came into their heads.

The next day the Company set out to do its best to provide whatever might be needed in the way of bus services to help the war effort.

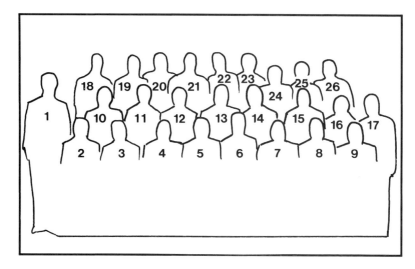

1 H. H. Merchant, Chief Divisional Manager England. Later Traffic Manager.
2 G. K. Palmer, Assistant Engineer. Later Acting Engineer.
3 Exide.
4 Wally Wright, Chief Engineer.
5 Exide.
6 W. J. Crosland Taylor.
7 Exide.
8 H. Eckersley, Chief Accountant. Later Secretary.
9 S. Hughes, Divisional Manager North Cambrian (Caernarvon).
10 H. W. Mills, Divisional Manager Bangor. (Prev. with Midland Red/Royal Blue).
11 W. M. Wynn, Divisional Manager Rhyl. (Prev. with Silver Motors).
12 H. Jones, Divisional Manager Wirral and South West Lancashire.
13 Capt. E. Roberts, Chief Divisional Manager Wales & Divisional Manager Wrexham.
14 R. C. Cowmeadow, Architect.
15 S. M. Johnson, Divisional Manager Chester and Licensing Officer.
16 Exide.
17 Exide.
18 D. S. Deacon, Divisional Manager South Cambrian. Later Divisional Manager Crewe, then Rhyl/Llandudno.
19 J. Grandon, Publicity.
20 W. L. Baynham, (Formerly asst. to General Manager Western Transport).
21 J. F. Burnley, Assistant Engineer.
22 C. Wise, Assistant Engineer.
23 W. Meachin, Divisional Manager Crewe.
24 J. M. Hudson, Private Hire Manager.
25 A. H. Martin, Traffic Assistant.
26 A. W. Smith, Company Secretary.
    C. R. Taylor, Divisional Manager Llandudno (Formerley General Manager Royal Blue) unfortunately missed this outing and is thus not included in the group.

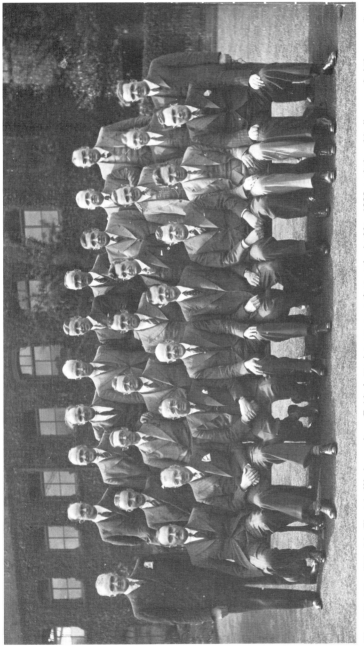

We visited the Chloride Electric Works—where Exide batteries are manufactured—in May 1939 and they kindly recorded the occasion by having a group photograph taken for us. It gives me pleasure to include it since it includes many of our management team at that time.

1939-1948

When I got to the office at Crane Wharf on Monday, 4th September, things were much as usual but there was a sort of expectancy in the air. What was our part going to be in the war? The fact was that nobody could tell us, though we felt ready for anything. We were almost at the end of what had been a very busy summer, and in the ordinary course of events would very shortly be reducing mileage ready for the winter. The coming of war cut short the season, and this was lucky, because a number of drivers and others were in the Reserve and had been called up a few days previously. They had been paid a few pounds a year which was easy money during peace time, but now they had to keep their side of the bargain, so off they had gone, and their places were taken by men who otherwise would have been out of work. Many of these reservists were first class drivers with long experience and it was a blow to lose their services. Good drivers, and good conductors too, are worth their weight in gold. They are the backbone of any bus company and get the money on which we all live, although they in their turn could not do without the rest of us who keep them on the road. Still, nobody is indispensable in this world and so we continued to function.

I wrote to Mr. Wreathall to tell him how things were and got a reply from Mr. J. S. Wills to say the Chairman was not well and was away from business. On 21st September, 1939, he died. He had been associated with the B.E.T. Company for many years—even before the 1914-1918 war, I believe—and during that war had served with the R.O.D. about which he had often told me tales. He had been closely connected with the Wrexham and Llandudno Companies; perhaps that is why he became Chairman of the new Crosville Company in 1930. For over nine years he had been behind the scenes guiding our destinies with a judgment that was absolutely sound. His decisions were always made quickly and with few words; he had an uncanny ability in putting his finger on the points that mattered and asking questions that required an absolute knowledge of one's subject. His mental arithmetic worked like lightning, but I used to think he was highly strung and nervy at times. Perhaps the war upset him—I know he had thought a lot about it during the last year. It was a pity he did not live to see the achievements of his own particular industry, but there it was. I went to the funeral feeling that we had lost a good friend.

J. S. Wills

J. S. Wills
Chairman, 1939-1942

After the split of 1942, John
Spencer Wills, always a BET
man, rose to become Managing
Director of that group in 1946.

J. S. Wills became Chairman, and E. R. Soames took the vacant seat
on the Board.

Preparations had been made to convert 32 single-deckers into
ambulances for ten stretchers each, and we got on with the work. They
were to be held at the disposal of the Ministry of Health for air raid
casualties, but of course they were not used at that time. We stored
their blankets and other equipment, and forgot about them, except
that the engines were run every now and then, to make sure they
would be able to function if wanted.

Petrol rationing was to take effect during September, and we were
asked to cut what services we could down to about 80 per cent. of
normal, but factory services must not be touched. This was a golden
opportunity to get things sorted out, since we had a lot of superfluous
mileage that had to be kept going in normal times but that was really
not required. Some routes had always been too thin and should never
have been started, but uncontrolled competition in the past had
saddled them on to us. There were complaints from people who
expected special buses for about two passengers, but they soon died
down. Many busy routes suffered no reduction at all—some were even
increased, because in this new war there was at least one thing about
which everybody was certain—they were restless and wanted to
travel. In fact the whole population had an urge to move somewhere
else and do something different. This need for movement soon affected
our services. The receipts per mile began to rise—even during the

187

winter. We had struggled for the last four years to gain hundredths of a penny a mile and now we were given whole pennies, without doing anything. There were plenty of seats to fill, and the spare capacity went on absorbing traffic which much more than offset the increased costs per mile.

In October the standing limit of five passengers was raised to eight, and later in the war to twelve. Finally by arranging the seats along the sides of a single decker we got up to thirty standing passengers in that type of machine.

All wars bring a rise in the cost of living followed by a rise in wages which brings a further rise in the cost of living and so on *ad infinitum*. Our first rise in wages was 4/- per week on 20th December, 1939.

To deal with the wages question on a national basis the Ministry of Labour and National Service had got the employers and the Trade Unions to agree to the formation of the National Council for the Omnibus Industry. The Omnibus Owners' Conference nominated employer members to this Council and the several Unions concerned supplied an equal number of members. I well remember the first Council meeting in Montagu House, Whitehall, in 1940, when we were addressed by Ernest Bevin in his usual able manner, and personally I felt glad that wage negotiations were going to take place on that level and not locally. Up to now the practice had been to play one company off against another. We would be told that Ribble do this, or Lancashire United do that. Those companies in turn would be asked for something "because Crosville have given it to us."

We dealt with the Salford office of the Transport and General Workers' Union. Tom McLean was the Passenger Trade Group Secretary and we had known him for many years, but he was getting older and also was not well. Too many midnight meetings—rowdy ones too. Coyle had gone to London to join the Union headquarters, so it fell to J. G. Dickie gradually to take McLean's place, which he did very effectually.

One of the first things the National Council did was to conclude what was called the "Standstill Agreement" under which it was arranged that during the war basic rates would remain the same, and any adjustments of war wage would be fixed by the Council and recommended to their members. This was to prevent the individual local applications by the Unions which might prejudice the proceedings of the Council. Later on the Unions wanted to do away · with this Agreement and there was a lot of argument about it, but on the whole the system worked well.

We were obviously going to have to do a great deal of factory contract work, and I began to think about vehicles. Normally we sold a number of old ones in the autumn and arranged a replacement programme, but in 1939 we kept what we had got and it was decided to put in an order for 102 new Leyland chassis including 66 double-deckers, even though we might have no chance of getting them. The order would be there and we should have some priority when the war was over.

The winter was cold, and we had a problem at Wrexham, where a large number of vehicles were being gathered together to service a large Royal Ordnance Factory that was now nearing completion. A field at the back of Mold Road Depot was covered with hundreds of tons of macadam well rolled in, and there we parked nearly 150 buses that could not be got under cover. Imagine the difficulties in the black-out during the long winter nights, and they nearly all had to get in and out at the same time. There was hot water in tar boilers in time of frost and luckily the field was on gravel so that surplus water drained away fairly rapidly, although large puddles were unavoidable and many a man did his work with wet feet and wet clothes too when it rained.

Tar boilers being used to produce hot water at Wrexham.

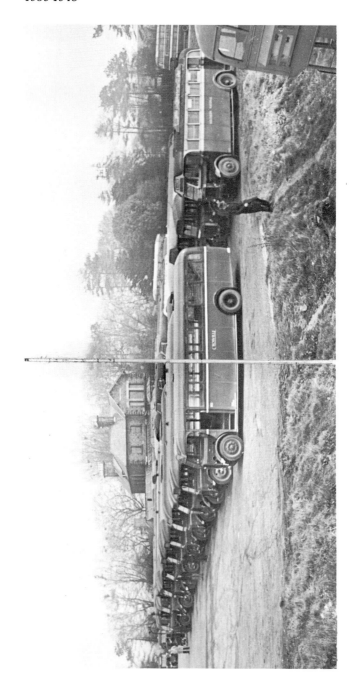

Mold Road, Wrexham, with a motley selection of vehicles including Leylands and Tilling-Stevens from our own fleet (the latter ex-Wrexham Transport) and hired vehicles from Western National and Wallasey. The long winter is drawing to a close and the birds are accurately forecasting a good summer with their high nests.

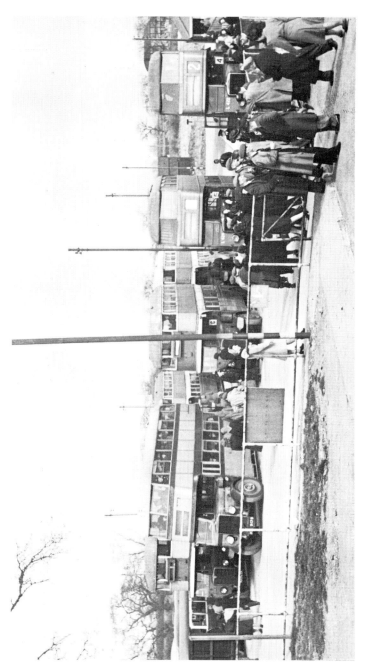

Double-deckers from Wallasey and London and a Ribble Leyland Tiger loading for the homeward trek. L424, visible on the bus second from the right, is our fleet number identifying it as a petrol-engined Leyland machine.

Humphreys, the Depot Superintendent, was there early and late, and when I say early I mean 5 a.m. every morning. Chief Inspector Morris also was a tower of strength, but there are so many names one could mention that it is impossible to do justice to them all. The leadership was good, and that made it possible for the main body of men to back them up. I do not know what we should have done without the Club which was so handy to the Depot. As for Watson, the Area Engineer, nothing disturbed his habitual calm, but he must have been hard put to it to keep things going, especially the hired vehicles, because we had been forced to get buses on loan—as many as 134—and no sane operator lends his best machines.

I think the Manchester Corporation buses were the best, but there was nothing under twelve years old and even if they were given the lightest mileage they were not easy to keep going. Of course, we ought to have bought them and gradually rebuilt them, especially the bodies, because the day of reckoning would come when we would have to send them back and not be able to get anything to replace them.

The operators in the North Western Traffic Area had formed themselves into a sort of mutual aid society with the idea that if one of us got into trouble through bombing or anything else, the others would rally round and help. It applied to spare parts and other stores too, and Mr. Bennett of Manchester Corporation acted as Secretary in no uncertain manner. We obtained help in many cases from the others and, I hope, we in turn did the same for them. Later on the idea was changed a little and the association developed into a sort of maintenance committee to pool engineers' information.

As everybody knows, it was not until April, 1940, that the war really started, and during that month it was decided to pay small maintenance allowances to wives of our people who were serving in the Forces. There were no hard and fast rules but each case was considered on its merits by a special committee formed at all Depots, and a recommendation put forward. The amounts were only small because we did not know how far the thing would go, but there were many letters of appreciation and every little bit was a help to the wife who had so many expenses to meet and such a small pay packet to meet them with.

When the Red Cross Penny-a-Week Fund started nearly everybody became a subscriber and 3,000 pennies a week amount to £650 per annum.

There were no conductresses until about April, after which they

Mold depot with its rolled macadam, puddles, hired buses, and, a brighter note, one of our first conductresses. By this time photographic materials were in extremely short supply, aerial reconnaissance being one obvious area which took priority. Even professionals had difficulty in obtaining their requirements and picture quality often suffered accordingly. This Manchester Titan has clearly seen better days and yet these were among the **best** of the hired vehicles, having received new bodies around 1936. This one was with us from 1940 to 1945.

began to appear everywhere. There was only one thing for it—we must have a Lady Supervisor to look after their interests, and Mrs. Valdes appeared on the scene. She must have interviewed nearly every girl who came and applied for a job, and spent many weary hours travelling from place to place. The result was that there was very little trouble considering such a radical change. I never asked her how she did it but she must have had some strange experiences. We backed her up to the best of our ability. In any body of men there are good ones and bad ones and it was exactly the same with the women. As the numbers increased forewomen were appointed at the larger places and we settled down to the new conditions. There were several cases of man and wife working the same bus. Driver Lloyd of Nantwich was one. I sat in his bus on Crewe Square one day and talked to both of them. It was grand, they said, to be able to work together, and come home to meals together. Lloyd was an old servant and I wished all our people could be as happy as they were.

It was fun being on the Square again. So many old faces and old friends amongst the men. A word with this one and a handshake with that one—and always smiles. Buses came and went like bees visiting their hive. Queues formed and melted like spring snow. No sooner were they formed up than a bus arrived and took them away. My mind flashed back to the days of the Queen's Park Fête when I used to act as Controller all afternoon and evening, shouting myself hoarse, while the bus crews worked like demons till after midnight. There was always a procession about a mile long, the Square was thronged with people the whole day long, and cashing-up at Nantwich did not finish until 2.0 a.m. Crewe depot did not exist then. We used to get extra buses from Chester to help out. Yes, I liked visiting Crewe Square where people were so friendly.

The summer of 1940 would have been a gay season in ordinary times, but in that year they were anything but ordinary. Excitement followed excitement until we were in a more or less dazed condition. Of course holidays were cancelled, not only for us, but for everybody in the country—and just as well because our factory commitments were such as to leave no margin of staff for our usual seasonal work.

A Dennis single-decker with snow plough attached receives some coaxing at Wrexham. Some of the 'visitors' can be seen in the background. WA1 was an oil-engined Lancet II with Dennis body ordered by J. R. Lloyd, Bwlchgwyn, but delivered to us after we had taken over his business in 1938.

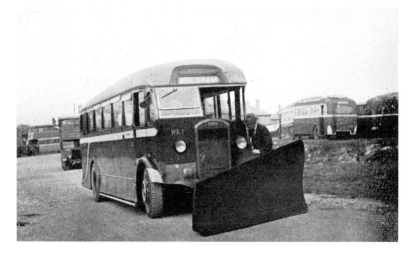

The weather was grand and seemed to have been specially provided to compensate us for the hard frosts of January when the Dee had been frozen over, and the river view from Crane Wharf was just a mass of pack ice moving up and down with the tide, making strange noises as it was pressed and crushed together. Now there was day after day of sunshine whilst the invasion of France was rapidly accomplished by Germany.

Our own Crosville Staff worked hard and did what they were told—and we were told plenty. The Government was grinding out Statutory Rules and Orders at the rate of over 2,000 every year. Each Order had the effect of an Act of Parliament and became the law until it was altered or cancelled by another one. Who could keep pace with them? The only organisation that had a hope of doing so was Butterworth's Emergency Legislation Service, and so we became subscribers and began to fill my bookcase with neatly bound volumes of the new laws. Not so many affected us, but they were there for reference in case they were wanted. One of them issued in 1940 concerned the immobilisation of vehicles. A petrol engine was easy to deal with, but what must one do with a diesel engine if one wanted to leave it for half an hour? Nobody knew, and, of course, there is no answer short of removing a part that would take quite a long time to put back. A detachable steering wheel was one suggestion , but what if it came off by mistake as one was going along?

I referred to heated petrol and strong men with a rope on the starting handle in the early days. That was one way—this was the other!

Even the North Wales coast had elaborate anti-invasion devices since it was seriously thought in some quarters that the Germans would attempt a long sea journey before landing. The late Chief Constable of Caernarvonshire took every precaution. The degree of headlight illumination was laid down, but he would have even less light on the Llandudno sea front. It was dangerous and really impossible to drive down from Penrhyn to Llandudno with no lights, so we said that the service would be suspended if we were not allowed to adhere to the proper regulations; as this would have produced heavier complaints from the public than the war headlights had done, Mr. Pritchard gave in. He told me that many residents were quite sure that the bay was full of submarines, so he felt that he had to do something.

In 1935 we had five grades of wages and it was our policy gradually to level these up by eliminating the lower grades. It was perhaps hard luck on Grade I who were the highest paid men in the English area,

Some enthusiasts managed to continue taking pictures during the war and recorded scenes we would otherwise have missed. This Tiger single-decker hadn't been with us very long before it succumbed to white edging to the mudguards and chassis dumb-irons. One look at the tyres says it all as far as rubber supplies were concerned. The slots in the headlamps' masks gave all the light we were allowed — Chief Constables notwithstanding. We took delivery of twelve of these TS8s in 1940, plus a further four with coach bodies by Burlingham. The final three arrived at Chester as bare chassis — evacuation of the Lowestoft factory at 24 hours notice during the invasion scare had stopped ECW body production completely. We could see no chance of getting bodies for these chassis and so we gave them the rear-entrance bodywork fitted in 1936/7 to former Brookes Bros TS2s in the big rebodying programme. Better to have spare TS2 chassis than brand new TS8s. We were going to get plenty of opportunity to show our talents in this direction over the next decade.

because they had to remain more or less stationary at a time when the trend of wages for the country as a whole was in an upward direction. Any spare money that could be allocated to wages was immediately applied to the bottom dogs, which was quite right really, but there was no doubt that the thin Welsh areas could never have stood by themselves and paid the wages that our people there were now getting. On 6th June, 1940, in the middle of all the excitement, we found time to move Rhyl and Denbigh from Grade II to Grade IA, and this was only one of a series of adjustments that culminated in December, 1942, in one grade for everybody. It cost a lot of money and was a big step for us to take. We are two-thirds Welsh and one-third English, and I am sure that the Welsh element will realise how much was done for them when grading was abolished. It is not their fault that Anglesey, for instance, is so very poor for bus services, or that so many places are apparently dead during the long winter months. Higher fares would make things still worse, and why should Welsh people pay more for their travel than anybody else? And why should they receive less wages than others doing similar work elsewhere? No, the prosperity of Wales lies in linking up with England in these matters, so that we can see that it was a wise fate that built up the Crosville services in such a way as to link the thick with the thin into one financial whole.

The turn of events that summer made it obvious that our big Leyland order for 102 vehicles would have to remain in abeyance indefinitely, and when an opportunity presented itself to acquire ten new double-deckers that were not wanted by the East Kent Company we welcomed

One of the 'diverted' East Kent Titans, new paint still gleaming, crosses the tramway on its way to Llandudno. The destination layout identified these vehicles' intended owner, as also, of course, did the BFN registration marks.

Although the 'highbridge' Southdown vehicles differed quite considerably in appearance from the 'lowbridge' East Kent machines, both batches had been built by Park Royal in London. This was the sort of variety of style which, as far as ECW at least was concerned, would become a thing of the past. M115 and KA146, both fitted with the later 'hooded' headlamp masks, are seen in Bangor in October 1942.

them with open arms. Services in the south-east had been very much curtailed, and many people had left the district. The same thing happened a few months later in the Southdown Company's area and we obtained another sixteen buses. They were of the highbridge type that we would not have chosen in the ordinary way, but it did not really matter—we wanted as many as we could get because the factory services were growing all the time and it was a point of honour to fulfil every demand made on us.

Ellesmere Port Oilworks had become immense—how they ever escaped serious bombing always astounded me. Vickers-Armstrongs needed a special organisation, so did the Wrexham R.O.F. and many others.

We gradually persuaded the factories to realise that it was not possible to change their working hours or take on hundreds of new people without considering how they would get to and from work. Also, there must be staggering of hours in order to save vehicles. In 1940 it was still fairly easy to get enough staff for all these activities as the original age reservation groups had not been touched, but once Dunkirk was over one could foresee that the war would have to be taken much more seriously and there would be a comb-out everywhere.

On 7th July the war bonus was increased from 4/- to 7/- per week, and the next month we arranged to pay extra money for spreadover duties over 11 hours. The ordinary man in a factory works 8 or 8½ hours more or less straight off and then finishes until next day, but our industry is cursed with having to work at all hours intermittently. Not only is this wasteful, but it is also exasperating to those who have to do it. One works say from 7 a.m. to 10 a.m. and then there is nothing to do until 5 p.m. Is a man to go home? Perhaps so—it depends how far away he lives. But once he is home he cannot put on his old jacket and settle down to whatever he wants to do. He has got to turn out again and go all the way to work and back just for a couple of hours' pay. Blessed is the straight turn of duty, but it is a physical impossibility to have them all straight, and so we must bear with at least some split duties. By keeping to a 48-hour week they can be minimised but they can never disappear.

That fateful summer passed, and as the nights drew in it became evident that Merseyside and its surroundings were going to be seriously troubled by bombing. People simply did not go out after dark. There was nowhere to go, and one might have to remain out all night. It was no use running about empty, so late trips were cancelled and all buses came in very early. Mileage was saved, too, which was important.

Our premises and vehicles were so spread out that it was hardly possible for us to escape unscathed. On the other hand this very dispersal was a safeguard in that a major disaster was unlikely. And so things turned out. I went to Rock Ferry Depot one morning to find pretty well all the roof glass on the floor, windows out, and the Depot at one end looking as if a giant had leaned against it or a typhoon had struck the sheeting. A land mine had fallen in the field behind the boundary fence and in one split second about £4,000 worth of damage had been done. But it was nearly all superficial and no vehicles were damaged beyond repair. The Engineer's and Architect's squads were already on the scene and great energy was being applied to clearing up. The services were running well in spite of serious personal difficulties endured by our employees, many of whose homes had been hard hit. A special team of men from Chester was always held in readiness for just such an event. It consisted of men of all trades and their tools and equipment, so that they could get things working pretty quickly without waiting for outside contractors who had far too much to do anyway. It was no use replacing the glass which might have been broken again at any time, so the roof lights were covered with anything we could get. Another night at Rock Ferry a bus was set on fire by an incendiary bomb that fell through the roof. It was put out quite quickly and did no harm. Fire-watching was in force by then. We had these people in most Depots with their camp beds, rugs and insatiable thirst for tea. It was hard to find accommodation for them, but it was done somehow.

In November, 1940, many factories in and around Coventry were damaged and as a lot of them were working on aeroplane parts they had to find other premises as soon as possible. It fell to the Ministry of Aircraft Production to do this for them. A man named Lord Beaverbrook was the Minister at the time and he had no consideration for anything but the work of his own organisation. Quite right, too, but one must beware of such people and be prepared to resist them if necessary. He would have this building and that building, quite regardless as to whether such action would upset industry to a greater degree than the advantage he would gain.

What better for his purpose than a few bus garages? Before we knew what was happening he had prevailed on Sir Arnold Musto, Regional Transport Commissioner in Birmingham, to give him our Oswestry Depot without any arrangements being made to find us other accommodation. We stuck fast, and were told to find a yard somewhere. We still hung on and asked the Commissioner for an actual date on which he would like the Oswestry bus services to stop running as we could not carry on without some premises. I had made up my mind that we would not go until an order was made in court or the bailiff arrived to throw us out. Finally the G.P.O. vans were turned out of a garage just up the road and we took it over.

A similar thing was happening in North Wales and we lost part of Bangor before we could get our Transport Ministry's full support. They wanted nearly all the other Depots as well, but by now the

Commissioners had realised the importance of Bus Depots and no more were allowed to be taken. At Bangor I was more or less told by Daimlers that if we could not have our premises in working order in three weeks we might as well give in to Germany. In point of fact it was months before they made a start. Thus we lost all Oswestry and part of Bangor, but after that we held everything.

One of the L.M.S. Directors was Mr. O. Glynne Roberts, C.B.E. His name was familiar to many people who travel on the L.M.S. Railway because it appeared written up over all places where that Company sold drink or tobacco. That, of course, was because he was Secretary and, therefore, the licences were in his name. He was a quiet man, never saying much, but always ready to help people, especially in his own County of Anglesey. He had been with us since the formation of the new Company in 1930 and was now to retire, which he did in February, 1941. I mention this because this was the first retirement we

Bus production had virtually ceased by 1940. Subsequently the need to provide vehicles to move war workers was recognised and limited production of vehicles 'frozen' in build, or able to be constructed from components in stock, was authorised. Bodywork was to a design prepared by the Ministry of Supply, austere to say the least, and known as Utility in the nomenclature of the times. This Leyland TD7 carries bodywork by Willowbrook—the harsh outline reflects the lack of domes or other items which would have been produced by skilled panel beaters. Semi-skilled labour was to be used instead.

had had from the Board of Directors. I asked him where he was going to live. "Menai Bridge, of course," he replied. "In that case then," I said, "we shall meet from time to time." His brother Dick Roberts was L.M.S. District Goods and Passenger Manager for Chester and North Wales and a good friend of ours at all times. This made a vacancy on the Board and the L.M.S. nominated Mr. G. Royde Smith, their new Secretary—another man of few words but full of delightfully dry humour when one got to know him.

There was snow in January, 1941. Never have I seen it so deep in Cheshire, but it did not last more than a week, and then everything started to grow and spring had arrived. After May there was a lull in air raids, in fact a complete cessation as far as the north-west was concerned, and we turned our thoughts towards a very limited holiday traffic. Fuel had again been cut, so we could not do very much. 38 vehicles had suddenly been requisitioned in April and we simply had to let them go. There was no work for them and they were chiefly coaches and 20-seaters unsuitable for factory services. One had a special experimental five-speed gear box and after a terrific amount of struggling against red tape we got it back in exchange for another one. As for compensation, it was difficult to know how to base a claim—so difficult, in fact, that even now, six years later, we have not received a penny, and the amount is to be fixed by arbitration.

The usual annual war bonus claim was settled on 23rd July, and became 11/- per week after a full-dress enquiry in London, although everybody knew the answer before it started. The country as a whole was beginning to feel the financial strain and War Savings schemes were being pushed everywhere. I had a talk with Mr. Wills as to what we could do. He suggested some sort of bonus scheme, as the Treasury had indicated unofficially that anything reasonable would be allowed as an expense of the business. Something sure plus something with a bit of a gamble such as a direct contribution and a periodic draw for free certificates. I said I would prepare a plan on those lines. So in October, 1941, we launched our scheme whereby deductions could be made from wages and the Company would make up the fifteenth shilling on each Savings Certificate. Added to this they put in one free certificate for every sixty in the scheme, and these were drawn for every three or four months. The draw was quite an event and was made at the Queen Hotel, Chester, by about a dozen of our Depot Savings Organisers who got a free lunch and a day off at the same time. Once we invited the Mayor, and another time Mr. S. E. Shrapnell-Smith

Overhauls and repairs became more and more difficult with shortages of staff and spares; vehicle shortages increased mileages far beyond normal standards. The B-class Lion, left, appears to have had the roof repainted already, before completion of the overhaul. Behind the Fordson tractor is a Cub, and behind that one of the Manchester buses. Engines are being re-assembled on the right.

came and addressed us.

Some Bus Companies gave still better terms, notably the Red & White, who were extremely generous. The actual bonus cash was really paid by the Government because they received just that much less Excess Profits Tax, and so it amounted to issuing certificates at a discount to a certain section of the people. Quite wrong in principle, but it achieved its object, which was more money saved and lent to the country.

At about the same time, 22nd October to be exact, we were scheduled under the Essential Work Order which meant that in theory nobody could leave us without special permission, and that we could not dismiss an employee without similar permission. This worked fairly well, but if a man had made up his mind he wanted to go his standard of work suffered badly if he was forced to stay. On the other hand, it put an end to people just walking out because they had their eye on another job round the corner where pay was higher. Somehow or other about two of our people left us every day on the average in spite of the Order, but it might easily have got out of hand otherwise. The labour question was getting worse all the time, and a number of elderly people began to appear, to whom we were very grateful for their stepping into the breach, but who were often referred to by the more disrespectful members of the Staff as the venerable old gentlemen. Venerable they may have been, but the point was that they came when they were wanted, and it must have been hard for some of them. There were also the very young who stayed until they were called up. Yes, nobody needed to be out of work.

The advent of Russia into the war had heartened us considerably, and when U.S.A. came in too it seemed that it would only be a matter of time before the end came.

Clothes rationing meant coupons for uniform. The number to be given in for a full outfit was twelve per annum out of the then total issue of sixty-six. It was good value and we took the line "No coupons—no uniform." There were a few hard cases who refused to give them in, but the Board of Trade congratulated us on the response, and in their turn gave us all the buying coupons we wanted without question, so that we could look after our uniformed staff properly as far as the supply position would allow.

Early in 1942 we found that some sort of canteen facilities must be provided at Liverpool Pier Head. There had been a place in the Goree but that no longer existed after the raids in May, 1941. Since then we

In the months leading to the Munich crisis we had considered our future very carefully. The need for more vehicles seemed undeniable, and in 1939 we held on to everything we had. We also purhased some PLSC Lions from Ribble Motor Services— twelve with original bodywork and dating from 1927/28. They were virtually identical to some of our own examples sold in 1938, some of which had been rebodied by Eastern Counties in 1933. We still had a substantial number in service and plenty of spares to keep them going. One of the Ribble vehicles was later converted for use as a canteen, as shown.

had run the mobile canteen down to the stand every day and taken it away at night, but it was not really large enough. There was a house in the G.W.R. yard in Irwell Street which had been damaged but was repairable. It was suggested that we might turn this place into a canteen of some sort, so I saw the Railway people, who said "Certainly," but that they would not pay for the repairs. All right then, provided the rent was low we would do the repairs and fit the place up. They let us have it at a very low figure and a canteen committee ran it, with some success. This sort of place is always best run by the employees themselves. We have tried it, but human nature is too strong and there is naturally much more interest taken in a place owned by the customers. If a man throws the cups about or steals the cutlery—well, he will get into trouble from the other owners who are present, and in any case he is also harming himself. It was surprising what was accomplished by this and other similar canteens at our various Depots. Breakfasts are important. Many a man will not be late if he knows that he can get a bite of something at the Depot just before going out. Also it saves the rations, and that means quite a lot. Flint was and is noted for its breakfasts—Liverpool for its dinners and so on.

The Clubs generally prospered during war time. In many of them men in uniform were allowed to use their facilities and, of course, there was more money about than ever before. But we suffered a little from inexperience in certain matters, such as limitation of outside membership. The Company had invested a considerable sum of money for the benefit of employees. Rents were cheap and they did not have to find money for rates. It was a little disturbing, therefore, to find in one case that there were more outside members than Crosville men, and in another that outside people were actually on the Committee. All this could have been provided for on the lease if we had only known.

Then again it was intended that committee membership should embrace all branches of employees and thus be truly representative, but there was a tendency in some places to try and exclude some branches and create a monopoly amongst one particular set of men. Meetings for any other purpose than club activities were strictly prohibited, and that was good, although there was often a temptation to use the premises for other things such as political or religious functions.

One thing we did find out, and that was that such premises are a bad fire risk. Caernarvon nearly had a fire when a cigarette end dropped down the side of an armchair. In February, 1942, the Chester Club was nearly burnt out through a mysterious fire in the fire-watchers' sleeping quarters! It occurred early in the morning in the interval between the watchers going off duty and the day staff coming on, and the reason was the obvious one of the neglected cigarette end. Lastly there was the disastrous fire at Rhyl in July, 1945, about which more will be said later.

On 25th March, 1942, the war bonus went up from 11/- to 15/- and one began to look on this rise as an annual affair, but if money was easier to come by, petrol was not, and there were signs of much tightening up. Certain companies were experimenting with gas producers and in the Tilling Group in particular much progress had been made by the Eastern National and Eastern Counties Companies. I discussed all this with J. S. Wills and it was decided to get three of these machines, or whatever one called them, and I arranged to go to Chelmsford, Norwich and Cromer to have a look at what was being done there. Palmer came with me and we duly called on Mr. Worssam, the General Manager of Eastern Counties. When we had explained the real reason for our visit he was very helpful but quite candid. "You know how it is," he said, "we don't like the things, but necessity is the mother of invention, and the alternative is to lose quite a lot of mileage." That visit was before we were ordered to put 10 per cent. of our fleet on to producer gas, but Sir J. F. Heaton, Chairman of Thos. Tilling Ltd., had seen it coming and was well ahead with his group of Companies.

"I'll tell you what would be the best thing to do," Worssam went on. "Go to Cromer as passengers this morning to try one for yourselves, and then have a good look at the Depot and stay the night. I will come along next morning and then you can tell me what you think." So off we went to Norwich Bus Station, which was a very fine place adjoining a large Depot. We waited on the Cromer stand and there appeared a Bristol single-decker with the usual trailer. All I can say is that we left to time and arrived to time too. There were no hills to speak of and once she got really warmed up we really got along in fine style. Cromer was a small Depot of about 15 vehicles, all on gas, and we had a good look round. The main impression I got was that it was a distinctly dirty and messy job, but that it was certainly possible to keep

In 1943 utility single-decker bodywork became available — if justified — and we obtained three for fitment to the former Brookes Bros TS2 chassis which had been used for trials with gas producer units since their replacement bodies had been transferred to the TS8 chassis mentioned on page 196. K37, DM 6231, with Burlingham 34-seat bodywork, waits its duty at St. George's Square, Wrexham.

going and above all that everybody was genuinely keen. They had had so many visitors that they felt they were pioneers. We took a light bus round a fairly hilly route. After one long rise the driver got out and poked the fire into renewed activity as it was getting blocked with clinker. Otherwise all went well.

That night we slept at an almost empty hotel and looked out of the windows along the coast at miles of dreary barbed wire. What a prospect, but the breakfast was good—bacon and eggs!

The next day Worssam picked us up and put us on the train for Chelmsford, where Mr. Pickett of Eastern National took us out on a special bus with the gas producer mounted on the back of the vehicle itself. This one had a more powerful engine and we were much more impressed by its performance. Pickett told us that he had had the Minister of Transport down with Sir Frederick and given them a satisfactory ride on it. We came back to Chester ready to face up to it and soon after that were told to buy 101 trailers at about £100 each.

The conversion of the bus itself was quite a job and took time, especially as our staff was already inadequate for ordinary needs. And then again, special buildings would be required with improvised machinery for mechanising the process of servicing the producer units. I talked it over with Palmer and we decided to concentrate on Depots at Chester, Rhyl, Wrexham and Crewe, using Leyland Tiger petrol-engined vehicles. Our private opinion was that the war would be over before we could get the programme completed, and I think there is no harm in saying that we fervently hoped that it would be, because we already had all the work we could manage without having to become Heath Robinsons. Indeed, the producers themselves, and the queer apparatus for hoisting and weighing the anthracite, might well have been designed by that famous artist.

We had about fifty on the road before the order was cancelled overnight by one of those sudden strokes of the pen for which the Government was famous. But I am forgetting—we had a gas car too—it was Claude's eight-cylinder 32 h.p. Chrysler, and Palmer used it quite a lot, travelling to Plymouth in one direction and Darlington in the other. He used to take a stoker and a few sacks of coal in the back, together with a surreptitious supply of petrol to help out when necessary. Wear and tear was heavy with the trailers and we used most of our spares whilst others were being repaired, so it was just as well that we did not do our full number of conversions. We should never have kept them on the road.

The producer gas trailers were mainly attached to our Leyland Tiger single-deckers — their six-cylinder engines had sufficient power to make up losses resulting from the lower efficiency of the set-up. Fleets throughout the country were similarly equippped by Government decree — 10% of the fleet had to be converted. Fortunately we managed to avoid having to involve too many TD1s and TD2s where reserves of power were less. On our visit to Eastern Counties we had seen and sampled Bristol vehicles with similar trailers to this one. The national target was 10,000 conversions, though I believe slightly less than 10% of *that* figure was achieved.

When it was over we lined them all up on the old tennis courts at Sealand Road and wondered what to do. Perhaps they would be useful to farmers as trailers. So an advertisement was put in the local papers, and in a week or two they had all gone at £13 each. The tyres were the attraction. A "dealer" from the Manchester area offered to buy the lot at that price and save us the trouble of dealing with individuals, but we preferred to let local people have them.

Sealand Road works had been invaded by Vickers-Armstrongs who were using two out of the seven bays to turn out certain aeroplane parts. We worked amicably together, but one day in 1942, Mr. Duncan, the Manager of their Broughton Works, came along and said that they wanted a third bay very badly — in fact there would be a serious bottle neck if they didn't get it. I pointed out that it was just as important to us to keep it since we must carry the majority of his people to work, and we couldn't do it without a certain minimum standard of maintenance. It was a logical argument, and I suggested that if the M.A.P. would build us two new bays at the other end of the works then we would release the bay that Duncan wanted. This was a shot in the dark but it worked, and I went to the M.A.P. in London with our Solicitor, Mr. Herington of Sydney Morse & Co. There we met the appropriate official and hammered out an agreement under which they would build us our two bays and we would each pay half the cost.

Eventually we could buy the second bay at whatever it might be worth to us at the time. It was the best part of a year before the work was finished, but we got a brand new paint shop twice the size of the old one, and indeed big enough to suit our needs for many years. Vickers got their extra bay, but didn't use it very much as by that time their plans had changed.

Repairs and maintenance during the war became more and more difficult, and I sometimes wondered how we kept on the road at all. Many vehicles didn't, and we could no longer say that at week-ends during the summer the only machines not on the road were those that had had serious accidents. There were, of course, two main handicaps—the continued famine of spare parts and the everlasting labour question. The Regional Transport Commissioner's technical staff were as helpful as they could be, but a system of certificates of need does not help much. We used to say that if all the controllers were put on productive work the country would have produced more goods. As it was one had a continual headache wondering if one was breaking one of the new Statutory Rules and Orders which were still being ground out by the Government departments at the rate of over two thousand each year—six or seven every day! The ability to survive was measured by the ingenuity of those who had to do the work in scrounging—yes, that is the best word—scrounging what they could where they could get it. Welding old parts became an art. Palmer, our Engineer, came with me to a demonstration of this sort of work in Liverpool and we did a lot of it. One woman was particularly good and we lent samples of her work to a travelling exhibition of salvage methods. Needless to say, they never sent them back.

There were other women in the shops too,—good people, but above all there was Maude,—I don't know her real name. She still drives the small motor truck between the shops with consummate skill, and on occasion can shovel coke with any man. Short, stout, and immensely strong, she has done much good service.

Palmer had a bright idea of painting the machinery in the shops a pleasant shade of blue, and keeping it nice and clean. Every now and then there was a grand week-end clean up—in fact a spring-clean. Some thought it a waste of time, but the vast majority were pleased to work under tidier conditions, and probably worked better in consequence. Overtime was unavoidable. Our five-day week was a thing of the past and the men in the shops worked pretty long hours. But the mileage done by engines before overhaul went up and up until many of them had done 180,000 miles before they received attention. Quite a number failed before they were brought in, and things like crankshafts suffered from fatigue as well as being ground down to too small a size. But this is not the place to go into all these details. What we could do was to try and keep up the spirits of those who had to do the work, and this was done in various ways. One idea was to try and introduce a team feeling, and to this end we organised visits of all types of employees to Headquarters, where they saw everything, including the maintenance side, on a personally conducted tour. They must see what the other members of the team had to do in order to understand their own place in the game. The visits were popular enough. It meant a day off, free food, and indeed an interesting time. I saw most of them before they went back to their Depots, and they seemed pleased with the efforts we had made to entertain them.

In 1942 there were rumours of a change of control. Since 1930 we had been one of the Companies of the Tilling and British Automobile Traction Group which meant that both Thos. Tilling Ltd. and the British Electric Traction Co. Ltd. had an interest in us. It was said that this joint arrangement was going to be terminated and the constituent companies would be apportioned to one main group or the other. In a way this had always been so in that each of the Companies was under a Chairman of one house or the other. In order to avoid cash payments being made, the accountants recommended amongst other changes that the North Western Road Car Company should go over to the B.E.T. and Crosville should become part of the Tilling organisation. This meant a change of Chairman and Directors, and so on the 3rd December, 1942, we sat down with Mr. J. S. Wills in the chair, and got up with Sir J. Frederick Heaton occupying that position. Additional Tilling nominees on the Board were Messrs. P. J. Stone Clark and J. H. Mills. G. Cardwell and F. P. Arnold of course remained and the railway Directors were not changed.

Sir J. Frederick Heaton
Chairman 1942 onwards.

John Frederick Heaton
was awarded a knighthood
in 1941, acknowledging
his contribution to
wartime economy by the
use of producer gas,
thereby conserving petrol.

Thus in a twinkling of an eye, as it were, we became a Tilling company. I had not met Sir Frederick before, although he told me he knew Claude, and we had a short talk on other matters. I explained our system of wage grading at Depots and how we had gradually reduced the number of grades. "How much would it cost to put them all on one rate?" he asked. I told him, and it was a large amount. "Would it help you if we do it?" I said that it would be the final solution of a problem that had worried us for years, and then and there he told me to go ahead as he thought that differential rates were bad in principle. He also asked me to look around for any likely property that might interest the Company—land or buildings, or both. It was to be in preparation for future developments, and to be regarded as an investment, since property was a rising market. There were to be other policy changes also which would bring us in line with the Companies in the Group, some of them immediate, and some gradual. I had the impression that my new Chairman had very definite ideas formed on many years of experience in the industry. There would be no more meetings at 88 Kingsway, that homely and familiar building over the Holborn tube station with its three board rooms, all of which I had been in from time to time. Instead of that it would be Crewe House in Curzon Street with its more dignified appearance and its very fine board room with the oval table and rather nice chairs. I was a member of the English Speaking Union just round the corner in Charles Street, and found it conveniently near to Crewe House. Bombing of London had ceased on a large scale and many of the Tilling staff had been able to come back from Bovingdon Grange whither they had gone during the height of the raids. Crewe House itself was cracked and damaged, but not too badly, and the destruction of the houses on the corner of Queen Street and Curzon Street had effected a great improvement in its outlook. Yes, we were now in Mayfair, and I think it is a good thing that one of the main organisations of the passenger road transport industry should be housed in the best part of London.

In the meantime the war went on. We had 134 hired buses, making 1,166 in all, and very few new ones were available. Guy Motors of Wolverhampton had been allowed to build a few double-deck chassis, and we obtained our share of them, but it was only a handful, and we

After the 'unfrozen' Leyland vehicles with their austerity bodywork came the first of the true 'utilities'. Guy Motors of Wolverhampton produced the chassis, a simple, rugged, no nonsense, Gardner-engined product which was very reliable. The bodywork was built by any one of several concerns, (this one is by Roe) all working to the same MoS specification. The responsibility for preparing this had been given to the National Federation of Vehicle Trades and Operators Joint Technical and Advisory Committee, whose President, W. R. Black, was Director and General Manager of Park Royal Coachworks Ltd. Here we had a true professional who took a personal interest in the scheme. Wooden slatted seats replaced the normal upholstered type in some of these vehicles from the end of 1943, and so we put our allocation to work in Crewe where the short journeys involved would cause least discomfort.

put them at Crewe on the town services. The Chairman suggested that I should get rid of as many hired machines as possible, but that was easier said than done. We would have done better to buy them in the first place, but I doubt if many of the owners would have been willing to sell. We sounded them on this point, and one or two did part, but the vast majority said "No, we may want them at any time." From then onwards we determined to buy what second-hand machines we could, and so gradually release the hired ones. Before the war single-deckers fetched £10-£15 and double-deckers from £20-£25, but it was a different story now. Double-deckers fetched anything up to £500 and were soon to cost more, but we kept getting a few.

Our needs did not diminish, and it became evident that many single-deck routes had permanently changed over to the use of double-deckers—if we could get them, and we began to prepare a long-term programme to achieve this purpose. Even Anglesey was to have them—poor, thin Anglesey, but the island was more flourishing now, and the reconstructed Menai Bridge was to play an important part in its development. I often visited Holyhead, Amlwch and Llangefni, usually staying two nights at the Station Hotel at the former place. There were a number of Dutch Naval men there, and other interesting people as well. One night I remember, there were two British officers from a destroyer with a large brown paper parcel. They came in about 6-30 p.m. and had drinks in the lounge. After we had had dinner they were still there, but something had happened to upset their equilibrium. It was not only the drinks, which had been numerous enough, but they were upset about something else too. We watched them with interest. About 10-30 p.m. the one who had done most of the talking and who was in civilian clothing, got up and with some difficulty came over and spoke to my wife. Would she accept the brown paper parcel as a favour? They had brought it from the ship as a contribution for a party, but unfortunately they had been recalled that night and so there would be no festivities and they were fed up. There was a bottle of vermouth and other things, but unfortunately, a bottle of gin had fallen on the quayside at the feet of a dock policeman who had conveniently turned the other way while they kicked the broken bits into the water. It was *verboten* to bring drink ashore that had paid no duty, and they made it a rule never to take back what had once been brought ashore. This was a long tale, told most carefully, and with great effort. It was in vain that we said that they ought not to give it to *us* of all people—what about paying for it— wasn't there anybody we could send it to? No, they had seen us there all that evening and were sure we were not Customs Officers in disguise. All they wanted was to give us the parcel and if we were up at dawn perhaps we would wave them goodbye as they left the harbour. When we got to our room, we took off the brown paper, and behold a bottle of American vermouth (very powerful), two pounds of Naval brown sugar and a pound of butter—valuable contraband indeed when things were so short. I told Miss Thompson, the Manageress, about it next morning. She smiled. "We get all sorts here," she said, "and they do all sorts of things too." These little episodes certainly relieved the dullness of those left at home during the war.

March 1943 saw an important innovation in our methods of organisation. It was arranged to form a Traffic Department, and H. H. Merchant was made Traffic Manager. He and Capt. E. Roberts had worked things between them for some years, and as he was a few years senior to Roberts, he was duly appointed with the latter as his chief assistant. These two made a strong team which took over Licensing and Publicity as well as all the ordinary work. At the same time the latest wage system was installed under Mr. Eckersley and a central Wages Department was established. This change-over entailed an immense amount of work at a time when staff was much too short, and it speaks volumes for Eckersley's ability in doing it so smoothly.

One of the activities of the Tilling Association was advertising on vehicles, and we had to consider what we could do about it. Our only experience of this sort of thing was an unfortunate one and dated right back to 1918 or 1919, when we were persuaded by a Mr. Abraham to enter a contract with him to exhibit certain advertisements on the back panels of our then small fleet. These advertisements were on enamel plates and were supposed to appear in specified districts, but we were soon in trouble because buses were changed round in the ordinary course and the advertisement for "John Smith's Boots" which were only sold, shall we say in Crewe, appeared in Mold where that commodity meant nothing to the inhabitants. John Smith was rightly incensed and complained bitterly to Mr. Abraham, who had artfully put a penalty clause into the advertising agreement, and now threatened to make us pay. There had been only one thing to do—ask him how much he wanted to cancel the whole business. The answer was £100, so we paid but felt very sore about it. From then onwards we always refused advertising offers, except on the backs of tickets where there was just one advertisement, and we could not go wrong.

Now, however, it was different, and I went to see Miss Dowsett at Crewe House to explore the possibilities. She showed me figures that we could not afford to ignore and which outweighed the aesthetic objections because costs were still rising and anything that would bring in revenue must be made use of. We divided our territory into districts and told Crewe House that they could make a start. There were little troubles at first, but a proper organisation soon came into being. When asked why we were doing it, we told enquirers the truth—namely, that it kept the fares down.

Our move to the Tilling group involved many changes — some of the most obvious to our passengers are seen here. Green replaces the former maroon paint scheme. The advertising contracts were more carefully handled this time — no problems with complaints about local content would result from *Albatross Flour, Tintex Dyes* or the all pervading *Bisto*. Titan L12 carries its wartime white markings.

The single-deck 'utility' body was not so markedly austere in its frontal appearance—interior comforts were few and far between, however. Six of these bodies, built by Burlingham of Blackpool in 1943, were fitted to selected chassis from the 1939 batch of PLSC Lions we had purchased from Ribble, in addition to the Brookes Bros Tigers mentioned on page 207.

The availability of Bristol K chassis in 1944, the Tilling group's standard double-decker in wartime AEC-engined form, meant we needed to apply for no more Guy utilities. Between then and the resumption of peacetime construction at Lowestoft 22 such chassis were purchased, with utility bodywork as shown, built by Strachans. The finished result was a far cry from our handsome pre-war standard but even so we were very glad to get our hands on them. MB 184 stands at the Pier Head amongst Liverpool's own buses and trams.

On 7th July, 1943, the war bonus had its annual rise from 15/- to 20/- per week, arranged or recommended by the National Council for the omnibus industry. It did not much matter whether there was a full scale arbitration or not—the local authorities always gave way to pressure fairly easily, and so were the first body to be approached through the Joint Industrial Council. Then the Unions tackled the Companies, who were more inclined to show fight. Reasons were put forward which really did not hold much water, but we knew what the outcome would be. No tribunal had the courage to call a halt to the process of paying more money whilst the goods it was supposed to buy became fewer. The Government would not give a lead for fear of upsetting the war effort, and so wages must go up more than the cost of living, which they did quite regularly. That is the penalty of war. We could pay it at the moment, but what would happen afterwards was only too obvious.

Thus 1943 passed on. Grandon, our Publicity Officer, left in September, and we did not replace him since Lee, his assistant, who had long experience of the printing trade, was well able to look after that branch which had now merged into the Traffic Department. Our ordinary publicity activities had ceased, but in 1942 we had started a series of announcements in the local press in order to try and make the public understand why buses were so overcrowded and travelling was so uncomfortable. It was also necessary to tell them how they could help to make things better, the idea being that some constructive propaganda must be put forward rather than just say "Things are very bad," and leave it at that. When this had been going on for some weeks I thought that it was all very dull, and surely people were sick of reading the same old tale week after week. We were getting nowhere. Perhaps a little humour, or a funny drawing or something like that, and it must be human! We wanted to talk to our public as individuals, so that they would realise that it was not just an advertisement, but something interesting and new to be looked forward to every week. "What is Crosville telling us this week?" Yes, that was what they must say to themselves. I thought this over and suddenly had an idea. Would he do it? I would ask him anyway.

In the spring of 1940 my boy, Paul, was in the Middlesex Hospital, having a skin graft operation on his face after a disastrous encounter with some molten caustic soda. In the next room to him was the artist who illustrates the charivaria page in *Punch*. It was in fact Mr. Douglas England. When Paul was on his feet again and able to walk along the passage to the bathroom he struck up an acquaintance with Mr.

"JUMP ON, MOTHER"

This little poem is assigned
To that poor creature much maligned
The woman shopper, bless her heart!
Please don't forget she plays her part
In feeding every girl and fellow
Who work to make Old Hitler bellow
As he's never done before,
That there shall be an end to war.
Her feet are wet, her hands are cold.
The queues are long, the goods all sold.
No canteen, no unrationed meal
Rewards her labours. Yet no squeal
Is heard from her; so please don't shout
"She must not travel, throw her out."

Bulletin No. 98

'STANDING ON OUR OWN FEET'

PRIVATE ENTERPRISE

Our Staff has been called up, our buses taken away, and our garages turned into factories.

Our petrol is cut down, our spare parts used and not replaced, our paper for time-tables is no longer to be had.

New buses are fairy tales.

Our finances are not subsidised or guaranteed in any way by the Government.

BUT

Fares remain at pre-war level and we continue to stand on our own feet (or is it wheels?) and to prove that well-managed private enterprise is equal to any emergency.

Don't forget all this when we ask for your patronage after the war.

England, and in the end he came away with a drawing of himself complete with dressing gown, head bandages and a tuft of hair sticking out at the top. This sketch was duly framed and much treasured, and I thought that if I wrote the wording of a series of advertisements perhaps Douglas England would do an appropriate drawing. It was exactly what he did for the charivaria page. Yes, he would do it, and I was to send him two sets of wording every fortnight about a month in advance of publishing time, and then we would get a block made and send it to the numerous local papers in our area. This was the happy beginning of over a hundred illustrated bulletins. I used to write them up in the train, at home, in the office—in fact anywhere as they occurred to me. Some were in prose—some in rather bad verse. The chief thing was that the drawings were always full of humour and that was what people needed during the war. We had many nice letters from fans who said that they always looked forward to the weekly paper because our bulletin was so refreshing.

At the end of 1943, we had a fire in the body shop at Sealand Road, which burnt out one bus and would have been much worse but for timely warning given by the night staff at Vickers-Armstrongs who happened to see it in the early stages. It started at or near the batteries and we presumed that it originated through a short circuit, but cigarette ends are possible causes almost anywhere, and the destruction was so complete in this case that it might have been either. By some mischance the fire-watchers were not told until it was all over, but that was not their fault.

Small fires on buses are not infrequent, but rarely serious. Perhaps there is a backfire, a short circuit, or a faulty exhaust joint under the body. A hot and dirty oil-covered engine burns in a tenacious sort of way, and sand is a better remedy than extinguishers. One wonders what is burning, but it is the oil vapour and not the actual metal. Petrol is dangerous and goes up quickly, but fuel oil tanks are much more stable and will almost boil before they start to burn. At Rhyl in 1945, fuel oil was found afterwards in tanks of vehicles that had been in the thick of the flames.

At the end of 1943 also, D. S. Deacon went to the Forces in a special transport branch of the Civil Control Commission. He had been Divisional Manager at Crewe for two years, but he was comparatively young and so had to leave us for a time. He had had a special course of training before being commissioned, and I could not help thinking that it was good to see proper uses made of a man's previous occupation.

The winter was passing, and troops and material were gathering for some great happening, but not a word leaked out. We did not perhaps see so much of it in our area, but one was told that many of the Eighth Army were home. Peculiar-looking concrete contraptions were being built and launched at Deganwy. One day they would be there and the next they had disappeared—launched and towed away at midnight. Parts of Mulberry Harbour, they were, but we never guessed.

North Wales, too, was a centre for broadcasting. Bangor Theatre and the Grand Theatre at Llandudno were used. I often used to see the Happidrome at the latter place on Sunday evening at 8 p.m., and at Bangor there was Sam Jones who ran many of the Welsh features in his own inimitable way. Once, in December, 1943, we were asked to stage a broadcast in the Bridge Builder series, to be relayed later to the United States. What tremendous preparation for a 20-minute programme, and on the great night itself what excitement, and fun too,

D. S. Deacon

Crosville has always been strong on loyalty and Deacon's departure from Aberystwyth in March 1940 illustrates this. He was moving to Crewe and the entire staff at Aberayron and Aberystwyth depots turned out to see him off and wish him well – although this was a Sunday morning and none of them would have been on service, everyone donned uniform so that a proper record could be made by the photographer. There was no doubt also a feeling that many of the younger men would soon be off to war and so it was doubly worthwhile recording the event. Seated in the centre row, not in uniform, from left to right are H. Jones, Tours Superintendent Aberystwyth; J. I. Jones, Depot Clerk Aberystwyth; E. W. Baker, Depot Superintendent Aberystwyth; D. S. Deacon, Divisional Manager South Cambrian area; C. H. F. Kent, Area Engineer South Cambrian area; W. D. Jones, Depot Superintendent Aberayron; J. Parry, Assistant Tours Superintendent Aberystwyth. Kent's son, later to be an inspector, stands tenth from the left in the back row.

221

with Sam Jones running in and out, rehearsing each item until at the appointed time we were ready, and whole thing went off without a hitch! We were told that it went by land line to Manchester, where a recording was made, and that we would receive twenty guineas for our trouble. Truly a bus company earns its money in strange ways! It was there that I first heard our Caernarvon male voice choir, conducted by Richard Jones. They sang well—a Welsh song, and I wished I could hear more. A year or two later they came to Chester one Sunday and gave a fine performance in the Town Hall. Amongst other things they chose "Llef"—a Welsh hymn of extraordinary beauty, and I am sure that many of the listeners were thrilled and probably felt lumps in their throats—I know I did. Claude would have been pleased, but in his day we did not run to male voice choirs. My brother, Edward, heard the broadcast in his home in America in due course, but reception was not too good. Still, he did hear it, so it wasn't wasted.

The buying of property continued, and early in 1944 there came an opportunity of acquiring 6 acres right in the middle of Wrexham—the Vicarage estate. A large house and rather nice grounds right up against the shopping centre. I went to Cardiff with Dennis Clarke of Drivers Jonas, estate agents, and we called on the Representatives of the Church in Wales. They were very nice to us and a reasonable price was mentioned. I worked it out and found that I could recommend my Chairman to go ahead, which we did. The Vicar was provided with a house much more to his liking, but for the moment he stayed where he was, as his new vicarage was under requisition. He showed me round the place. What a house! He was glad that it was sold. It was originally built of stone and then, perhaps fifty or sixty years ago, somebody had put on an outside shell of Ruabon brick so that the walls were now two feet thick and the place looked ugly. The original must have been rather nice. Wrexham Corporation were not pleased. We asked them if they would object to our making part of it into a bus station for all services in order to consolidate the existing four or five stands in various parts of the town. No, they wouldn't have it. They had missed buying the place years ago, and now nobody else must do anything with it. We prepared drawings to show how it could be done, but they were quite adamant. They could have had the most modern bus station in the country, set in beautiful surroundings and dealing with 1,000 departures a day, but they wouldn't have it—even the benefit to the rates did not seem to count, and that in a town where every penny was of value.

The first Crosville buses were grey, but it was a bad colour for wear and soon became shabby, so we changed to red—not the Post Office red of the Midland Red buses, but almost a maroon. This colour remained with small variations for many years. There were cream lines later to provide a relief, and then we painted coaches green and grey to distinguish them from buses. Some Tilling Companies were green, and some red, but I think it was the bad quality red paint that first made us try a few green ones, and at the end of 1944, the Board agreed that we should become green. Palmer had an artistic eye and tried various shades, often using two different ones on the same bus. He also did a coach in green and cream. It looked fine, so we set to work on the fleet of 1,100 at the rate of about thirteen a week. Chester Corporation were alarmed and annoyed. We had usurped their colour, and the poor passenger would now board one of our vehicles when his real allegiance was to the Corporation! We pointed out that it was an ill wind that blew nobody any good, and Warrington would be delighted, because hitherto our colour had been exactly the same as theirs. In any case a passenger should look at the indicator. All buses in London were the same colour, but there was no trouble there. Chester had their own ideas, however, and started to change their paint. They were going to be different.

The post-war green and cream coach livery seen on a 1937 Harrington-bodied Leyland TS7. K6 identifies it as still being petrol-engined. We had virtually standardised on Harrington coach bodies from about 1936.

Dear old Coventry died on 24th July, 1944. He had been a Director of the Company since 1933, and those of us who had come in contact with him had very pleasant memories of his geniality and humour as well as his extraordinary memory for detail. I think he must have been one of the characters of the G.W.R. like Mr. Cope, Chief Accountant, and Mr. Nicholls, the Superintendent of the Line. He had retired, but remained a Director right to the end. He was replaced by Mr. C. R. Dashwood, the railway company's Chief Accountant.

Mr. Mosley retired in January, 1945, and was replaced on the Board by Mr. J. Shearman, whom I knew quite well. He was the Chief Road Motor Engineer for the L.M.S.

We had now entered a year when there were to be many changes of all sorts. The war was nearly over, and there was every indication that it would be finished within twelve months. One felt like a diver who has held his breath under water for as long as possible, but has come to the surface and is able to breathe again. We were going to be all right now. There was going to be a change after that under-water effort of the last six years. One's mind instinctively turned to the future and plans began to form. During the war years we had worked as a team, particularly the senior officials of the Company. There had been no changes, and I think we understood each other fairly well. One day in January, Sir Frederick Heaton asked me if we could recommend a suitable man as Assistant Traffic Manager for Eastern National. After thinking it over I put forward H. W. Mills' name and sent him up for interview. He had been Divisional Manager at Bangor since 1933, and before that was at Llandudno as Chief Assistant to C. R. Taylor. Always bright, sometimes a little too anxious over small things, but with a sound training and a good mixer, he seemed to be the man they wanted. He was, and it was arranged for him to leave on 20th March. One does not like to lose good men, but promotion must never be interfered with for selfish reasons, and he went with the Company's blessing and good wishes for his future. I remembered many Anglesey journeys in his company and many meetings at the Holyhead Station Hotel. He knew the complex road system of the island backwards, and though not Welsh, he understood their needs which were sometimes difficult to meet. For the moment we did not replace him.

Mills had not been gone long before we were asked to recommend somebody as General Manager for the Caledonian Company, and I was glad to put forward H. H. Merchant's name. He came to us in 1920, I think it was, and established himself at West Kirby, gradually taking

We were not unhappy to see the end of producer trailers. This picture will bring back memories to all those involved in their operation but no one mourned their passing.

over the whole of Wirral and South Lancashire. His work in starting and developing the Liverpool routes was invaluable, because they had the highest receipts of any, and were correspondingly important. In 1935 he had come to Chester as Traffic Manager of the whole of the English area, and worked in close co-operation with Capt. E. Roberts, who held the same position for the Welsh area. In 1943 he had become Traffic Manager for all services, as he was slightly senior to Roberts. Did he want to go to Scotland? No, not very much, but it was promotion, and when he was offered the job he took it. After all, he had managed with the Welsh, and surely that was a good precedent for tackling the Scots! He left on 18th June, 1945, and Roberts took his place, whilst Harold Jones came in from the Wirral and Lancashire to be Assistant Traffic Manager.

This was a golden opportunity to re-organise our Divisions and reduce them from nine to seven, at the same time giving promotion to a number of people who richly deserved it for their loyalty and good work during the hard years. Bangor and Caernarvon were fused into one area, so also were Rhyl and Llandudno. Barmouth and Dolgelly Depots were taken from Caernarvon and put on to the South Cambrian

Division. Stanley Hughes thus got further responsibilities at Caernarvon, and D. S. Deacon was promoted, whilst absent in Holland, from his old Crewe Division to Llandudno and Rhyl. W. M. Wynn left Rhyl for Aberystwyth, whilst W. Meachin came from Aberystwyth to Headquarters to look after the new Schedules Department. This latter job was very important, and he set to work to get together a first-class team of Divisional Schedules Clerks. C. R. Taylor came to take charge of Chester, which now included Flint and Mold, and S. M. Johnson left Chester for Wrexham. Finally, J. C. Niblock from Rock Ferry went to Llandudno to look after Deacon's Division for the time being.

All this sounds very complicated, and was indeed a big change. The housing shortage did not make it any easier for those concerned, but we could not wait. The war was drawing to a close and unless our staff was properly placed we would not be ready for any developments that would be sure to take place. New brooms sweep clean, too, and however good a man may be in a certain position he becomes blind to some things which are probably spotted immediately by his successor. I was glad when it was all over, and hoped that we had not made any mistakes, but it seemed to work all right and everybody settled down to their new jobs.

The next to go was G. K. Palmer, acting Chief Engineer since 1939, when Goodhall had left so suddenly owing to the war. The Brush Company evidently thought very highly of him, because they offered him a position as Assistant Managing Director of their Body Works and, of course, he could not afford to refuse. This happened in September, and funnily enough coincided with Goodhall's return from India where he had been doing a variety of interesting work, being lent by the Royal Engineers for that purpose. However, at last he was back after six years' absence. I told him that he would find things very different, and he replied in his downright way that he quite expected it.

Hird, our Stores Officer, left at the same time. He had come out of retirement from the B.M.O. to help us out during the war, and felt that he wanted to go and settle down again now it was over. Everybody liked Hird, I think. He had been in the jewellery trade in Birmingham. A shy but lovable character, we made him a bit of a presentation as we had done for Merchant and Palmer. He was quite touched about it.

A. W. Smith retired as Secretary on 1st October, his place being taken by H. Eckersley, our Accountant, who now combined both jobs, and finally R. C. Cowmeadow, Architect and Surveyor, told me that he must leave, as his uncle was retiring from the family practice, and he must

Just how difficult it was to obtain vehicles may be judged from this picture—in 1945 we actually purchased six of these open-staircase vehicles, dating from 1931, from the Brighton company. Venerable old gentlemen? Certainly. And that open staircase. Well, we shall see. Plans are in hand to rehabilitate these six vehicles next year, with a complete chassis overhaul and brand new bodywork.

As services were restored we began to buy second-hand vehicles to augment our fleet. In this area, at least, we were our own masters and we purchased many Leyland TD1 and TD2 Titans which we knew we could rehabilitate. Amongst the first to arrive were six from Leigh in Lancashire—within a few months two of them had been destroyed in the blaze at Rhyl. One of the remaining four waits by the railway station at Colwyn Bay prior to setting off to Abergele.

take his place. This was rather a blow, as Cowmeadow had looked after our buildings and designed all the new ones for the last eighteen years. He had a unique knowledge of a bus company's requirements—so much so that Mr. Wreathall had asked him to do quite a lot of work for the other companies. He had an uncanny flair for estimates which must have impressed Wreathall, and a quiet but firm way with contractors that resulted in a high standard of work. We gave him a lunch and something to remember us by, and he gave me an old iron bullion box weighing about 3 cwts., probably about 200 years old, and with a sevenfold handmade lock that was a work of art. I showed it to Harper, our Works Manager, as Cowmeadow had no key and had never opened the box. "Can you open it?" I said. It took him all one day and the next, but he was a man who never owned himself beaten at anything and he eventually got it open and we admired the fine workmanship of the handmade levers. It was said that it had been used to send valuables between this country and Ireland. Cowmeadow had got it from some solicitor's office in Anglesey. R. D. Dowell carried on, but our policy of having only three departments, i.e., Engineering, Secretarial and Traffic, caused the Architect and Surveyor's Department to become Engineering (Buildings) and he became responsible to the Chief Engineer for our very extraordinary and diverse property up and down the country. We had things like tea houses, shops, houses, flats, a tannery, a woodland estate, and at one time even a public house as well as our ordinary offices and garages. Dowell was also asked to prepare all sorts of traffic maps and engineering drawings, buy furniture and other things too numerous to mention. The tannery, by the way, was in Warrington, about 200 yards from the centre of the town. One day it may be the central bus station there, but there are now so many regulations and controls that it is impossible to be certain of anything.

On the 26th March, 1945, there was an event at Bangor which marked an important stage in our development. Ever since 1826 there had been a rather beautiful road suspension bridge over the Menai Straits, this being the only road bridge leading to Anglesey, but unfortunately there was a weight limit which prevented heavy vehicles from getting across. One cannot help feeling convinced that this was one of the reasons, if not the main one, why the island had never had much chance, commercially, of competing with the mainland. But on the above date we organised a celebration luncheon to mark the completion of the bridge reconstruction, and the inauguration of the first double-decker bus service to run across it. The party of local authority representatives, and other notables, was taken over the bridge to the Anglesey Arms Hotel and brought back again to the Castle Hotel at Bangor for lunch. Afterwards they were each presented with an illustrated brochure to mark the occasion. Inside the brochure was the following short article:-

"DOUBLE DECKED BUSES AND ANGLESEY

"What is the connection between these two utterly different things, and why this lunch?

"Cast your mind back to the Roman times when the chief industry of Anglesey was undoubtedly copper mining on Parys Mountain. The Romans wanted copper as well as tin and lead, and they made their usual straight drive across country towards their object. One road at least led across Bwlch-y-ddeufaen and down through Rhiwian to the shore—across the Lavan Sands to the ferry below Beaumaris.

"Menai Straits were much narrower then. Some say there was only the river Ogwen flowing into an estuary which led past Beaumaris and out to sea between Penmon and Puffin Island. They say, too, that one night early in the sixth century there was a sudden sinking of coast level which engulfed Llys Helig and other properties. Perhaps the sinking covered a period of years, but sink it did and the Straits became wider and more difficult to cross.

"The Romans had gone by then, and for another 1,300 years Anglesey was only visited by boat across a dangerous stretch of water. The land was poor and it was too windy to grow timber, but in 1826 Telford's Bridge was opened, no doubt with suitable celebrations. In 1850 the railway also bridged the gap and a new era commenced for the island.

"Telford's Bridge was elegant, but unfortunately had a weight limit, so that modern heavy motors could not cross, although an apparently unlimited number of individual vehicles could be on the bridge at the same time provided each weighed less than 4 tons 5 cwt. A bus and its passengers could cross together but the passengers must walk.

"Specially built light 20-seaters had to be used and we shall only realise how much the development of Anglesey was retarded when fuel restrictions are removed and road transport gets into its stride again.

"One night there was a terrific gale from the west. The bridge always swayed a little in the centre if the wind was strong, but this time things came to a head when the holding bolts on the Caernarvonshire side snapped, and that end began to move from side to side in relation to the fixed piece of road on the approach viaduct. A bus came across from Menai Bridge. The driver saw the danger and waited the exact moment when he managed to get his vehicle on to the solid portion of the roadway. No more vehicles crossed that night, or for several days, until the swinging end was secured by some new bolts.

"It is an ill wind that blows nobody any good, and this wind brought things to a head, with the result that the long-delayed plan of reconstruction was put in hand. By a marvel of engineering the new bridge of steel gradually replaced the old iron bridge with no cessation of traffic. From a distance it looks exactly the same but there is now no weight limit or toll. The war started during the reconstruction but the work was carried through to completion.

Before—the toll booth and prominent posters outlining the 4¼ ton weight limit and other restrictions serve as a reminder of the problems which used to face us at Menai.

"Double deckers in other places have established a permanent trade up-lift. Can they do so here? Can this milestone in the affairs of Anglesey be firmly planted? and trade built up on it? The answer is Yes, but only with your help. As a team we can do it, and so we asked you to come along as our guests on this rather special occasion, and join the team, and incidentally be the first passengers to travel over the bridge on a really full-size motor bus.

"This brochure is meant to remind you of our earnest request for your help in our efforts to promote the post-war welfare of North Wales in general, and perhaps Anglesey in particular."

It was a happy gathering, and I hope that it helped to show that Welsh interests are Crosville interests and *vice versa*.

After — M88, one of our faithful ECW-bodied Titans, on the rebuilt bridge in 1944, becoming the first full-sized bus to cross into Anglesey. Now we could make proper arrangements to serve the island.

The party of local authority representatives outside the Anglesey Arms Hotel.

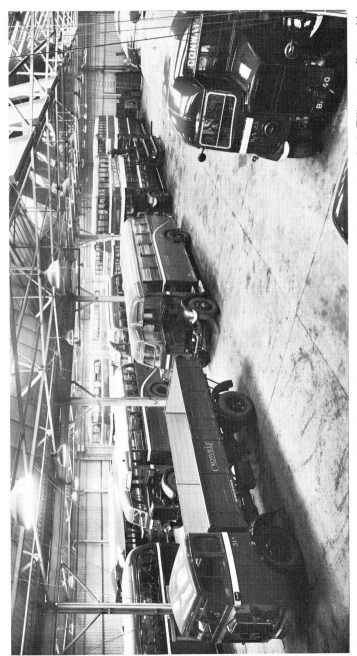

The new paint shop at Sealand Road in 1944 with a good selection of vehicles in view. They all seem to be in Tilling green livery with the exception of the vehicle having advertisements applied, which would appear still to be in maroon. We reckoned to paint about thirteen vehicles a week at this time. The lorry in the foreground was a wartime conversion of a Dennis Mace 26-seat bus.

Something happened in 1945, however, which was not so pleasant. I went to bed on the night of the 16th July and was roused about 1 a.m. the next morning by the telephone ringing. Who could it possibly be at that hour? But I was very soon wide awake. Capt. Roberts' voice came through. "Crescent Road Depot at Rhyl is ablaze from end to end. It started in the Club. The N.F.S. have issued a district call but can't say yet what will be saved—if anything." "All right," I said, "meet me there in an hour's time. Wake up Palmer and tell him to start mobilising fifty spare vehicles to stand by—a few from each division." It was the only thing to do—get over there at once and see how things were. 49 buses at Crescent Road, and the height of the season! What appalling bad luck, and as for the Club—well, we would see about that. The roads were deserted and I got there before 2 a.m. to find that the worst was over. Some ten buses had been got out before the office and club floor collapsed and between twenty and thirty had been saved inside by the firemen's efforts, but thirteen had been destroyed beyond all hope. The whole place was a mass of red hot and twisted steel work with gas mains burning like torches in several places. The safe containing some

The aftermath of the disastrous fire in July, 1945, at Crescent Road, Rhyl. There were thirteen buses under this heap of concrete and steel.

Crescent Road depot had originally belonged to Brookes Brothers — this is how it used to look before it was gutted by fire.

£700 had been in a comparatively cool corner and was still there, and an overhead fuel oil tank containing 2,000 gallons had not exploded, but its contents had poured out through a melted pipe and had been burned with everything else. Fuel oil does not burn easily. As I have said before, we found some still in the tanks of completely burnt out vehicles. About 4 a.m. it was nearly finished and we went inside, but it was not light enough to see much. The gas had now been cut off, and Hughes, the Divisional Engineer, invited us to his house for a welcome cup of tea.

The police had kindly put their telephone at our disposal and we had arranged for a complete set of equipment to come up from Wrexham. Roberts had set the night staff preparing this before he came along. It was now nearly 5 a.m. and buses began to arrive from all parts until there were at least sixty lined up in the streets. It was evident that the services were going to be normal, and so they were. The Rhyl men put up with untold inconvenience to do this, and the drivers who had brought buses from other depots in the middle of the night should also be mentioned. Flint Depot gave them breakfast on their way back, and we started clearing up. All the saved buses were got out through a side entrance and demolition of the débris was comenced, but the Depot was quite unusable for the rest of the year — the damage amounting to £30,000.

The Club was upstairs, above part of the Depot. It had a reinforced concrete floor, and was well alight before the cleaning staff downstairs were told by a passer-by. We learned one or two lessons. Don't have clubs above garages, but in any case, all closed premises should be visited by the night staff several times each night. Clubs are a bad fire risk because of cigarette ends, which get into all sorts of peculiar places. This fire was almost certainly started by one.

The European war had ended on 8th May, 1945. I went to Nantwich on that day and listened to the broadcast at 3 p.m. with Arthur Bevan, our old solicitor friend. I don't suppose we realised the full significance of that moment, but we were sufficiently impressed to open a bottle of champagne that he insisted we should share and which he had kept for the occasion. Then I went on to Crewe Square of many happy memories. It was difficult to get on to the place at all and everybody was dancing to loud speakers. Indeed they continued to do so till late that night. I left the car and found many friends amongst the drivers, conductors and other staff. Need I say more? We were all feeling very benevolent and it was an unforgettable occasion — much more so than the end of the Japanese war in August. We didn't look ahead. Sufficient to the day was the goodwill thereof, and I was glad to be back at that moment on the old spot where I had received most of my training in the years that were past.

But the strain of war had frayed people's tempers, and unofficial strikes were breaking out in all directions. The slightest thing seemed to set them off, and they usually only lasted a few days or even a few hours. We were not immune, but as a public utility concern any such action by our people only penalised the public who had done nothing to warrant such treatment, and indeed who had put up with a good deal of hardship on the universal excuse of there being a war on. It made no financial difference to the Company, but we lost much goodwill that had patiently been collected drop by drop — so hard to come by and so easy to lose is that elusive thing that makes or mars the fortune of a Company like ours. In other words, our people were hitting themselves by injuring the goose that laid our golden egg, but many of them couldn't see it. They thought they were putting pressure on the Company, forgetting that they themselves were an essential part of that Company and made their living from that very goodwill which they were undermining.

Suspicion of the possible bad employer is rooted in the minds of most men, and it was only too often well founded in the old days, with the result that it will take several generations of people to remove it. Most Irishmen distrust the English for the same reason, although the bad days are gone for ever.

Strikes had not been common things with us. Except for the Crewe incident back in the twenties, we had had no trouble until Friday, 22nd July, 1938, when Wrexham, Oswestry and Johnstown stopped work at midnight because the Company would not immediately raise them from Grade IA to Grade I which was paid 1d. per hour more. I went to a midnight meeting in Wrexham at which I was invited to put forward the Company's point of view. The atmosphere of the crowded room was so thick that I could hardly see the men at the back, but I got a fair hearing and there were many questions. It was no good—they had already made up their minds, and so the garage doors were closed on Saturday morning and there was a strange silence and a feeling of deadness in the building that had always been so active. All that day nothing was done, but by Sunday everybody had cooled off sufficiently for the Trade Union to win their argument that the negotiations were at a standstill because nobody could be expected to negotiate under the threat of a strike or a lock-out. It was, therefore, decided to go back to work that very evening and so we were back where we started, but grading could not be abolished just then, and it was not until the end of 1942 that we were able to pay the same rates to everybody.

On 7th April, 1945, there was trouble at Llandudno because a conductor had been told off by the Depot Superintendent for running early. The Superintendent must be dismissed at once and then they would go back to work. However, as Alderman H. T. Edwards of the Transport and General Workers' Union rightly pointed out to them, the Company could not even hold an enquiry whilst a strike was taking place, and so it was agreed to go back that very afternoon and let the matter take its normal course.

There is no doubt that 1945 was a difficult period owing to excitement about the end of the war, because we had more trouble on 6th June, this time at Bangor, where a combination of circumstances produced a 48-hour stoppage that spread right down to Barmouth although the latter place had no idea what it was all about. A meeting was held which the local Union offical said was a Special Depot Committee—at which stage the Traffic Manager and a Union official should attend—but in point of fact it was not a special meeting, and therefore the Traffic Manager did not come. The men thought they were slighted and decided to strike. The women supported this and many welcomed the time off. The management had not handled the affair too well in its first stages, nor had the Union, but once again H. T. Edwards obtained a resumption of work so that things could be straightened out.

After that there was a respite until 21st January, 1947, when a difference of opinion between two groups of men at Crewe caused a 24-hour strike. The older men there had always had the best turns, leaving the odd ends for the junior people. The latter thought that it ought to be share and share alike, and they were right. The Company pointed out that a reduction from a 51-hour to a 48-hour week would make things better for everybody and there would be fewer spreadovers. On the other hand, our hands were tied until work was resumed. There was an immediate return to work, but what a pity to let ourselves down in the public opinion over a matter that was purely internal!

During the bad weather in February, 1947, the news somehow got round at Mold that there was to be short pay. They stopped work, but of course the whole tale had not been told. Even at that moment we were arranging for all men who offered themselves for their normal duties to be guaranteed a 48-hour week. I went and told them so and there was an immediate resumption that very hour.

Finally, Easter of 1947 saw a bad stoppage of four days at Wrexham. I say bad, because something was wrong with the leadership. The reason given for the strike was the fact that the existing arrangement did not provide for an 8-hour guaranteed day during the Easter holiday period. There was no official request through the normal channels for such a guarantee, and no notice was taken of the fact that the week was guaranteed at 48 hours in any case. It was simply resolved that there should be no work from Good Friday to Easter Monday inclusive. One would have thought that if four days extra holiday were required they could have been taken at another time, but those who organised the strike had it in the back of their minds that the Company could ill afford to be idle over Easter. It was, of course, the public who suffered, and the Company actually benefitted through not having to pay overtime rates or make up any guarantee. The employees as a whole only followed blindly and nobody dared take on himself to demand an inquiry as to exactly how work was to be stopped and what would be gained by doing so. The following week-end another attempt was made on the Friday night to get everybody out on Saturday and Sunday if the Company did not take off a late trip recently started, and submit all proposed late trips to the Depot Committee before putting them on. A resolution had previously been passed to that effect. The Union and the Company refused to budge and required the resolution to be withdrawn in general meeting — also it was Friday and two days' pay had already been lost, with another two the following Friday. The only thing to do was to wash out the resolution and proceed on more orthodox lines.

When will our people learn that our working life no longer consists of a game called "Men versus Management" and that we have now changed to one team called "Crosville United"? I know that the old ideas die hard, but die they must or we shall continue to upset the public and ourselves by quite useless stoppages. We all play on the same side of the field now and the game is against the difficulties of our particular industry, and the deadweights of the controls that are like the barnacles on a ship's side. But there is no need to lose heart. Once we do that we shall lose the game. I have often thought that there is one big thing missing in our organisation and that is some sort of profit-sharing scheme. An employee of whatever grade should have his proper wage plus a percentage of any profits that may be available for shareholders after everything else has been provided for. This could be made very realistic by giving each employee a certificate when he entered the service to say exactly what his interest is. Making a profit for others, even if they have provided the necessary capital, is not so much fun, but if you know that both capital and labour are to receive a just reward you work much harder and see that others do the same. Employers may have been too greedy in the past, but they now see where the mistakes have occurred. Unfortunately bad deeds are much harder to forget than good ones.

1945 also saw the beginning of restoration of services and mileage, not to speak of private parties and tours, though it was not until 1946 that the real boom came and we had more work offered than we could possibly do. We had steadily returned hired buses as they could be replaced, so that try as we would we could not achieve a nett increase in our fleet. The Chairman agreed that we must enter the secondhand market, and we did so, buying double-deckers at prices ranging from £25 to £1,200. In 1946 we just managed to get through the summer, but with mileage at 38,000,000 per annum as against 33,000,000 pre-war it was obvious that more vehicles were required. For 1947 we had arranged to mortgage every source of vehicles to see us through the

When the war finished, thankfully, in 1945, our vehicles were very run down by comparison with 1939. Petrol rationing and a slow return to normal peacetime standards of travel, particularly in respect of private motoring, were two factors which increased the demand for the items we had least of — smart new coaches to take people to the country or the seaside. What to do? We painted some of our Cubs in coach livery and they joined other veterans in the 'thin cream line' holding the fort until replacements could be obtained. Not until we'd updated our elderly bus fleet and got back to something approaching normality could we think about buying new coaches.

month of June. July and August provided some new deliveries and so eased the strain, but we had an even worse struggle than in the previous summer. Surely 1948 will be better, but one never knows.

There were great peace celebrations in London in June, 1946. I went there to attend the Savings Movement garden party at Buckingham Palace on 6th June, and on the 8th joined the crowd in Park Lane to see the mechanical transport procession headed by Field Marshal Montgomery and consisting of every type of vehicle that was ever made. After all the service types there were four double-deck buses, including a Manchester Corporation machine, newly painted, but still with our identification number left to mark the fact that it had run for us for some three or four years. I was duly thrilled — so we were not forgotten in the great procession after all, and quite by chance I had been privileged to be there to see it as the Crosville representative. One of our youthful fans who write in about bus numbers had spotted it in the illustrated papers, and asked if it was really there. I was able to say that I had seen for myself.

There were lots of things to do. I wrote up the "Crosville in Wartime" brochure and got it printed.

Leyland Titan TD2 models were about the most modern second-hand double-deckers that could be found in the months immediately after the war. Plymouth Corporation's disposal of most of its fleet of such buses was eagerly snapped up by about eight of the Tilling companies, even though they were then about thirteen years old. We took eight, including this one with a Mumford body, which looked quite modern for a 1932 bus, and all of them have been fitted with Leyland oil engines. The varied collection of destination blind styles on these and other buses constituted quite a problem and the Tilling group has in any case been urging standardisation on its lavish and expensive new layout. These displays are much bigger than anything we have had before and permit decent-sized lettering, even with those long Welsh place names. So our engineers have been fitting them during the inevitable body overhauls needed on such old buses, though I must confess the end result on a body style like this is somewhat overpowering. I'm getting reports of problems with the mechanisms too, because the blinds are so long. The destinations are arranged alphabetically and a turn on say Chester-Warrington involves much winding at each end, very unpopular in itself. I suspect we shall have to take a hard look at the whole business before long.

Our requisitioned buildings were gradually released, and there was a very full programme of renewals and improvements to premises. Poor Dowell was really worked to distraction, but he remained calm in spite of everything. Contractors were so slow and there seemed to be a thousand snags in all he touched.

This clearing up after a long war was inevitable, but to make it easier we re-designed the "family tree" in such a way that Depot Super-intendents really had charge of their Depots. Some of them revelled in it, but others found it difficult to change from the old routine after twenty years. Nevertheless we shall get it right and the effort will be worth while.

On the other hand, here we are two years after the end of the war, and we seem to be worse off in many respects. The shadow of nationalisation of everything is hanging over us, and the young people who are to carry on are thinking in terms of emigration to any place where you are not immediately stopped as soon as you have found something good to do. A rich man in the old days could only spend a small sum on himself. The rest he put back into industry and employed more people. But the rich are no more. It is the State which is going to own the businesses, but the trouble is that they don't make a profit because there is no incentive. Yet when the time comes we shall give very loyal service.

That is why there should be some record of the forty odd years that have just gone by—at least as far as the Crosville Company is concerned. Soon we may be carved up into bits of Traffic Boards, or perhaps other bits will be added to us. It is all in the lap of the gods, but we shall never be quite the same. 1929 saw the end of the best period of all, though there has been some good fun since then. It is all so much bigger than it was, and size can be a help or a hindrance according to how you make use of it. But it is no use speculating about the future. I remember some negotiations with the Transport and General Workers' Union which took place at the Crewe Arms Hotel. Old man Wreathall was there, and when the requests had been discussed, we were being told the usual tale about the temper of the men being very uncertain, and that the slightest thing might precipitate trouble. The old man had listened to all the arguments very carefully and said nothing, but now he looked up with his rare smile. "Whatever you or I do, Mr. McLean," he said, "we may rest assured that the wheels which we started turning years ago will go on merrily long after we are dead. They may stop locally for a short time, but that is all." Yes, whatever happens as regards nationalisation or anything else, nobody—not even the politicians—can stop the wheels for long.

And is that the end? Well, no, not quite.

In common with other industries in 1947, we had to consider a request for a shorter working week of 44 hours instead of 48, for drivers, conductors and certain other grades of employees. Wage rates had been gradually increasing right through the war until February, 1946, a substantial advance was given, which was awarded in such a way that it looked as if we had reached some stability for at least two or three years. There was, however, still another way to do it, and that was by shortening the hours to 44, but still paying the 48-hour rate for those 44 hours. No doubt the Transport and General Workers' Union were only following the lead of the other unions in this respect, and they could not very well do otherwise.

It was agreed that the whole question of hours and other conditions should go before an independent tribunal under Sir John Forster as Chairman. It should be appreciated that during the war years it had become a practice for the Union to approach the Municipalities first on these matters because they had the rates behind them and, therefore, they did not drive so hard a bargain as the Companies, who had to stand on their own feet. Once something had been obtained from the Local Authorities it was much easier to come to the Companies and present a *fait accompli.*

In this case both sides agreed to abide by the Tribunal's decision, whatever it might be, and all seemed well. On 6th June, 1947, the award was given. The 44-hour week was granted but the other items were refused. This immediately brought on a crop of unofficial strikes in various parts of the country—mostly in places where there were municipal services running alongside Company services. The National

Our need for extra vehicles, and intention to rebuild many of them with new, standard, bodies brought several unusual types into the fleet. Many of them found their way to Rhyl and this former Rawtenstall double-decker is one such example, being of highbridge design. As there are no low bridges in the area no problems would arise, of course. Here, for once, the Tilling display looks quite at home but someone wasn't going to wind from R to A, and back, each trip.

Council for the Omnibus industry accepted the award officially, but it made no difference. Mass meetings were easily influenced by the show of hands method of voting where many men felt a natural reluctance to vote the way they felt. There was a readily understandable feeling of frustration amongst many of our people that they had not got what the municipal men had obtained, but one cannot always be on the winning side. There was a sort of shock effect, too, in that the sequence of increases granted over a series of years had received a check that was bound to come sooner or later.

Strikes occurred at all our English Depots, except Liverpool, but only at two Welsh Depots, namely Mold and Flint. Every day the position was different — some places came in, others went out, and so it went on for a fortnight in June. The long-suffering public did not say very much. They were tired of saying things about unofficial strikes. Over £11,000 of good wages were lost to our employees, and in the end work had to start again before the dispute could be carried any further.

A new request was made by the Union for a National Conditions Agreement, and a new tribunal was set up under Mr. William Gorman, K.C. On 18th August, 1947, they made an award of most of the things asked for, but not all, and this was accepted as a basis for a National Conditions Agreement. A number of points will still be left for local settlement, but the main items are now fixed.

Early in the year we had eight weeks of snow and frost like everybody else. Conditions of working were appalling, especially at those places which had to leave vehicles in the open. The British character is a peculiar thing. We must have more production, so we immediately cut our hours of work, and the very men who so easily stopped work for some small reason were the first to put their backs into it when adversity came along in the shape of deep snow and frost for such a long period! No wonder foreigners think we are mad. Men who lived four or five miles away would walk in through the snow on the off chance of being able to help in some way. Those who did work must have been wet through and half frozen most of the time. Volunteer crews went out with the snow ploughs and kept important routes open so that others could be brought to work, and the team spirit which we have tried so hard to bring about was never nearer to the surface than it was under those adverse conditions. The Company was duly grateful, and for each week of that period, 48 hours pay was assured for all those who helped us so well.

In the end the thaw came as it was bound to do, and when we had

The post-war single-decker Tilling design became available in 1946 and the lower radiator position on the Bristol chassis is certainly an improvement. This reversed livery is applied to vehicles intended for express services, of course. KB1 had been built as a prototype by ECW and arrived after having been their property for quite some time, and having received coach seating.

We have started a full scale rebodying programme based on this ECW body design, and many pre-war chassis will thus be given a new lease of life, oil engines also being fitted to improve fuel economy. This Tiger TS6 was new in 1933 and joined our fleet from Seiont Motors.

got over the flood difficulty, we settled down to the final preparations for the summer season. There did not seem to be enough vehicles—an old tale—but this time I had some anxiety that there really would not be sufficient to meet our commitments. Every Monday morning, Mr. Goodhall, our Chief Engineer, and Capt. Roberts, the Traffic Manager, came to my office and we had endless discussions as to how it was to be done. It was plainly necessary for both Traffic and Engineering to contribute something towards the deficiency, and in the end we worked things out to an exact balance for 5th July, which was our critical date.

Early in the year I had forecast our difficulty to Sir Frederick Heaton, pointing out our increased commitments. He was most helpful and we were immediately given an extra allocation of 35 new Leyland double-deckers, of which 20 were to be the first that were delivered to the group. I went to Leyland on the strength of this and found them well up to date with their chassis programme. It looked as if we should have them in time for the high season, and in fact we did. The public little knew how near we were to a breakdown in our summer arrangements, and I hope that we shall never have to scrape through like that again. Next year it will be different, but there, we always say. that. The fact remains that we hired too many buses during the war instead of buying them, and when they were called in we could not get enough new ones to replace them and also bring about a nett increase to run our extra mileage.

On journeys along the Welsh coast early in the year, we heard that the boarding houses and small hotels were not doing too well with their bookings. The truth was that prices were too high, but one felt that day trips would be still more popular, and so they were, but we did not seem to suffer, and the grand weather in August tried our resources to the utmost. It might be the last summer before national-isation, so we determined that it should be a good effort. During the second week in August the wheels spun round at the rate of a million miles a week which, if you work it out, is some six thousand miles an hour, and the dear old public got in or out of our vehicles at no less than thirteen every second of the day and night.

Those who have been with the Company many years will be pleased to hear about this, and I am sure they will feel a great pride in the fact that our last harvest has been so good. I hope that many of the younger generation will think the same. I do know that old George Woodyatt of Llandudno, who retired from our Clonmel Street office last

The standard double-decker body was intended for the Bristol K chassis but looks well on our Leylands. We managed to get 35 of the new PD1 model and have put them to work in Rhyl and Llandudno areas.

All good things come to an end, of course, and we will be seeing many more of these Bristol K types. In the background is a single-decker L type. Now, throughout the country, Tilling group buses will present a uniform appearance with only the livery, red or green, and the advertisements giving any variation.

Christmas at the age of 80, will feel his head swell inside his famous bowler hat when he reads these words. I was told the other day that he had been busy helping with the hay harvest and that his bicycle had been much in evidence. It is nice to think that we have had the services of such men.

But now the summer has passed and we must look to our receipts and expenses, because the recent wage increases have made that very necessary. We must make our estimates and use our accumulated experience and knowledge to the utmost to keep at bay the spectre of raised fares which often seems very near. Can we do it? Only time will tell. Our experience of nationalisation of other industries had been unfortunate in this respect. The transport industry will have to pay for the additional army of civil servants that will be set up to run it, and the outlook is not too good, but the old Crosville need never be ashamed of its forty-one odd years, the history of which I have humbly tried to record in these pages.

No one person could carry in his head all the facts and incidents mentioned in this book, and I should like to record my grateful thanks to everybody who has contributed material towards it. First of all there is the Board of Directors who kindly gave their permission for the Company's Records to be used, their photographs to be reproduced, and their Publicity Department to organise the distribution. Then there are the members of the Staff, past and present, whose names are too numerous to mention, but who gave me almost too much information, and whose forgiveness is asked because it has not been possible to include everything submitted.

Some members of the public, too, were very good in unearthing the records of the Wrexham Tramway of 60 years ago and more.

Finally, may I mention Edmund Vale who wrote the foreword. His advice as an old friend and an experienced author has proved invaluable.

W. J. CROSLAND-TAYLOR

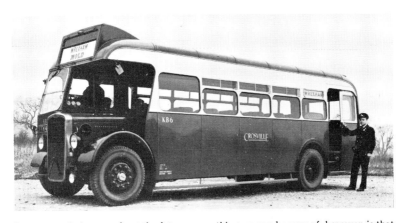

One can rarely be sure about the future—one thing we can be sure of, however, is that the days of the scene below are already numbered. Future orders will be for Bristol chassis with Eastern Coach Works bodies, single-decker buses as seen above, express versions as seen on page 245 and double-deckers as on page 247. Standardisation will replace the wide variety we now see. Our long association with Leyland, dating from 1922, has already been brokem. Whether this new policy will play a big enough part in stemming the tide of rising costs remains to be seen but whatever the future holds we shall be ready for it. The scene below, at Rhyl, includes Leylands, AECs and a solitary Bedford. Prominent is one of the rebuilt Tilling AECs we obtained from Brighton as shown on page 227. Whether we shall ever again need to go to such lengths is debatable but what is certain is that without these skills we should not be where we are today.

APPENDICES

This piece of strategically-placed advertising—on the rear of Prestatyn Depot—is seen by thousands of railway passengers as they look out of their carriage windows.

APPENDIX 1
GENERAL STATISTICS

CROSVILLE MOTOR SERVICES LTD.

NOTE.—Authorised Capital 31.3.47 £1,200,000.

Year Ending Date	Issued Capital £	Loans £	Traffic Receipts £	Gross Div. £	Profit as per Bal. Sheet £	Pence per Car Mile	Div. %	Miles	Passengers	No. of Vehicles
31.7.06	3,199	—	—.	—	—	—	—	—	—	—
31.7.07	6,000	1,000	—	—	—	—	—	—	—	—
30.4.08	6,000	4,000	—	—	—	—	—	—	—	—
30.4.09	3,500	4,000	—	—	− 2,531	—	—	—	—	—
30.4.10	3,550	4,000	—	—	− 1,526	—	—	—	—	—
30.4.11	3,550	4,100	1,000	—	+ 432	18·00	—	13,300	80,000	2
30.4.12	3,550	5,478	1,200	—	− 2,094	18·50	—	15,600	82,000	3
30.4.13	3,550	6,500	4,000	—	− 21	18·90	—	51,000	360,000	5
30.4.14	3,550	5,350	6,041	177	+ 1,302	18·90	5	78,000	480,000	9
30.4.15	3,625	5,350	9,022	272	+ 2,746	19·50	7½	110,000	720,000	12
30.4.16	5,775	6,650	14,985	577	+ 3,166	19·70	10	182,000	1,200,000	18
30.4.17	10,000	5,700	17,100	1,000	+ 2,795	19·40	10	212,000	1,300,000	20
30.4.18	15,000	3,500	27,522	750	+ 1,605	20·50	5	322,000	1,500,000	21
30.4.19	25,000	3,500	29,002	1,875	+ 3,237	22·25	7½	313,463	1,800,000	22
30.4.20	50,000	3,500	56,353	5,000	− 7,673	20·00	10	675,000	2,500,000	32
30.4.21	71,000	3,500	90,763	7,100	+ 12,950	18·20	10	1,190,000	4,000,000	45
30.4.22	77,900	3,500	106,368	7,790	+ 19,918	16·60	10	1,535,915	4,532,957	57
30.4.23	100,000	3,500	124,112	10,000	+ 23,999	14·50	10	2,025,491	6,309,798	72
30.4.24	140,000	3,500	157,499	14,000	+ 36,767	14·00	10	2,699,984	8,914,240	93
30.4.25	145,000	3,500	224,021	14,500	+ 52,063	13·50	10	4,003,322	12,816,297	133
30.4.26	200,000	3,500	289,833	20,000	+ 57,008	12·75	10	5,453,762	17,250,150	179
30.4.27	233,000	3,500	349,308	23,300	+ 68,587	13·08	10	6,389,077	21,595,356	200
30.4.28	253,500	3,500	408,403	25,350	+ 72,617	11·76	10	8,280,830	27,967,396	265
30.4.29	297,000	3,500	445,147	29,700	+ 75,182	11·28	10	9,532,858	32,091,707	298
L.M.S. Year	—	—	511,887	—		10·61	Nil	11,661,837	37,896,476	402
30.4.31	800,000	25,000	729,290	32,000	+ 123,760	9·72	4	17,412,024	49,868,841	580
30.4.32	800,000	25,000	820,149	32,000	+ 141,341	9·46	4	20,789,335	56,904,044	668
30.4.33	800,000	50,000	827,789	32,000	+ 169,099	9·13	4	21,688,203	57,382,373	680
30.4.34	955,000	50,000	938,008	47,750	+ 207,313	8·93	5	26,343,086	69,079,089	794
30.4.35	955,000	50,000	1,041,431	71,625	+ 224,806	8·79	7½	28,379,111	74,002,539	857
30.4.36	1,100,000	—	1,114,711	88,000	+ 235,037	8·70	8	30,688,089	80,868,872	943
30.4.37	1,100,000	—	1,158,047	88,000	+ 233,271	8·69	8	31,879,611	86,310,208	942
30.4.38	1,100,000	—	1,218,919	88,000	+ 256,853	8·91	8	31,201,419	89,918,948	971
30.4.39	1,100,000	—	1,250,349	88,000	+ 261,689	8·98	8	33,465,636	94,455,182	995
30.4.40	1,100,000	—	1,394,659	88,000	+ 320,063	11·00	8	30,418,510	100,526,812	1,101
30.4.41	1,100,000	—	1,741,220	88,000	+ 243,783	14·74	8	28,348,053	115,900,317	1,204
30.4.42	1,100,000	—	2,083,945	88,000	+ 159,486	16·78	8	29,806,946	134,549,315	1,198
31.3.43	1,100,000	—	2,043,560	88,000	+ 80,904	18·34	8	26,737,791	129,835,585	1,186
31.3.44	1,100,000	—	2,263,161	88,000	+ 115,433	19·40	8	28,000,481	141,346,210	1,186
31.3.45	1,100,000	—	2,366,401	88,000	+ 110,133	19·68	8	28,859,102	148,544,258	1,188
31.3.46	1,100,000	—	2,353,439	88,000	+ 127,562	18·75	8	30,160,920	149,420,087	1,155
31.3.47	1,100,000	—	2,654,875	188,000	+ 319,428	17·43	8+5 (F.T.)	36,726,787	158,490,453	1,156

Estimated Mileage for year ending 31.3.48 is 41,000,000.   F.T. denotes " Free of Tax."

APPENDIX 2

SERVICE COMMENCING DATES

Date Started or Acquired	Service No.	Route	Origin
1911	1	Chester—Birkenhead via Ellesmere Port and Little Sutton	C.M.S.
1911	2	Chester—Kelsall	Lightfoot Bros.
1934	3	Chester—Ashton—Helsby	C.M.S.
1925	4	Chester—Northwich (Joint with N. West Road Car Co. Ltd.)	C.M.S.
1920	5	Chester—Crewe—Newcastle	C.M.S.
1921	6	Chester—Rhyl (Holywell—Rhyl by Brookes till 1930)	C.M.S.
1924	7	Chester—Shotwick	C.M.S.
1921	8	Chester—Mold (All Services)	C.M.S.
1928	9	Chester—Clatterbridge	C.M.S.
1909	10	Chester—Wrexham via Farndon and Saighton (Farndon 1909, Wrexham 1934)	C.M.S.
1921	11	Chester—West Kirby via Puddington	C.M.S.
1919	12	Chester—Hoole—Chester	C.M.S.
1921	13	Chester—Upton	C.M.S.
1935	14	Chester—Upton—Hoole	C.M.S.
1923	15	Chester—Guilden Sutton	C.M.S.
1935	16	Chester—Piper's Ash Circular	C.M.S.
1923	17	Chester—Ince	C.M.S.
1919	18	Chester—Warrington	C.M.S.
1927	19	Chester—Tilston—Malpas—Whitchurch	C.M.S.
1934	20	Chester—Bunbury	T. O. Maddocks
1922	21	Chester—Tattenhall—Bickerton	C.M.S.
1922	22	Chester—Caergwrle	C.M.S.
1930	23	Chester—Stapleford—Old Moss	C.M.S.
1931	24	Chester—Waverton—Burton	Z. Woodfin
1931	25	Chester—Barrow	Z. Woodfin
1931	26	Chester—Tarporley—Northwich	H. C. Pascoe
1932	27	Chester General Station—Sealand Road	C.M.S.
1939	28	Connah's Quay—Vickers-Armstrongs	J. Pye
1940	29	Mold—Vickers-Armstrongs	C.M.S.
1919	30	Mold—Northop—Flint	C.M.S.
1919	31	Mold—Shotton via Northop and Northop Hall (Workpeople)	C.M.S.
1919	32	Mold—Llanarmon—Ruthin	C.M.S.
1922	33	Mold—Denbigh	C.M.S.
1939	34	Mold—Flint via Connah's Quay	C.M.S.
1939	35	Buckley—Llay Main (Workpeople)	H. Stanley
1919	36	Mold—Shotton Ironworks (Workpeople)	C.M.S.
1925	37	Flint—Mancot—Sandycroft	C.M.S.
1919	38	Flint—Holywell	C.M.S.
1919	39	Flint—Garden City (Workpeople)	C.M.S.
1928	40	Flint—Sandycroft (Workpeople)	C.M.S.
1928	41	Mold—Rhesycae—Lixwm—Holywell	C.M.S.
1943	42	Greenfield—Point of Ayr	C.M.S.
1930	43	Mold—Rhosesmor—Halkyn—Milwr—Holywell	C.M.S.
1927	44	Holywell—Pantasaph—Brynford	C.M.S.
1923	45	Holywell—Afonwen	C.M.S.
1924	46	Mold—Erryrys	C.M.S.
1924	47	Mold—Cilcain	C.M.S.
1924	48	Mold—Pantymwyn	C.M.S.
1924	49	Mold—Nerquis—Treuddyn—Leeswood	C.M.S.
1938	50	Flint—Queensferry—Buckley—Mold—Llangwyfan Sanatorium	C.M.S.
1919	51	Garden City—Hawarden—Flint	C.M.S.
1925	52	Chester—Football and Greyhounds	C.M.S.
1927	*53	Chester—Blackpool	C.M.S.
1932	54	Chester—Parkgate Road—Saughall	C.M.S.
1930	55	Holywell—Whitford—Mostyn—Halendy	C.M.S.
1943	101	Woodside—Loggerheads	C.M.S.
1924	102	Woodside—Parkgate	J. Pye
1930	103	Woodside—Burton	C.M.S.
1924	104	Woodside—Ruthin—Denbigh	C.M.S.
1922	105	Woodside—Meols	C.M.S.
1920	106	Liscard—West Kirby—Meols	C.M.S.
1922	107	New Ferry—Meols	C.M.S.
1920	108	West Kirby—Park Station	C.M.S.
1920	109	Warrington—Runcorn	C.M.S.
1924	110	Warrington—Walton Local	C.M.S.
1923	111	Runcorn—Locals	C.M.S.
1925	112	Transporter Bridge—Helsby	C.M.S.
1919	113	" " —Chester	C.M.S.
1924	114	Heswall—Birkenhead	C.M.S.
1924	115	Heswall—Banks Road	C.M.S.
1923	116	Liverpool—Roby—Huyton—Prescot	C.M.S.
1922	117	Liverpool—Widnes via Tarbock	C.M.S.
1922	118	Liverpool—Widnes via Halewood	C.M.S.
1921	119	Liverpool—Prescot—Warrington	C.M.S.
1922	120	Liverpool—Widnes—Warrington	C.M.S.
1932	121	Liverpool—Hunts Cross	C.M.S.
1930	*122	Woodside—Burntwood Sanatorium	C.M.S.
1943	123	Liverpool—Cronton Colliery	C.M.S.
1944	124	Runcorn—Clatterbridge	C.M.S.
1928	125	Runcorn—Northwich (Joint with N. Western Road Car Co. Ltd.)	C.M.S.
1940	126	Birkenhead—Vickers-Armstrongs (Broughton)	C.M.S.
1928	*127	Liverpool—Caernarvon (A Service)	C.M.S.
1930	*128	Liverpool—Caernarvon (B Service)	C.M.S.
1945	129	Eastham—Clatterbridge	C.M.S.
1944	130	Birkenhead—Cranage	C.M.S.
1927	*131	Liverpool—London	Brookes Bros.
1928	*132	Liverpool—London via Crewe	C.M.S.
1938	*133	Warrington—Rhyl	C.M.S.
1924	134	Heswall—Storeton—Birkenhead	J. Pye
1937	135	Birkenhead—Holywell	C.M.S.
1928	*136	Wallasey—Llandudno	C.M.S.

* Indicates Express Service.

Date Started or Acquired	Service No.	Route	Origin
1946	137	St. Helens—Speke (Joint with St. Helena Corporation)	C.M.S.
1947	138	Liverpool—Pwllheli	C.M.S.
1947	139	Liverpool—Amlwch	C.M.S.
1947	140	St. Helens—Warrington	C.M.S.
1913	201	Nantwich—Willaston—Shavington—Middlewich Road—Crewe	C.M.S.
1923	202	Crewe—Sandbach via Ettiley Heath	J. Gibson
1929	203	Crewe—Willaston via Valley Road	S. Jackson
1915	204	Nantwich—Audlem—Drayton	C.M.S.
1934	205	Nantwich—Swanbach via Aston and Audlem	Lowe
1924	206	Market Buses	C.M.S.
1915	207	Crewe Town (Service)	Ward Bros.
1919	208	Crewe—Tarporley via Beeston	C.M.S.
1913	209	Crewe—Sandbach—Middlewich—Over	C.M.S.
1923	210	Crewe—Audley	J. Gibson
1915	211	Crewe—Aston—Whitchurch	C.M.S.
1920	212	Newcastle—Madeley	C.M.S.
1924	213	Newcastle—Woore—Audlem—Whitchurch	C.M.S.
1940	214	Crewe—Radway Green	C.M.S.
1943	*215	Crewe—Oswestry (Hospital)	C.M.S.
1930	*216	Crewe—Burntwood Sanatorium	C.M.S.
1937	217	Nantwich—Woore via Blakenhall	C.M.S.
1931	*218	Newcastle—Blackpool	C.M.S.
1931	*219	Newcastle—Llandudno	C.M.S.
1928	220	Sandbach—Middlewich—Chester	C.M.S.
1933	301	Chester—Wrexham—Acrefair—Llangollen	Western Transport
1933	302	Mold—Wrexham	W.T.
1935	303	Wrexham—Cymmau	J. Price
1940	304	Wrexham—Vickers-Armstrongs	C.M.S.
1940	305	Wrexham—Ellesmere (Train Service)	C.M.S.
1933	306	Wrexham—Farndon—Broxton—Nantwich	W.T.
1933	307	Wrexham—Farndon—Shocklach—Stretton Circular	W.T.
1933	308	Wrexham—Penycae	W.T.
1933	309	Wrexham—Oswestry	W.T.
1933	310	Wrexham—Malpas—Whitchurch	W.T.
1933	311	Wrexham—Gresford Colliery	W.T.

Date Started or Acquired	Service No.	Route	Origin
1933	312	Wrexham—Llay Main	W.T.
1936	313	Wrexham—Bradley	G. Roberts
1933	314	Wrexham—Coedpoeth—Minera	W.T.
1933	315	Wrexham—Brymbo	W.T.
1933	316	Oswestry—Welshpool	W.T.
1933	317	Wrexham—Ruthin	W.T.
1933	318	Wrexham—Bryneglwys—Corwen	W.T.
1938	319	Wrexham—Gwynfryn	J. R. Lloyd
1938	320	Bwlchgwyn—Coedpoeth—Llay Main	J. R. Lloyd
1933	321	Wrexham—Pentre Broughton	W.T.
1933	322	Wrexham—Pentre Broughton—Llay Main	W.T.
1933	323	Wrexham—Rhos	W.T.
1939	324	Wrexham—Chirk—Llangollen—Glyn	A. Wright
1933	325	Llay—Chester	W.T.
1933	326	Wrexham Town Services	W.T.
1933	327	Wrexham—Llanfynnyd—Treuddyn	W.T.
1933	328	Wrexham—Caergwrle—Leeswood—Treuddyn	W.T.
1933	329	Wrexham—Clwt—Bryn and Penylan	W.T.
1935	330	Wrexham—Tanyfron	J. Price
1935	331	Oswestry—Sodylt Bank—New Marton	W. B. Jones
1935	332	Oswestry—Dudleston Heath—Ellesmere	W. B. Jones
1935	333	Ifton Heath—Chirk Hospital	W. B. Jones
1935	334	Oswestry—Nant Mavr.	D. H. Tyler
1935	335	Oswestry—Sychtyn	D. H. Tyler
1935	336	Oswestry—Bryn	J. B. S. Platt
1933	337	Johnstown—Rhos—Penycae—Cefn	W.T.
1933	338	Wrexham—Acton—Trevalyn	W.T.
1933	339	Wrexham—Wern—Minera	W.T.
1933	340	Wrexham—Rhos Ucha	W.T.
1940	341	Wrexham—Isy-Coed	C. W. Shone
1933	342	Welshpool—Llanfair Caereinion	W.T.
1933	343	Oswestry—Llangynog	W.T.
1933	344	Oswestry—Llanfair Caereinion	W.T.
1933	345	Corwen—Llangollen	W.T.
1933	346	Corwen—Bettwsy-Coed	W.T.
1939	347	Wrexham—Red Wither (Workmen's)	C.M.S.
1933	348	Johnstown—Rhos Colliery Services	W.T.
1933	349	Wrexham—Overton—Ellesmere	W.T.
1933	350	Oswestry—Llangollen	W.T.
1933	351	Oswestry—Weston Rhyn	W.T.

Date Started or Acquired	Service No.	Route	Origin
1933	352	Corwen—Bethel—Bala	W.T.
1933	*353	Wrexham—Birkenhead	W.T.
1933	*354	Wrexham—Llandudno	W.T.
1935	*355	Rhos—Blackpool	J. Price
1935	*356	Rhos—Rhyl (Convalescent Home)	J. Price
1933	*357	Wrexham—Rhyl (Convalescent Home) via Southsea and Bradley	W.T.
1933	*358	Wrexham—Blackpool	W.T.
1933	359	Corwen—Llandrillo—Bala	W.T.
1946	360	Wrexham Industrial Estate	C.M.S.
1933	361	Oswestry—Kinnerley	W.T.
1946	362	Plas Coch—Smithfield Rd. (Wrexham)	C.M.S.
1947	363	Wrexham—Garden Village (Strange)	F. W. Strange
1947	364	Wrexham—Pandy (Strange)	F. W. Strange
1922	401	Llanrwst—Rhyl	C.M.S.
1922	402	Llanrwst—Cerrig—Ruthin	C.M.S.
1926	403	Llanrwst—Penmachno—Cwm	C.M.S.
1931	404	Llanrwst—Gwytherin	Llandudno Blue
1937	405	Llanrwst—Llanddoget	C.M.S.
1931	406	Llandudno—Conway—Penmaenmawr—Bangor—Caernarvon	Ll. Blue
1931	407	Llandudno—Glan Conway—Eglwysbach	Ll. Blue
1931	408	Llandudno—Rhos-on-Sea—Colwyn Bay—Penmaen Head	Ll. Blue
1931	409	Llandudno—Colwyn Bay—Abergele—Rhyl and St. Asaph	Ll. Blue
1931	410	Colwyn Bay—Bettws-yn-Rhos	Ll. Blue
1931	411	Colwyn Bay—Llystaen	Ll. Blue
1930	412	Llandudno—Deganwy—Conway—Llanrwst—Bettwsy-Coed	Silver
1941	413	Colwyn Bay—Bryn-y-Maen	Owen Roberts
1930	414	Colwyn Bay—Conway	Silver
1934	415	Llanrwst Square—Capel Garmon	R. T. Jones
1931	416	Llandudno—Colwyn Bay—Bettws-y-Coed	Ll. Blue
1936	417	Llandudno—Pydew	C.M.S.
1930	418	Rhyl—Holywell	Brookes Bros.
1930	419	Rhyl—Trelogan—Holywell—Flint	Brookes Bros.
1930	420	Prestatyn—Llanasa—Trelogan	Brookes Bros.
1930	421	Rhyl Circular via Prestatyn, Rhuddlan and Dyserth	Brookes Bros.

* Indicates Express Service.

Date Started or Acquired	Service No.	Route	Origin
1930	422	Rhyl—Kinmel—St. George	Brookes Bros.
1930	423	Rhyl—St. Asaph—Rhuallt—Tremeirchion	Brookes Bros.
1930	424	Rhyl—St. Asaph—Cefn Glascoed	Brookes Bros.
1930	425	Rhyl—Abergele—Petryal	Brookes Bros.
1930	426	Rhyl—Llansannan Circular	W. Edwards
1930	427	Rhyl—Denbigh—Ruthin—Corwen	W. Edwards
1940	428	Rhyl—Rhydymwyn	C.M.S.
1930	429	Denbigh—Llansannan—Llanfair T.H.	Brookes Bros.
1930	430	Denbigh—Llansannan via Bylchau	W. Edwards
1930	431	Denbigh—Peniel—Nantglyn	W. Edwards
1930	432	Denbigh—Henllan—Llannefydd—Plas Hari—Abergele	W. Edwards
1930	433	Denbigh—Prion—Saron	W. Edwards
1930	434	Denbigh—Tremeirchion	W. Edwards
1930	435	Denbigh—Waen—Bodfari	W. Edwards
1930	436	Ruthin—Clawddnewydd—Clocaenog	W. Edwards
1930	437	Ruthin—Gyffylliog—Hiraethog	W. Edwards
1930	438	Denbigh—Ruthin—Penire Goch—Rhewl Smithy	W. Edwards
1930	439	Denbigh—Ruthin via Llangynhafal	W. Edwards
1943	440	Newmarket—Point of Ayr	C.M.S.
1930	441	Pendyffryn Circular	Brookes Bros.
1930	442	Rhyl—Pen-y-fordd	Brookes Bros.
1930	443	Rhyl—Gwaenysgor	Brookes Bros.
1930	444	Rhyl (Marine Lake)—Grosvenor Avenue	Brookes Bros.
1930	445	Rhyl—St. Asaph—Waen—Tremeirchion	Brookes Bros.
1930	446	Rhyl Toast Rack Services	Brookes Bros.
1935	447	Prestatyn Toast Rack Services	C.M.S.
1946	448	Weaverton (Country Club)—Brynhedydd	C.M.S.
1935	449	Colwyn Bay—Seafield Road	C.M.S.
1937	450	Conway—Pant-y-Tan	C.M.S.
1924	451	Conway—Sychnant Pass	Ll. Blue
1926	452	Llandudno Circular	C.M.S.
1937	453	Llanrwst-Nebo	C.M.S.
1934	454	Llanrwst—Melin-y-Coed	R. T. Jones
1947	455	Colwyn Bay—Denbigh	C.M.S.
1947	456	Cefn—Denbigh	
1929	501	Holyhead—Llanfairynghornwy—Amlwch	Mona Maroon
1929	502	Holyhead—Amlwch, via Llanrhyddlad	Mona Maroon

Date Started or Acquired	Service No.	Route	Origin
1929	503	Holyhead—Amlwch, via Llanddeusant	Mona Maroon
1929	504	Holyhead—Amlwch, via Llanerchymedd	Mona Maroon
1929	505	Holyhead—Trearddur Bay—Holyhead Circular	Mona Maroon
1929	506	Holyhead—South Stack	Mona Maroon
1929	507	Holyhead—Bodedern—Llangefni	Mona Maroon
1930	508	Llangefni—Pentraeth—Llanbedrgoch	U.N.U.
1931	509	Llangefni—Newborough—Bangor	Ll. Blue
1931	510	Bangor—Holyhead	Ll. Blue
1929	511	Llangefni—Benllech	Mona Maroon
1933	512	Llangefni—Aberffraw	C.M.S.
1931	513	Llangefni—Llanerchymedd—Amlwch	Ll. Blue
1935	514	Anglesey—Llangefni Market	Mechell Maroon
1931	515	Amlwch—Llanellian, Bull Bay—Llys Dulas and Llwyn Arth	Ll. Blue
1931	516	Bangor—Beaumaris—Llangoed—Penmon Priory—Llanddona	Ll. Blue
1931	517	Bangor—Bethesda—Llanrwst	Ll. Blue
1931	518	Bangor—Bethesda Local	Ll. Blue
1931	519	Bangor—Llanberis	Ll. Blue
1931	520	Bangor—Amlwch—Cemaes Bay	Ll. Blue
1932	521	Bangor—Gerlan	Bethesda Grey
1932	522	Bangor—Tregarth—Bethesda	Bethesda Grey
1932	523	Bangor—Mynydd Llandegai	Bethesda Grey
1932	524	Bethesda—Mynydd Llandegai	Bethesda Grey
1934	525	Bangor—Rhiwlas	Wm. Morris
1944	526	Bangor—Maes Geirchen	C.M.S.
1944	527	Bangor—Maes Tryfan—Bangor (Circular)	C.M.S.
1924	528	Bl. Festiniog—Portmadoc—Pwllheli	C.M.S.
1937	529	Bl. Festiniog—Tanygrisiau	C.M.S.
1924	530	Bl. Festiniog—Llanrwst	C.M.S.
1924	531	Bl. Festiniog—Dolgelley	Ll. Blue
1926	532	Bl. Festiniog—Llan Festiniog	C.M.S.
1928	533	Portmadoc—Morfa Bychan and Borth-y-Gest	C.M.S.
1930	534	Bl. Festiniog—Penrhyn (Workmen's Service)	C.M.S.
1925	535	Caernarvon—Portmadoc, via Garn	C.M.S.
1934	536	Caernarvon—Penygroes—Nantlle	Seiont
1925	537	Caernarvon—Portmadoc via Bedgelert	Busy Bee
1925	538	Caernarvon—Pwllheli	Busy Bee
1925	539	Caernarvon—Llanberis	Busy bee

Date Started or Acquired	Service No.	Route	Origin
1925	540	Caernarvon—Dinorvic	Busy Bee
1931	541	Caernarvon—Bangor	Ll. Blue
1932	542	Caernarvon—Groeslon—Deiniolen—Dinorwic	Rhiwen
1932	543	Caernarvon—Crawiau—Deiniolen—Dinorwic	Rhiwen
1932	544	Caernarvon—Dinas Dinlle	Caernarvon Bay
1936	545	Caernarvon—Carmel—Cilgwyn	J. Hughes
1936	546	Caernarvon—Bethesda	D. M. Prichard
1928	547	Criccieth—Caernarvon	C.M.S.
1933	548	Pwllheli—Nevin—Llangwnadl—Aberdaron	W.T.
1935	549	Edeyrn—Nevin—Llithfaen—Caernarvon	Tudor Evans
1933	550	Pwllheli—Nevin—Edeyrn	W.T.
1934	551	Pwllheli—Four Crosses—Criccieth	Tocia
1934	552	Pwllheli—Abersoch—Sarn Bach—Ysgubor Hen	Tocia
1934	553	Pwllheli—Abersoch—Llangian	Tocia
1934	554	Pwllheli—Llanbedrog—Mynytho	Tocia
1934	555	Pwllheli—Aberdaron (via Rhydyclafdy)	Tocia
1934	556	Pwllheli—Llaniestyn—Brynmawr	Tocia
1934	557	Pwllheli—Aberdaron (via Llanbedrog)	Tocia
1930	558	Pwllheli—Rhiw—Aberdaron	W. J. Jones
1938	559	Caernarvon—Menai Bridge—Newborough—Llangaffo	U.N.U.
1938	560	Pwllheli (Stn. Sq.)—West End	C.M.S.
1939	*561	Pwllheli—Morfa Garreg	C.M.S.
1938	562	Caernarvon—Aberystwyth	C.M.S.
1929	563	Bangor—Llandegfan	C.M.S.
1931	564	Holyhead—Rhosneigr	Mona Maroon
1931	565	Bangor (Town Clock)—Bangor (Pier)	Ll. Blue
1931	566	Caernarvon—Llanberis—Capel Curig	Ll. Blue
1931	567	Llanfairfechan (Vict. Gdns.)—Llanfairfechan (Nant School)	Ll. Blue
1947	569	Foel Ferry—Aberffraw	Ll. Blue
1924	601	Aberystwyth—Devil's Bridge via Ponterwyd	C.M.S.
1924	602	Aberystwyth—Devil's Bridge via Penparcau	C.M.S.
1925	603	Aberystwyth—Aberayron—Cardigan.	Jones Bros. and Hooker
1933	604	Aberystwyth—Aberayron—Lampeter	Jones Bros.
1925	605	Aberystwyth—Pontrhydfendigaid	C.M.S.
1933	606	Aberystwyth—Borth—Ynyslas—Tre'rddol	W.T.

* Indicates Express Service.

Date Started or Acquired	Service No.	Route	Origin
1933	607	Aberystwyth—Tregaron—Lampeter	Jones Bros.
1934	608	Aberystwyth—Cwm Woods—Clarach	C.M.S.
1925	609	Aberayron—New Quay	D. M. Jenkins
1931	610	Aberystwyth—Capel Bangor—Glyn Rheidol	
1924	611	Llanidloes—Newtown	C.M.S.
1924	612	Llandrindod Wells—Builth Wells	C.M.S.
1924	613	Llandrindod Wells—Kingston	C.M.S.
1925	614	Llandrindod Wells—Rhayader	C.M.S.
1933	615	Machynlleth—Corris—Aberllefenny	W.T.
1933	616	Machynlleth—Dinas Mawddwy	W.T.
1933	617	Machynlleth—Towyn	W.T.
1933	618	Machynlleth—Aberystwyth	W.T.
1933	619	Machynlleth—Aberhosan	W.T.
1933	620	Machynlleth—Talywern	W.T.
1939	621	Cardigan—Pardilyn	C.M.S.
1939	622	New Quay—Llangranog—Aberporth	C.M.S.
1925	623	Barmouth—Harlech—Maentwrog—Bl. Festiniog	
1924	624	Barmouth—Dolgelley	C.M.S.
1933	625	Dolgelley—Dinas Mawddwy	C.M.S.
1933	626	Dolgelley—Llanfachraeth	W.T.
1933	627	Dolgelley—Corris—Towyn	W.T.
1933	628	Dolgelley—Hermon	W.T.
1933	629	Dolgelley—Hywel Dda—Bala	W.T.
1935	630	Towyn—Bryncrug—Llanegryn—Rhoslefain	W.T.
1933	632	Newtown—Carno	J. A. Richards
1929	*633	Aberystwyth—Birmingham	W.T.
1935	634	Towyn—Caerbellan	B.M.O.
1935	635	Machynlleth—Llanwrin—Mathafarn	J. A. Richards
1946	636	Aberystwyth—Cwm Erfin	C.M.S.
1933	637	Towyn—Dolgelley	Primrose
1946	638	Rhayader—Elan Valley	W.T.

* Indicates Express Service.

ORGANISATION CHART

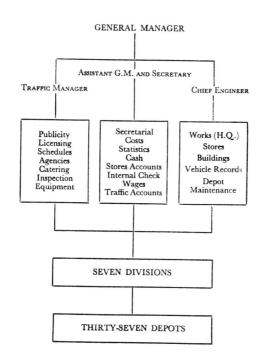

GENERAL MANAGER

ASSISTANT G.M. AND SECRETARY

TRAFFIC MANAGER

CHIEF ENGINEER

| Publicity Licensing Schedules Agencies Catering Inspection Equipment | Secretarial Costs Statistics Cash Stores Accounts Internal Check Wages Traffic Accounts | Works (H.Q.) Stores Buildings Vehicle Records Depot Maintenance |

SEVEN DIVISIONS

THIRTY-SEVEN DEPOTS

APPENDIX 3
LOCATION OF DEPOTS AND VEHICLE ALLOCATIONS
AS AT 31st MARCH, 1947

Place	Date	Vehicles
Aberayron	1929	4
Aberdaron	1934	2
Aberystwyth	1934	28
Amlwch	1935	11
Bangor	1931	54
Barmouth	1924	4
Birkenhead	1932	68
Bl. Festiniog	1926	11
Bryn Crug	1935	3
Caernarvon	1932	44
Cardigan	1941	2
Chester	1927	78
Corwen	1934	8
Crewe	1926	54
Criccieth	1927	5
Denbigh	1930	21
Dolgelley	1934	5
Flint	1937	47
Heswall	1924	27
Holyhead	1930	9
Johnstown	1933	19
Llandrindod Wells	1928	4
Llandudno Junction	1931	47
Llandudno	1931	21
Llangefni	1930	7
Llanfaircaereinion	1933	2
Llanrhaiadr	1936	1
Llangynog	1933	1
Llangybi	1934	1
Llanidloes	1925	2
Llanrwst	1931	13
Llanrug	1936	4
Liverpool	1928	67
Machynlleth	1934	8
Middlewich	1934	4
Mold	1923	42
Nantwich	1915	17
Nevin	1933	4
Newcastle-under-Lyme	1932	5
Oswestry	1933	14
Portmadoc	1936	6
Pwllheli	1934	15
Rhyl	1930	55
Runcorn	1942	37
Warrington	1924	23
West Kirby	1923	27
Wrexham	1933	103

West Kirby.

Llanrwst.

Liverpool Edge Lane.

Denbigh before entrance altered for double-deck access.

Criccieth.

Pwhelli.

APPENDIX 4
ROAD AND RAIL STANDING JOINT COMMITTEE

This Committee first met on 3rd June, 1930. The first members were :

ROAD .. .. Claude C. Taylor (*Chairman*).

W. J. Crosland-Taylor.

RAIL (L.M.S.) F. H. Cowell.

W. P. Bradbury.

In 1933 when the G.W.R. acquired an interest in the Company, J. R. Morris joined the Committee as their representative.

The main objects were and still are to decide, control and maintain :—

(1) Reciprocal advertising and display of facilities.

(2) Interavailability arrangements for return ticket holders.

(3) Combined road and rail travel, both for ordinary journeys and for excursions and tours and private hire.

(4) Connections at railway stations between road and rail.

(5) Reciprocal service in enquiry offices.

(6) Agreement where possible on time table, fare and route alterations before they are put into force.

(7) Road and rail combined parcels services.

In addition to the above, we could discuss any other items that might be of joint interest, but we could only recommend and not bind our respective Companies to do anything. We were there to advise and naturally we saw to it that our advice was sound.

The Committee met about twice a year and there have been thirty-three meetings since it started.

Contact of one sort or another was effected at nearly 200 stations and hundreds of time table connections were arranged up and down the area. Interavailability was useful in many places where last buses were overcrowded and people could be put on a still later train. Road/Rail tours gave us £2,900 of entirely new traffic in 1937.

These were the more tangible advantages of the arrangement, but there were other things too. By agreeing alterations beforehand we were able to go before the Traffic Commissioners with practically no railway opposition. This saved endless time—and time is money. Finally, we really got to know our opposite numbers in the railway camp, and they got to know that we were ordinary human beings like themselves. We always have lunch together and in the Summer we go down the coast and see things for ourselves.

APPENDIX 5

BUSINESSES PURCHASED AND DATES OF ACQUISITION

Name	Place	Date	Main Routes Only
Lightfoot	Kelsall ..	-. -.11 ..	Kelsall—Chester.
Gregory	Crewe ..	-. 1.15 ..	Nantwich—Crewe—Sandbach.
Ward Bros.	Crewe	-. -.15 ..	Crewe Town.
J. M. Hudson	Ellesmere Port	27. 1.22 ..	Ellesmere Port—Chester.
J. Pye	Heswall ..	1. 1.24 ..	Birkenhead—Heswall.
			Birkenhead—Parkgate.
D. M. Jenkins	Aberayron ..	21. 2.25 ..	Aberayron—New Quay.
J. Gibson	Crewe	6. 4.25 ..	Crewe—Audley.
			Nantwich—Crewe—Sandbach.
Gauterin Bros.	Farndon ..	26.10 25 ..	Farndon—Chester.
Richards (Busy Bee)	Caernarvon ..	9.11.25 ..	Caernarvon—Pwllheli.
A. Harding	Birkenhead ..	-.11.25 ..	Birkenhead—Heswall.
Hooker	Aberayron ..	-.11.25 ..	Aberayron—Cardigan.
Abraham Lloyd	Queensferry ..	11. 3.26 ..	Queensferry—Chester.
Trevor Garner	Runcorn ..	10. 2.27 ..	Runcorn Local.
Joseph Rogers	Malpas ..	10. 2.27 ..	Malpas—Chester.
Hugh Jones	Penmachno ..	10. 2.27 ..	Llanrwst—Penmachno.
A. & R. Motors	Criccieth ..	1.10.27 ..	Portmadoc—Pwllheli.
J. Lewis Owens	Caernarvon ..	10.11.27 ..	Nevin—Edeyrn.
A. V. Peach	Haslington ..	10.11.27 ..	Haslington—Crewe.
Don Taylor	Haslington ..	10.11.27 ..	Haslington—Crewe.
Peris Motors	Caernarvon ..	-.10.28 ..	Caernarvon—Llanberis.
Thos. John Edwards	Caernarvon ..	-.10.28 ..	Caernarvon—Bryn Refail.
Cynfi Motors	Deiniolen ..	11. 7.29 ..	Caernarvon—Dinorwic.
Holyhead Motors (Mona Maroon) ..	Holyhead ..	4.11.29 ..	Holyhead—Valley.
			Holyhead—South Stack.
			Holyhead—Rhoscolyn.
			Holyhead—Cemaes—Amlwch (four route
			Holyhead—Llangefni—Benllech.
U.N.U.	Llangefni ..	1. 1.30 ..	Caernarvon—Beaumaris.
			Bangor—Holyhead.
			Bangor—Newborough.
			Bangor—Llangefni.
			Caernarvon—Birkenhead.
			Caernarvon—Bangor.
			Caernarvon—Menai Bridge—Newboroug
Brookes Bros.	Rhyl ..	1. 5.30 ..	All round Rhyl.
W. Edwards	Denbigh ..	31. 7.30 ..	Ruthin—Clocaenog.
			Ruthin—Hiraethog.
			Caerwys—Station.
			Denbigh—Llanrhaiadr.
			Denbigh—Tremeirchion.
			Abergele—Rhyl.
			Denbigh—Ruthin—Corwen.
			Denbigh—Bylchau.
			Denbigh—Prion Saron.
C. Burton	Tarporley ..	31. 7.30 ..	Chester—Tarporley.
N. Wales Silver	Llandudno ..	1. 8.30 ..	Llandudno—Colwyn Bay—Abergele.
			Llandudno—Conway.
			Llandudno—Alexandra Road.
			Llandudno—Bettws-y-Coed.
			Colwyn Bay—Llysfaen.
			Colwyn Bay—Bettws-yn-Rhos.
Llangoed Red	Beaumaris ..	1.10.30 ..	Bangor—Llangoed—Penmon.
Vincent Smith	Prestatyn ..	29. 1.31 ..	Hillside—Beach.
H. C. Pascoe	Tarporley ..	31. 1.31 ..	Tarporley—Northwich.

Name				*Place*			*Date*		*Main Routes Only*
Zacchaeus Woodfin	..	..	..	Tarvin	..	..	2. 2.31	..	Chester—Tarporley via Christleton.
									Chester—Burton via Huxley.
									Barrow—Chester.
Ribble Motors (Liverpool—London)			..	Preston	..	..	5. 2.31	..	Liverpool—London.
Llandudno Coaching	..	..	..	Llandudno	..	..	18. 2.31	..	Llandudno and Bangor Blue.
Bethesda Greys	..	..	..	..	Bethesda	..	..	1. 1.32	..	Rachub—Bethesda.
									Bangor—Gerlan (five routes).
									Bangor—Bethesda.
									Douglas Hill—Bethesda.
									Douglas Hill—Bangor.
J. W. Hughes	..	..	..	..	Rhiwen	..	..	15. 1.32	..	Caernarvon—Rhiwlas.
									Bangor—Llanberis.
									Caernarvon—Dinorwic.
Caernarvon Bay Motors		..	..	Caernarvon	..		6.12.32	..	Caernarvon—Dinas Dinlle.
Roses Tours	..	..	..	..	Rhyl	..	..	—. 2.33	..	Tours from Rhyl.
Western Transport	..	..	..	Wrexham	..	..	1. 5.33	..	All Wrexham, etc.
Jones Bros.	..	..	..	..	Aberystwyth	..	..	1. 5.33	..	Aberystwyth—Aberayron.
									Aberystwyth—Lampeter.
									Aberystwyth—Borth.
									Aberystwyth—Tregaron.
									Aberystwyth—Ponterwyd.
Wm. Lloyd	..	..	..	..	Beddgelert	..	..	14. 6.33	..	Beddgelert—Portmadoc.
Seront Motors	..	..	..	Caernarvon	..	..	1. 1.34	..	Caernarvon—Penygroes—Nantlle.
Jas. Rothwell	..	..	..	..	Holt	..	..	1. 1.34	..	Wrexham—Holt.
									Wrexham—Broxton.
Red & White	..	..	..	..	London	..	..	8. 1.34	..	London—Liverpool.
Wirral Motor Transport		..	..	Birkenhead	..	..	10. 2.34	..	Birkenhead—Bangor.
Nevin Blue	..	..	..	..	Nevin	..	..	15. 2.34	..	Pwllheli—Nevin—Edeyrn.
D. J. Williams (Mynytho)		..	..	Pwllheli	..	..	15. 2.34	..	Mynytho—Llanbedrog—Pwllheli.
Tocia Motor Co. Ltd.	..	..	..	Aberdaron	..	..	17. 2.34	..	Pwllheli—Criccieth—Abersoch.
									Aberdaron—Llanbedrog—Llangian.
Wm. Morris	..	..	..	..	Bethesda	..	..	23. 5.34	..	Bangor—Rhiwlas.
R. T. Jones	..	..	..	..	Llanrwst	..	..	1. 6.34	..	Llanrwst—Trefriw—Capel Garmon—Melin-y-coed.
S. Jackson & Sons	..	..	..	Crewe	..	..	26. 6.34	..	Nantwich—Wettenhall—Winsford.
									Nantwich—Crewe—Sandbach.
									Crewe—Valley Road.
T. O. Maddocks	..	..	..	Tattenha	..	..	1. 7.34	..	Bunbury—Chester.
									Broxton—Chester.
									Tattenhall—Chester.
									Tattenhall—Whitchurch.
W. J. Jones	..	..	..	..	Rhiw	..	..	2. 7.34	..	Pwllheli—Rhiw.
J. D. Davies	..	..	..	..	Llangybi	..	..	20. 7.34	..	Aberystwyth—Tregaron—Lampeter.
H. Lowe & Son	..	..	..	Audlem	..	..	1. 8.34	..	Audlem—Drayton.
									Audlem—Nantwich.
									Audlem—Whitchurch.
R. Jenkinson	..	..	..	..	Buckley	..	..	19. 9.34	..	Buckley—Chester Infirmary.
									Buckley—Mold.
									Buckley—Connah's Quay.
									Mold—Alltami.
Macdonald & Co.		..	..	Birkenhead	..	..	1.12.34	..	Birkenhead—Caernarvon, etc.
J. W. Garner	..	..	..	..	Runcorn	..	..	1. 1.35	..	Runcorn local and Helsby.
F. Watson	..	..	..	..	Runcorn	..	..	1. 1.35	..	Runcorn local.
R. Roberts	..	..	..	..	Pwllheli	..	..	11. 2.35	..	Pwllheli—Uwchmynydd.
									Pwllheli—Garn Chapel.
H. O. Owens	..	..	..	..	Pwllheli	..	..	11. 2.35	..	Pwllheli—Dinas.
Tudor Evans	..	..	..	Llithfaen	..	..	25. 2.35	..	Edeyrn—Nevin—Llithfaen—Caernarvon.
									Llithfaen—Pwllheli.
J. A. Richards	..	..	..	Towyn	..	..	11. 3.35	..	Towyn—Bryn Crug—Caerbellan.
A. W. Reeves	..	..	..	Oswestry	..	..	18. 3.35	..	Oswestry—Leighton.
									Oswestry—Bagley.
									Oswestry—Treflach.
D. H. Tyler	..	..	..	..	Oswestry	..	..	18. 3.35	..	Oswestry—Nant Mawr.
									Oswestry—Sychtyn.
J. B. S. Platt	..	..	..	Oswestry	..	..	18. 3.35	..	Oswestry—Trefonen and Bryn.

Appendix 5

Name	Place	Date	Main Routes Only
W. B. Jones	Oswestry	18. 3.35 ...	Oswestry—New Martin.
			Oswestry—Sodylt Bank.
			Oswestry—Duddleston Heath.
			Ellesmere—Duddleston.
			Ellesmere—Ifton.
New Blue	Llandudno Junction	11. 4.35	Conway—Llandudno.
			Conway—Colwyn Bay.
			Fforddlas Bridge—Colwyn Bay.
J. Price	Wrexham	15. 4.35	Rhos—Blackpool.
			Rhos—Rhyl.
			Wrexham—Llay Main—Caergwrle.
			Wrexham—Tanyfron.
			Wrexham—Cymmau.
H. Williams	Shop Uchaf	1. 5.35 ...	Rhydwen—Holyhead.
H. Williams	Glyn Afon	1. 5.35 ...	Glyn Afon—Holyhead.
Evan Owen	Garreglefn	1. 5.35 ...	Amlwch—Llangefni.
J. H. Roberts	Trevor	1. 5.35 ...	Llangefni—Holyhead.
J. Roberts	Gwalchmai	1. 5.35 ...	Llangefni—Holyhead.
G. R. Parry	Llanddeusant ...	1. 5.35 ...	Amlwch—Holyhead.
Pearson, Jones & Horn ...	Liverpool	25. 5.35 ...	Southport—Liverpool—London.
Mechell Maroon	Anglesey	5. 6.35 ...	Bangor—Cemaes.
			Holyhead—Cemaes, etc.
Albert Mates	Chirk	30.11.35 ...	Chirk—Cefn Mawr.
Iorwerth Evans	Llanrhaiadr ...	21.12.35 ...	Oswestry—Llanrhaiadr.
John Hughes	Carmel	25. 1.36 ...	Caernarvon—Cilgwyn.
G. Roberts	Southsea	28. 1.36 ...	Wrexham—Bradley.
			Wrexham—Rhyl.
G. A. Williams	Cefn	3. 2.36 ...	Cefn—Chirk.
			Cefn—Ellesmere.
D. M. Prichard	Llanrug	1. 3.36 ...	Caernarvon—Llanberis.
			Caernarvon—Bethesda.
W. D. Humphreys	Bethel	1. 3.36 ...	Caernarvon—Bethel.
S. Williams & Sons	Pentre Broughton ...	15. 6.36 ...	Wrexham—Pentre Broughton.
E. J. Hughes	Pen-y-groes ...	15. 6.36 ...	Pen-y-groes—Dinas Dinlle.
David Jones	Newborough ...	15. 6.36 ...	Llangefni—Newborough.
Jones' Motor Services... ...	Flint	15. 6.36 ...	Bagillt—Flint—Shotton.
Harold Roberts	Connah's Quay ...	6. 7.36 ...	Flint—Sandycroft.
Crowther & Co.	Shotton	12. 1.37 ...	Flint—Sandycroft.
Davies Bros.	Tanygrisiau ...	15. 3.37 ...	Festiniog—Tanygrisiau.
C. H. Williams	Rock Ferry ...	22. 7.37 ...	Tours from Birkenhead.
J. R. Lloyd	Bwlchgwyn ...	2. 5.38 ...	Wrexham—Bwlchgwyn.
			Wrexham—Gwynfryn.
Alfred Wright	Rhosymedre ...	1. 3.39 ...	Chirk—Cefn Mawr.
			Chirk—Glyn Valley.
H. Stanley	Buckley	1. 3.39 ...	Buckley—Shotton.
			Mold—Llay Main.
L. J. Roberts	Llanrug	30. 6.39 ...	Caernarvon—Ceunant.
C. W. Shone	Bangor Isycoed ...	1. 3.40 ...	Wrexham—Isycoed.
D. S. Rogers	Coedpoeth ...	15. 5.40 ...	Wrexham—Coedpoeth.
H. Hooson	Coedpoeth ...	15. 5.40 ...	Wrexham—Coedpoeth.
I. T. Roberts	Coedpoeth ...	15. 5.40 ...	Wrexham—Coedpoeth.
Owen Roberts	Colwyn Bay ...	1. 2.41 ...	Colwyn Bay—Brynymaen.
O. Glyn Parry	Benllech	11. 8.41 ...	Llangefni—Benllech.
Primrose Motors	Aberystwyth ...	-. 4.46 ...	Aberystwyth—Cwm Erfin.
F. W. Strange	Wrexham	9. 3.47 ...	Wrexham—Pandy.

APPENDIX 6

EXTENDED TOUR STATISTICS 1928-1939

Figures given are the number of TOUR DAYS to each general district in each of the above years.

	Devon	Scot-land	Lakes	Mid-lands	S. Coast	E. Coast	Total
1928 ..	14	7	5	10	---	---	36
1929 ..	84	84	7	7	—	—	182
1930 ..	91	84	14	—	—	---	189
1931 ..	173	112	—	---	42	—	327
1932 ..	112	159	—	---	42	---	313
1933 ..	211	267	—	---	91	---	569
1934 ..	211	258	—	---	86	—	555
1935 ..	144	261	30	—	77	42	554
1936 ..	202	281	35	25	82	56	681
1937 ..	214	366	30	30	229	56	925
1938 ..	233	402	35	30	217	56	973
1939 ..	238	486	55	—	174	42	995
	1,927	2,767	211	102	1,040	252	6,299

APPENDIX 7

THE 1935 RENUMBERING SCHEME

Firm's Old No.	Reg. No.	Group Letter	Group No.
1	EY 3133	S	1
2	EY 3301	S	2
3	EY 3541	S	3
4	EY 3538	S	4
5	EY 3537	S	5
6	EY 3449	S	6
7	EY 3539	S	7
8	EY 3540	S	8
12	FM 5242	K	1
13	FM 5243	K	2
14	FM 5244	K	3
15	FM 5245	K	4
16	FM 5246	K	5
17	FM 5247	K	6
18	FM 6391	L	1
19	FM 6392	L	2
20	FM 6393	L	3
21	FM 6394	L	4
22	FM 4817	B	1
23	FM 4818	B	2
24	FM 4819	B	3
25	FM 4820	B	4
26	FM 4821	B	5
27	FM 4822	B	6
28	FM 4845	B	7
29	FM 4846	B	8
30	FM 4847	B	9
31	FM 4848	B	10
32	FM 4849	B	11
33	FM 4850	B	12
34	FM 4829	B	13
35	FM 4830	B	14
36	FM 4831	B	15
37	FM 4832	B	16
38	FM 4833	B	17
39	FM 4834	B	18
40	FM 4835	B	19
41	FM 4836	B	20
42	FM 4837	B	21
43	FM 6395	L	5
44	FM 6396	L	6
45	FM 6397	L	7
46	FM 6398	L	8
47	FM 6399	L	9
48	FM 6400	L	10
49	FM 6401	L	11
50	FM 6402	L	12
51	FM 6403	L	13
52	FM 6404	L	14
53	FM 6405	L	15
54	FM 6406	L	16
55	FM 6407	L	17
56	FM 6408	L	18
57	FM 6409	L	19
58	FM 6410	L	20
59	FM 6411	L	21
60	FM 6412	L	22
61	FM 5226	B	22
62	FM 5227	B	23
63	FM 5228	B	24
64	FM 5229	B	25
65	FM 5230	B	26
66	FM 5231	B	27
67	FM 5232	B	28
68	FM 5233	B	29
69	FM 5234	B	30
70	FM 5235	B	31
71	FM 5236	B	32
72	FM 5237	B	33
73	FM 5238	B	34
74	FM 5239	B	35
75	FM 5240	B	36
76	FM 5241	B	37
77	EK 6285	B	38
78	FR 8419	B	39
79	EK 6286	B	40
80	EK 6287	B	41
81	CC 8166	B	42
82	CC 8167	B	43
85	CC 8516	T	1
86	CC 8517	T	2
87	MY 1415	T	3
88	UL 7229	R	1
93	CC 9578	U	1
99	VT 2653	R	2
100	CC 8607	R	3

Firm's Old No.	Reg. No.	Group Letter	Group No.
101	CC 8608	R	4
102	CC 8609	R	5
103	CC 8610	R	6
104	CC 8611	R	7
105	FM 6861	E	1
107	FM 6862	E	2
108	FM 6863	E	3
109	FM 6864	E	4
110	FM 6865	E	5
111	FM 6866	E	6
112	FM 6867	E	7
113	FM 6868	E	8
114	FM 6869	E	9
115	FM 6870	E	10
116	FM 6871	E	11
117	FM 6872	E	12
118	FM 6873	E	13
119	FM 6874	E	14
120	FM 6875	E	15
121	FM 6876	E	16
122	FM 6877	E	17
123	FM 6878	E	18
124	FM 6879	E	19
125	FM 6800	E	20
126	FM 6881	E	21
127	FM 6882	E	22
128	FM 6883	E	23
129	FM 6884	E	24
130	FM 6885	E	25
131	FM 6886	E	26
132	FM 6887	E	27
133	FM 6888	E	28
134	FM 6889	E	29
135	FM 6890	E	30
136	FM 6891	E	31
137	VR 8862	L	23
138	LG 2637	U	2
139	LG 2636	U	3
140	LG 2690	U	4
141	LG 7194	U	5
143	LG 2610	K	7
166	FM 6856	K	8
167	FM 6857	K	9
168	FM 6858	K	10
169	FM 6859	K	11
170	FM 6860	K	12
171	FM 5218	K	13
172	FM 5219	K	14
173	FM 5220	K	15
174	FM 5221	K	16
175	FM 5222	K	17
176	FM 5223	K	18
177	FM 5224	K	19
178	FM 5225	K	20
182	FM 6892	E	32
183	FM 6893	E	33
184	FM 6894	E	34
185	FM 6895	E	35
186	FM 6896	E	36
187	FM 6897	E	37
188	FM 6898	E	38
189	FM 6899	E	39
190	FM 6900	E	40
191	FM 6901	E	41
195	FM 6417	D	1
196	FM 6418	D	2
197	UR 3902	S	9
199	FM 4333	B	44
200	FM 4334	B	45
201	FM 3710	A	1
202	FM 3773	A	2
203	FM 3774	A	3
204	FM 3775	A	4
205	FM 3776	A	5
206	FM 3777	A	6
207	FM 3778	A	7
208	FM 3779	A	8
209	FM 3780	A	9
210	FM 3781	A	10
211	FM 6264	L	24
212	FM 6265	L	25
213	FM 6266	L	26
214	FM 6267	L	27
215	FM 6268	L	28
216	FM 6269	L	29
217	FM 6270	L	30

Firm's Old No.	Reg. No.	Group Letter	Group No.
218	FM 6271	L	31
219	FM 6272	L	32
220	FM 6273	L	33
221	FM 6274	L	34
222	FM 6275	L	35
245	FM 4281	A	11
246	FM 4282	A	12
247	FM 4283	A	13
248	FM 4284	A	14
249	FM 4285	A	15
250	FM 4286	A	16
251	FM 4287	A	17
252	FM 4288	A	18
253	FM 4289	A	19
254	FM 4290	A	20
255	FM 4291	A	21
256	FM 4292	A	22
257	FM 4293	A	23
258	FM 4294	A	24
259	FM 4295	A	25
260	FM 4296	A	26
261	FM 4297	A	27
262	FM 4298	A	28
263	FM 4299	A	29
264	FM 4300	B	46
265	FM 4301	A	30
266	FM 4302	A	31
267	FM 4303	A	32
268	FM 4304	A	33
269	FM 4350	A	34
270	FM 4351	A	35
271	FM 4486	B	47
272	FM 4487	B	48
273	FM 4488	B	49
274	FM 4561	B	50
275	FM 4562	B	51
276	FM 4791	B	52
277	FM 4792	B	53
278	FM 4733	B	54
279	FM 4794	B	55
280	FM 4795	B	56
281	FM 4796	B	57
282	FM 4797	B	58
283	FM 4798	B	59
284	FM 4799	B	60
285	FM 4800	B	61
286	FM 4801	B	62
287	FM 4802	B	63
288	FM 4803	B	64
289	FM 4804	B	65
290	FM 4805	B	66
291	FM 4806	B	67
292	FM 4807	B	68
293	FM 4808	B	69
294	FM 4809	B	70
295	FM 4810	B	71
296	FM 4811	B	72
297	FM 4812	B	73
298	FM 4813	B	74
299	FM 4814	B	75
300	FM 4815	B	76
301	FM 4816	B	77
302	FM 4823	B	78
303	FM 4824	B	79
304	FM 4825	B	80
305	FM 4826	B	81
306	FM 4827	B	82
307	FM 4828	B	83
308	FM 5027	B	84
309	FM 5028	B	85
310	FM 5704	C	1
311	FM 5705	C	2
312	FM 5706	C	3
313	FM 5707	C	4
314	FM 5708	C	5
315	FM 5709	C	6
316	FM 5710	C	7
317	FM 5711	C	8
318	FM 5712	C	9
319	FM 5713	C	10
320	FM 5714	C	11
321	FM 5715	C	12
322	FM 5716	C	13
323	FM 5717	C	14
324	FM 5206	L	36
325	FM 5207	L	37

Firm's Old No.	Reg. No.	Group Letter	No.
327	FM 5208	L	38
328	FM 5209	L	39
329	FM 5210	L	40
330	FM 5211	L	41
331	FM 5212	L	42
332	FM 5213	L	43
333	FM 5214	L	44
334	FM 5215	L	45
335	FM 5216	L	46
336	FM 5217	L	47
337	FM 5526	C	15
338	FM 5527	C	16
339	FM 5528	C	17
340	FM 5529	C	18
341	FM 5530	C	19
342	FM 5531	C	20
343	FM 5787	C	21
344	FM 5788	C	22
345	FM 5789	C	23
346	FM 5790	C	24
347	FM 5718	C	25
348	FM 5896	K	21
349	FM 5897	K	22
350	FM 5898	K	23
351	FM 5899	K	24
352	FM 5900	K	25
353	FM 5901	K	26
354	FM 5882	L	48
355	FM 5883	L	49
356	FM 5884	L	50
357	FM 5885	L	51
358	FM 5886	L	52
359	FM 5887	L	53
360	FM 5888	L	54
361	FM 5889	L	55
362	FM 5890	L	56
363	FM 5891	L	57
364	FM 5892	L	58
365	FM 5893	L	59
366	FM 5894	L	60
367	FM 5749	L	61
368	FM 5895	L	62
369	FM 5902	K	27
370	FM 5903	K	28
371	FM 5904	K	29
372	FM 5905	K	30
373	FM 5906	K	31
374	FM 5907	K	32
375	FM 5908	D	3
376	FM 5909	D	4
377	FM 5910	D	5
378	FM 5911	D	6
379	FM 5912	D	7
380	FM 5913	D	8
381	FM 5914	D	9
382	FM 5915	D	10
383	FM 5916	D	11
384	FM 5917	D	12
385	FM 5918	D	13
386	FM 5919	D	14
387	FM 5920	D	15
388	FM 5921	D	16
389	FM 5922	D	17
390	FM 5923	D	18
391	FM 5924	D	19
392	FM 5925	D	20
393	FM 5926	D	21
394	FM 5927	D	22
395	FM 5928	D	23
396	FM 5929	D	24
401	FM 6014	S	10
402	FM 6015	S	11
403	FM 6016	S	12
404	FM 6017	S	13
405	FM 6018	S	14
406	FM 6019	S	15
407	FM 6020	S	16
408	FM 6021	S	17
409	FM 6022	S	18
410	FM 6023	S	19
411	UR 6298	S	20
412	UR 6299	S	21
413	UR 6300	T	4
414	DM 6232	L	63
415	DM 5844	K	33
416	DM 5845	K	34
417	DM 5846	K	35
418	DM 6230	K	36
419	DM 6231	K	37
420	DM 5977	B	86
421	DM 5978	B	87
422	DM 5258	B	88
423	DM 5259	B	89
424	DM 5260	B	90
425	DM 5261	B	91
426	DM 5262	B	92
427	DM 5263	B	93
428	DM 5267	B	94
429	DM 5842	B	95
430	DM 5843	B	96
431	DM 6224	K	38
432	DM 6225	K	39
433	DM 6226	K	40
434	DM 6227	K	41
435	DM 6228	K	42
436	DM 6229	K	43
440	FM 6419	D	25
441	FM 6420	D	26
442	FM 6421	D	27
443	FM 6422	D	28
444	FM 6423	D	29
447	FM 6424	D	30
449	FM 6425	D	31
450	FM 6426	D	32
464	FM 6427	D	33
465	FM 6428	D	34
466	FM 6429	D	35
467	FM 6430	D	36
470	FM 6431	D	37
471	FM 6432	D	38
472	FM 6433	D	39
473	FM 6434	D	40
474	FM 6435	D	41
477	FM 6436	D	42
478	FM 6437	D	43
479	FM 6438	D	44
481	FM 6902	E	42
482	FM 6903	E	43
483	FM 6904	E	44
484	FM 6477	D	45
490	DM 6233	U	6
491	DM 6234	U	7
492	DM 6235	U	8
494	DM 5266	U	9
500	FM 6478	D	46
533	CC 8561	Q	1
534	CC 8562	Q	2
535	CC 8563	Q	3
536	CC 8564	Q	4
537	CC 8565	Q	5
538	CC 8566	Q	6
539	FM 6439	D	47
540	FM 6440	D	48
541	FM 6441	D	49
542	FM 6442	D	50
543	FM 6443	D	51
544	FM 6444	D	52
545	FM 6473	D	53
546	FM 6474	D	54
549	FM 6475	D	55
550	FM 6476	D	56
551	FM 6413	L	64
552	FM 6414	L	65
553	FM 6415	L	66
554	FM 6416	L	67
555	FM 6905	E	45
556	FM 6906	E	46
557	FM 6907	E	47
558	FM 6908	E	48
559	FM 6909	E	49
560	FM 6910	E	50
582	FM 8424	G	1
583	CC 6920	Q	7
584	CC 6921	Q	8
585	CC 7862	Q	9
586	CC 7863	Q	10
587	CC 9284	Q	11
588	CC 9285	Q	12
606	FM 6472	J	1
607	FM 6445	K	44
608	FM 6446	K	45
609	FM 6447	K	46
610	FM 6448	K	47
611	FM 6449	K	48
612	FM 6450	K	49
613	FM 6451	K	50
614	FM 6452	K	51
615	FM 6453	K	52
616	FM 6454	K	53
617	FM 6455	K	54
618	FM 6456	K	55
619	FM 6457	K	56
620	FM 6458	K	57
621	FM 6470	K	58
622	FM 6471	K	59
623	FM 6480	K	60
624	FM 6481	K	61
625	FM 6482	K	62
626	FM 6459	U	10
627	FM 6460	U	11
628	FM 6461	U	12
635	FM 6851	N	1
636	FM 6852	N	2
637	FM 6853	N	3
638	FM 6854	N	4
639	FM 6855	N	5
640	FM 6911	K	63
641	FM 6912	K	64
642	FM 6913	K	65
643	FM 6914	K	66
644	FM 6915	K	67
645	FM 6916	L	68
646	FM 6917	L	69
647	FM 6918	L	70
648	FM 6919	L	71
649	FM 6920	M	1
650	FM 6981	E	51
651	FM 6982	E	52
652	FM 6983	E	53
653	FM 6984	E	54
654	FM 6985	E	55
655	FM 6986	E	56
656	FM 6987	E	57
657	FM 6988	E	58
658	FM 6989	E	59
659	FM 6990	E	60
660	FM 6991	E	61
661	FM 6992	E	62
662	FM 6993	E	63
663	FM 6994	E	64
664	FM 6995	E	65
665	FM 6996	N	6
666	FM 6997	N	7
667	FM 6998	N	8
668	FM 6999	N	9
669	FM 7000	N	10
670	FM 7001	N	11
671	FM 7002	N	12
672	FM 7003	N	13
673	FM 7004	N	14
674	FM 7005	N	15
675	FM 7038	N	16
676	FM 7039	N	17
677	FM 7040	N	18
678	FM 7041	N	19
679	FM 7042	N	20
680	FM 7008	E	66
681	FM 7009	E	67
682	FM 7010	E	68
683	FM 7011	E	69
684	FM 7012	E	70
685	FM 7033	E	71
686	FM 7034	E	72
687	FM 7035	E	73
688	FM 7036	E	74
689	FM 7037	E	75
699	FM 7230	F	1
700	FM 7231	F	2
701	FM 7232	F	3
702	FM 7233	L	72
703	FM 7234	L	73
704	FM 7431	N	21
705	FM 7432	N	22
706	FM 7433	N	23
707	FM 7434	N	24
708	FM 7435	N	25
709	FM 7436	N	26
710	FM 7437	N	27

Firm's Old No.	Reg. No.	Group Letter	Group No.
711	FM 7438	N	28
712	FM 7439	N	29
713	FM 7440	N	30
714	FM 7441	N	31
715	FM 7442	N	32
716	FM 7443	N	33
717	FM 7444	N	34
718	FM 7445	N	35
719	FM 7446	N	36
720	FM 7447	N	37
721	FM 7448	N	38
722	FM 7449	N	39
723	FM 7450	N	40
724	FM 7451	N	41
725	FM 7452	N	42
726	FM 7453	N	43
727	FM 7454	N	44
728	FM 7455	N	45
729	FM 7456	N	46
730	FM 7457	N	47
731	FM 7458	N	48
732	FM 7459	N	49
733	FM 7460	L	74
734	FM 7461	L	75
735	FM 7462	L	76
736	FM 7463	L	77
737	FM 7464	L	78
738	FM 7465	L	79
739	FM 7466	L	80
740	FM 7467	L	81
741	FM 7468	K	68
742	FM 7469	K	69
743	FM 7470	K	70
744	FM 7471	K	71
745	FM 7472	K	72
746	FM 7473	K	73
747	FM 7475	K	74
748	FM 7474	K	75
749	FM 7476	K	76
750	FM 7477	K	77
751	FM 7478	F	4
752	FM 7479	F	5
753	FM 7480	F	6
754	FM 7481	F	7
755	FM 7482	F	8
756	FM 7483	F	9
757	FM 7484	F	10
758	FM 7485	F	11
759	FM 7486	F	12
760	FM 7487	F	13
761	FM 7488	F	14
762	FM 7489	F	15
763	FM 7490	F	16
764	FM 7491	F	17
765	FM 7492	F	18
766	FM 7493	F	19
767	FM 7494	F	20
768	FM 7495	F	21
769	FM 7496	F	22
770	FM 7497	F	23
771	FM 7498	F	24
772	FM 7499	J	2
773	FM 7500	F	25
774	FM 7501	F	26
775	FM 7502	F	27
776	FM 7503	F	28
777	FM 7504	F	29
778	FM 7505	F	30
779	FM 7506	F	31
780	FM 7507	F	32
781	FM 7508	F	33
782	FM 7509	F	34
783	FM 7510	F	35
784	FM 7511	F	36
785	FM 7512	F	37
786	FM 7513	F	38
787	FM 7514	F	39
788	FM 7515	F	40
789	FM 7516	F	41
790	FM 7517	F	42
791	FM 7760	L	82
792	FM 7761	L	83
793	FM 7762	L	84
794	FM 7763	L	85
795	FM 7764	L	86
836	UN 953	J	3

Firm's Old No.	Reg. No.	Group Letter	Group No.
840	UN 1914	R	8
841	UN 1916	R	9
842	UN 1915	R	10
843	UN 1917	R	11
844	FM 5268	R	12
845	FM 5270	R	13
846	FM 5269	R	14
847	FM 5271	R	15
848	FM 5782	R	16
849	FM 5783	R	17
850	FM 5784	R	18
851	FM 5791	R	19
852	FM 6523	R	20
853	FM 6524	R	21
854	FM 6525	R	22
855	FM 6526	R	23
856	FM 6527	R	24
857	FM 6528	R	25
858	UN 4479	R	26
859	UN 4480	R	27
860	UN 4481	R	28
861	UN 4482	R	29
862	UN 4483	R	30
863	UN 4484	R	31
864	UN 4485	R	32
865	UN 4486	R	33
866	UN 4487	R	34
867	UN 4488	R	35
868	UN 5390	R	36
869	UN 5391	R	37
870	UN 5392	R	38
871	UN 5393	R	39
872	UN 5394	R	40
873	UN 5395	R	41
874	UN 5396	R	42
875	UN 5397	R	43
876	UN 5398	R	44
877	UN 5399	R	45
878	UN 5400	R	46
879	FM 7057	R	47
880	FM 7058	R	48
881	FM 7059	R	49
882	FM 7060	R	50
883	FM 7061	R	51
884	FM 7062	R	52
885	FM 7063	R	53
886	FM 7064	R	54
887	FM 7065	R	55
888	FM 7066	R	56
896	UU 5014	U	13
897	UU 5013	U	14
898	UU 5012	U	15
899	UU 5010	U	16
900	FM 8133	G	2
901	FM 8134	G	3
902	FM 8135	G	4
903	FM 8136	G	5
904	FM 8137	G	6
905	FM 8138	G	7
906	FM 8139	G	8
907	FM 8140	G	9
908	FM 8141	G	10
909	FM 8142	G	11
910	FM 8143	G	12
911	FM 8144	G	13
912	FM 8145	G	14
913	FM 8146	G	15
914	FM 8147	C	16
915	FM 8148	G	17
916	FM 8149	M	2
917	FM 8150	M	3
918	FM 8151	M	4
919	FM 8152	M	5
920	FM 8153	M	6
921	FM 8154	M	7
922	FM 8155	M	8
923	FM 8156	M	9
924	FM 8157	O	1
925	FM 8158	O	2
926	FM 8159	O	3
927	FM 8160	O	4
928	FM 8161	O	5
929	FM 8162	O	6
930	FM 8163	K	78
931	FM 8164	K	79
932	FM 8165	K	80

Firm's Old No.	Reg. No.	Group Letter	Group No.
933	FM 8166	K	81
934	FM 6276	M	10
935	FM 6277	M	11
936	FM 6278	M	12
937	FM 6279	N	50
938	FM 6280	N	51
939	FM 6281	N	52
940	FM 6282	N	53
941	FM 6283	N	54
942	FM 6284	N	55
943	FM 6285	N	56
944	FM 6286	N	57
945	FM 6287	N	58
946	FM 6288	N	59
947	FM 6289	N	60
948	FM 6290	N	61
949	FM 6291	N	62
950	FM 6292	N	63
951	FM 6293	N	64
952	FM 6294	N	65
953	FM 6295	N	66
954	FM 6296	N	67
955	FM 6297	N	68
956	FM 6298	N	69
957	FM 6299	N	70
958	FM 8015	N	71
959	FM 8016	N	72
960	FM 8017	N	73
961	FM 8018	N	74
962	FM 8167	K	82
963	FM 8168	K	83
964	FM 8169	K	84
965	FM 8170	K	85
966	FM 8270	K	86
967	JC 1343	K	87
968	JC 200	K	88
969	CC 9401	K	89
970	CC 8531	C	26
971	CC 8532	C	27
972	CC 8021	B	97
973	CC 7449	A	36
974	CC 8879	S	22
975	CC 9592	U	17
980	BC 605	T	5
981	FM 8412	G	18
982	FM 8413	G	19
983	FM 8414	G	20
984	FM 8415	G	21
985	FM 8416	N	75
986	FM 8417	N	76
987	FM 8418	N	77
988	FM 8419	N	78
989	FM 8420	N	79
990	FM 8421	N	80
991	FM 8422	N	81
992	FM 8423	N	82
1000	AMD 256	L	87
...	FM 8974	J	4
...	FM 8975	J	5
...	FM 8976	J	6
...	FM 8977	J	7
...	FM 8978	J	8
...	FM 8979	J	9
...	FM 8980	J	10
...	FM 8981	J	11
...	FM 8982	J	12
...	FM 8983	J	13
...	FM 8984	J	14
...	FM 8985	J	15
...	FM 8986	J	16
...	FM 8987	J	17
...	FM 8988	J	18
...	FM 8989	J	19
...	FM 8990	J	20
...	FM 8991	J	21
...	FM 8992	J	22
...	FM 8993	J	23
...	FM 8994	J	24
...	FM 8995	J	25
...	FM 8996	J	26
...	FM 8997	J	27
...	FM 8998	J	28
...	FM 8999	H	1
...	FM 9000	H	2
...	FM 9001	H	3
...	FM 9002	H	4

Firm's Old No.	Reg. No.	Group Letter	No.
...	FM 9003 ...	H	5
...	FM 9004 ...	H	6
...	FM 9005 ...	H	7
...	FM 9006 ...	H	8
...	FM 9007 ...	H	9
...	FM 9008 ...	H	10
...	FM 9009 ...	H	11
...	FM 9010 ...	H	12
...	FM 9011 ...	H	13
...	FM 9012 ...	H	14
...	FM 9013 ...	H	15
...	FM 9014 ...	O	7
...	FM 9015 ...	O	8
...	FM 9016 ...	O	9
...	FM 9017 ...	O	10
...	FM 9018 ...	O	11
...	FM 9019 ...	O	12
...	FM 9020 ...	O	13
...	FM 9021 ...	O	14
...	FM 9022 ...	O	15
...	FM 9023 ...	O	16
...	FM 9024 ...	O	17
...	FM 9025 ...	O	18
...	FM 9026 ...	O	19
...	FM 9027 ...	O	20
...	FM 9028 ...	N	83
...	FM 9029 ...	N	84
...	FM 9030 ...	N	85
...	FM 9031 ...	N	86
...	FM 9032 ...	N	87
...	FM 9033 ...	N	88
...	FM 9034 ...	N	89
...	FM 9035 ...	N	90
...	FM 9036 ...	N	91
...	FM 9037 ...	N	92
...	FM 9038 ...	N	93
...	FM 9039 ...	N	94
...	FM 9040 ...	N	95
...	FM 9041 ...	N	96
...	FM 9042 ...	N	97
...	FM 9043 ...	P	1
...	FM 9044 ...	P	2
...	FM 9045 ...	P	3
...	FM 9046 ...	P	4
...	FM 9047 ...	P	5
...	FM 9048 ...	P	6
...	FM 9049 ...	M	13
...	FM 9050 ...	M	14
...	FM 9051 ...	M	15
...	FM 9052 ...	M	16
...	FM 9053 ...	M	17
...	FM 9054 ...	M	18
...	FM 9055 ...	M	19
...	FM 9056 ...	M	20
...	FM 9057 ...	M	21
...	FM 9058 ...	K	90
...	FM 9059 ...	K	91
...	FM 9060 ...	K	92
...	FM 9061 ...	O	21
...	FM 9062 ...	O	22
...	FM 9063 ...	U	18
...	FM 9064 ...	U	19
...	FM 9065 ...	U	20
...	FM 9066 ...	U	21
...	FM 9162 ...	P	7
...	FM 9163 ...	P	8
...	FM 9164 ...	P	9
...	FM 9165 ...	P	10
...	FM 9166 ...	P	11
...	FM 9167 ...	P	12
...	BG 207 ...	T	6
...	BG 208 ...	T	7
...	BG 209 ...	T	8
...	BG 210 ...	T	9
...	BG 613 ...	T	10
...	BG 614 ...	T	11
...	BG 615 ...	T	12
...	BG 616 ...	T	13
...	BG 617 ...	T	14
...	BG 618 ...	T	15
...	AMB 652 ...	U	22
...	LG 9466 ...	U	23
...	LG 6106 ...	U	24

APPENDIX 8
VEHICLE CLASSIFICATION LETTERS

A   Short wheel base Leyland 29 PLSC 1.

B   Long wheel base Leyland PLSC 3.

C   Leyland Lion LT 1.

D   Leyland Lion LT 2.

E   Leyland Lion LT 3.

F   Leyland Lion LT 5.

FA   Leyland Lion LT 5 with Albion 4 cyl. CI engine.

GA   Leyland Lion LT 5A with 6 cyl. CI engine.

H   Leyland Lion LT 7.

JA   Leyland Lion LT 7 with 6 cyl. CI engine.

JG   Leyland Lion LT 7 with 5 cyl. Gardner CI engine.

K   Leyland Tiger TS 1, 2, 3, 4, 6 and 7.

KA   Leyland Tiger TS 3, 4, 7, 8 and PS1/1 (CI engines).
KB   Bristol L6A (CI engine).
KC   Leyland Tiger TS 2 and 3 with 5 cyl. Gardner CI engine.

KG   Bristol L5G (CI engine).

KW   Bristol L6B (CI engine).

L   Leyland Titan TD 1 and 2, also A.E.C. Regent.

M   Leyland Titan TD 1, 2, 3, 4, 5, 7, PD1A and PD2/1 (CI engine).

MA   A.E.C. Regent (CI engine).

MB   Bristol K6 A (CI engine).

MG   Guy Arab (CI engine).

MW   Bristol K6 B (CI engine).

N   Leyland Cub KP2, KP3, 1KP2, 1KP2A.

O   Leyland Cub SKP3, 1SKP3.

P   Leyland Cub 1KPO2.

PC   Leyland/Beadle chassisless.

S.   Bedford WTL, OB (bus).

SC   Bedford-Beadle chassisless.

SL   Bedford OB (coach).

T   A.E.C. Regal.

TA   A.E.C. Regal (CI engine).

U   Shelvoke and Drewry.

APPENDIX 9

DEPOT ALLOCATION DOMES

Division	Depots	Coloured Dome on Vehicles
Chester	Chester Mold Flint	White
Merseyside	Rock Ferry West Kirby Heswall Warrington Runcorn Liverpool	Mauve
Crewe	Crewe Nantwich Middlewich Newcastle-under-Lyme	Red
Wrexham	Wrexham Oswestry Johnstown Corwen	Black
Rhyl and Llandudno	Rhyl Denbigh Llandudno Junction Llandudno Town Llanrwst	Blue
North Cambrian	Bangor Holyhead Llangefni Amlwch Caernarvon Criccieth Pwllheli Blaenau Festiniog	Yellow
South Cambrian	Aberystwyth Aberayron Machynlleth Llandrindod Wells Llanidloes Barmouth Dolgelley	Green

ACKNOWLEDGEMENTS

The work involved in producing this new version of W. J. Crosland-Taylor's much acclaimed work has, in many ways, been a labour of love. My memories of Crosville go back to about 1941/42, and from then until I started work in the 'fifties I went to Rhyl, where my grandparents lived close to the Botanical Gardens, four or five times each year during the school holidays. Grandad loved a bus ride, and we spent many happy hours together riding on petrol-engined single and double-decker Leylands. I can still hear the pop-pop of the TD1s in Rhyl bus station, and the distinctive surge of the toastracks as they started away from the stop around the corner from my bedroom window in Prince Edward Avenue.

I am grateful to those who have assisted me in this pleasurable task. First and foremost to Mr David Meredith, who has made me so welcome at Crane Wharf and introduced me to so many interesting people among present and former Crosville employees, and also traced surviving members of the family. Mr John Parker has also been most helpful in looking out particular items at my request. Mr Meredith and his 'opposite number' at Llandudno Junction, Mr Wroxborough, assisted in making sure that Crosville employees were aware of the work I was doing and that also is appreciated.

The Crosville Enthusiasts Club has played its part too. Members have been quick to support the venture and without that support publication would not have been so readily accomplished.

I must, of course, give particular thanks to John Carroll of the CEC who has made literally thousands of photographs and masses of data available to me to ensure that coverage was as thorough as possible. My own researches over the years have taken me to the photographic departments of many of Crosville's suppliers and Ron Hall at Leyland, John Bloor and Bernie Carr at Eastern Coach Works, 'Mick' Carolan at Park Royal, Martin Montano at Duple, Ray Braithwaite at Walter Alexanders, Andrew Whyte at Daimlers, Bob Smith, first at Willowbrook, later at Leyland, and John Symons at AEC have all helped in some way over the years, as did staff at Shelvoke & Drewry.

Among enthusiasts and photographers John Nickells, Eric Cope, Geoff Lumb, Bob Mack, Geoff Atkins, Eric Ogden, Robin Hannay, Bob Smith, Jack Barlow and of course, my good friend Alan Townsin, have all been helpful in providing material. My former neighbours and lifelong friends, Alan Drabble and Albert Meek, spent many hours with me on Crosville 'hunts' in the 1950s and I thank them for their companionship on the many treks we made. My apologies here to anyone I may have missed out.

Finally, but by no means least, I record my thanks to David Deacon, a gentleman who has provided so much first-hand information and looked out so many items which have always added just that little extra to the pages. In 1932 he joined Crosville, and from his first position as a management trainee appointed by Claude, he worked his way through the Company to become Divisional Manager, Crewe, and later for Rhyl and Llandudno, before moving to United Automobile Services in June 1950. I first met him, I believe, in 1947 or 48 at Albion Works, Rhyl. It has been a real pleasure to meet him again, to share his experiences and to come to understand why everyone always speaks of him so highly.

John A. Senior
Simmondley, Derbyshire.
February 1987

We hope you have enjoyed reading this book, and that it will have brought back happy memories to former Crosville employees, whilst giving others something of the flavour of a very special company. Work is well advanced on a similarly revised—but also extended—version of State Owned Without Tears. We particularly want to include pictures of people 'at work' and if you have any good sharp 'snaps' please let us see them. John Parker at Crane Wharf will be pleased to forward them to us for consideration, or you may send them to us at 128 Pikes Lane, Glossop, Derbyshire. A list of our other transport titles is available on receipt of a large stamped addressed envelope.
Thank you.

PHOTOGRAPHIC CREDITS

The Publisher wishes to record his thanks to the following for the use of their photographs as identified below, and apologises to anyone whose picture may have come from the Company's collection and therefore not been attributed correctly.

AEC	55
G. H. F. Atkins	138
J. Barlow	183
Brush	121, 123(lower), 127, 139(both), 162(both)
Mrs Bugge	5
John Carroll collection	12, 64(upper), 85(lower), 138, 178, 217(lower), 227(upper)
C. Carter	227(lower)
E. Cope	123(upper), 155, 169, 174(both), 176, 196, 197, 198
Crosville Motor Services	6(both), 10, 16, 17(both), 18(both), 19, 20, 21, 25, 27, 28, 33, 34, 35, 36, 37, 38, 39(both), 41, 49, 50, 64(lower), 65, 84, 88, 89, 91(both), 97(lower), 109, 119(both), 137, 147, 149(lower), 163, 165, 166, 179, 187, 189, 190, 191, 192, 193, 194, 195, 201, 203, 205, 209, 212, 213, 216, 219, 223, 225, 231, 232, 233, 234, 241, 247(upper), 249(both), 250, 257(all), 258(all), 267
D. S. Deacon	73, 85(upper), 107(both), 110, 126, 161, 171, 185, 221
Eastern Coach Works	113, 115, 117, 136, 159, 172, 173, 175, 177, 181
W. M. Evans collection	69
A. D. Jack collection	63
D. R. Kerrison	157(upper), 217(upper), 243, 245(lower), 247(lower)
Leyland courtesy BCVM	53, 66, 68, 75, 79, 81, 87, 94, 95(lower), 97(upper), 134, 135, 142, 144, 145, 149(upper), 151, 160
G. Lumb collection	77, 83(both), 98, 103, 111(upper), 230
John Nickels collection	95(upper), 104(both), 108, 111(lower), 129(both), 235
J. A. Senior	271
TPC Library	52, 61, 62, 70, 96, 140
A. A. Townsin collection	131, 143
P. Williams	157(lower), 207, 240, 245(upper)
R. L. Wilson	58